First Line Nursing Management

First Line Nursing Management

BRIAN LEMIN
SRN, RMN, HVOCert, NDNCert (Queens Nurse)

*Area Nurse (Personnel), Northumberland Area Health Authority
formerly Principal, The William Rathbone Staff College, Liverpool*

PITMAN MEDICAL

First published 1977
Reprinted 1979

Pitman Medical Publishing Co Ltd
PO Box 7, Tunbridge Wells,
Kent TN1 1XH, England

Associated Companies

UNITED KINGDOM
Pitman Publishing Ltd, London
Focal Press Ltd, London

USA
Pitman-Fearon Publishers Inc, California

AUSTRALIA
Pitman Publishing Pty Ltd, Melbourne

CANADA
Copp Clark Pitman, Toronto

NEW ZEALAND
Pitman Publishing NZ Ltd, Wellington

British Library Cataloguing in Publication Data
Lemin, Brian
    First line nursing management.
    1. Management   2. Nursing service administration
    I. Title
    658'.002'4613   RT89

    ISBN 0-272-79355-8

Text set in 10/11 pt IBM Press Roman, printed by photolithography
and bound in Great Britain at The Pitman Press, Bath

Contents

Preface

A popular radio quizmaster used to interview the contestants prior to them being asked the questions. One of his more frequent interviewing openings was to ask 'What is your most embarrassing moment?' From the management education viewpoint, I have two such incidents which have both embarrassed me, and (I hope) influenced me. The first incident occurred after I had given a lecture to a first line management course for nurses. A nurse in the audience said, 'You seem to know a little bit about our problems — what is your background?' To this day, I am ashamed to think that I could give a lecture to nurses and not have made it blatantly obvious by my concern for patients and for nursing, that I myself was a nurse. The second occasion was after I had given what I thought was an excellent lecture on management theory, and again a student from the back piped up and said, 'Mr Lemin, you have taken a great deal of time to tell us that *management is common sense with labels on it* !'

With these incidents still fresh in my mind, this book is an attempt by me — a nurse — to take a common sense look at management in order to remove some of the mystique out of the subject; to try to remove some of the barriers which the word 'management' arouses in many people.

The ideas I am presenting to you are stated in many ways throughout management literature. I have tried to bring together some of the fundamentals of management thought and action in order to give you an introduction to the subject in both theory and practice. I hope that it will be interesting pre-reading for your management course. I hope that during your course you will want to refer to it in order to see how to apply some of the industrial management concepts which may be presented to you; and after your course I hope that you will want to consult it for some clues as to how you might go about your particular management task.

B.L.

Acknowledgements

The material on pages 53–58 (including Table 3.1) was first published as 'Organisations and Their Processes' in the *Nursing Times* (1973), volume 69, number 24, and the section on Advertising (pages 89–94) (including Fig. 5.3) first appeared as an Occasional Paper, 'Recruitment Advertising', in the *Nursing Times* (4 June 1970). I am most grateful to the Editor for permission to reproduce this material, and repeat my thanks to the *Financial Times, Observer* and the *Sunday Times* for their guidelines to effective advertising.

For the four case studies, 'An Introduction to Peter's Ward' at the end of Chapter 6, 'Does She Exceed Her Duty?' at the end of Chapter 7, 'The Aggrieved Pathologist' at the end of Chapter 9 and 'But is the Report Fair?' at the end of Chapter 10, I am indebted to my friend and former colleague, Miss Vivien M. Jenkinson, DN(Lond), RegN, SRN, SCM, HonCert, Clinical Supervision (University of Toronto), now Senior Nursing Systems Analyst, The Hospital for Sick Children, Toronto, Ontario. My thanks are also due to Mr Alan Jones, Regional Training Officer, East Anglia Regional Hospital Board, for the case studies 'Tim' at the end of Chapter 4 and the Staff Selection exercises at the ends of Chapters 5, 11 and 12.

Figure 3.5 is from A. S. Tannenbaum (1968) *Control in Organizations,* New York and Maidenhead, McGraw-Hill, and I am most grateful to the author and the publishers for the permission to reproduce it here.

B.L.

Chapter 1

What is Management?

INTRODUCTION

It was quite a few years ago that I resolved never to introduce management to any group of students without first mentioning our patients. Since I originally made that resolution, on some occasions I have forgotten to do this, and without exception I have been brought down to earth very suddenly by a question or a challenge from some caring person in the audience about the relevance of management to her patients.

Here in its rightful place — the beginning of a book on management — I take the opportunity of not over-mentioning our patients, but putting them in their rightful place — which is at the pinnacle of the total management function.

Far too often diagrams and charts illustrating managerial relationships, or the structure of the hospital as an organisation, or even the delivery of health care to our patients and public, indicate that the highest, and apparently most important, person is some very senior member of 'the management', while the patient is relegated to the bottom of the page or not even mentioned!

How can this be in an organisation which owes its very existence to the prevention, control, curing or the eradication of ill health? The patient holds the top position in what I like to call the TRIANGLE OF CARE, about which the total management function revolves.

This trio holds the key to the reason for management, for it is here on the ward or in the patient's home that the process of caring is being enacted. Each member of that trio is playing her unique part in the healing process.

Were we considering just one of these trios, the need for management would hardly exist, but we are considering large numbers of these teams, and, if our patients are to get the best care we can offer within the resources at our disposal, we just have to organise it.

Not only do we have to arrange for the best doctoring and nursing of our patient, but we also have to make sure that he gets the right diet, that the ward is warm, that dressings are available, that he can be x-rayed, that he can be transported home . . . and I am sure you can add a great many other things that the patient, the nurse and the doctor need to enable them to do their job.

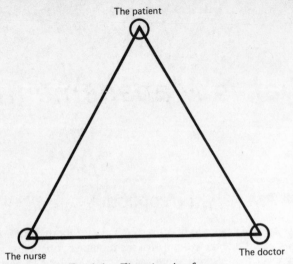

Fig. 1.1   The triangle of care.

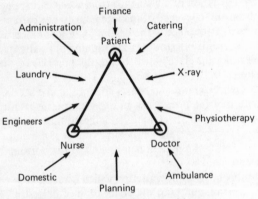

Fig. 1.2   A few of the enablers.

THE ENABLERS

We have now come to one answer to the question which this chapter heading posed: MANAGEMENT IS AN ENABLING PROCESS. The function of management is to enable our patient/doctor/nurse team to do their job as easily, as efficiently, as economically, as effectively and as humanly as possible.

While all three members of our caring team depend upon the whole range of supportive, enabling services, it would be true to say that nursing, more than any other profession in the Health Service, is dependent on its own enabling machinery to ensure that it functions effectively.

2

The main reason I put forward to justify this statement is the sheer numbers of nurses involved in delivering health care at the patient's bedside. Without organisation and coordination the nursing service would eventually collapse.

Let me illustrate by asking you to imagine that all nurse managers above Charge Nurse level just disappeared overnight! I wonder how long you could continue to work effectively without them? I think it would be quite a long time — certainly weeks, possibly many months — but eventually when groups of you met and started to discuss your work, you would soon decide amongst yourselves that to enable you to get on and do the work you like doing and are good at doing — patient care — it would be much better if one of you were appointed to do some of those tiresome jobs, such as sorting out holidays, replacing those nurses who left, organising a system with the X-ray Department which ensures you get the films in time for the Consultant's round; and in the course of time, she too would be asking for help, and before you know it, the old system of nurse managers would be back with you.

Management is an inevitable correlate of nursing numbers of patients. The second feature of the inevitability of nurse managers is related to TIME and DECISION MAKING.

The Ward Sister's pattern of decision making is such that she expects the results of decisions she makes to come to fruition almost immediately, or at least that day, with just a few exceptions. On the other hand, our senior nurse managers are making decisions related to the continuity of the nursing service which will only come to fruition in 1–2–3–5 or even 7 or 10 years' time!

While most of us had some reservations about the Salmon and Mayston Reports, one thing they did was to create two senior nursing management posts (Chief Nursing Officer and Principal Nursing Officer) whose holders not only had the time, but had the express brief, to represent nursing at the highest possible decision-making levels in the organisation, and to make plans for the continuing provision of patient care in the future.

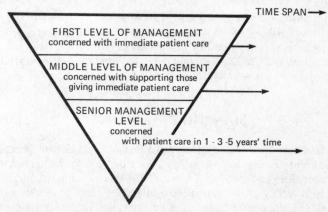

TIME SPAN →

FIRST LEVEL OF MANAGEMENT
concerned with immediate patient care

MIDDLE LEVEL OF MANAGEMENT
concerned with supporting those
giving immediate patient care

SENIOR MANAGEMENT
LEVEL
concerned
with patient care in 1 - 3 -5 years' time

Fig. 1.3   Concern for patient care related to time and level of management.

CASE STUDY — THE FIRST CHIEF NURSING OFFICER

The Chief Nursing Officer had not been in the post for more than three weeks, when one day the Group Secretary came into her office waving a sheaf of papers and exclaimed, 'Have you seen your student nurse recruitment figures?' (Incidentally, this statement shows the power which some Group Secretaries held before nursing management was fragmented.) 'You will have to get yourself over to Ireland for a fortnight, and bring back some nurses,' he continued.

'Yes, I have seen the figures,' the CNO replied. 'In fact, it was one of the first things I looked at when I came here, and I agree that we have to do something pretty quick to get our numbers up. What about sending Mr Bulloch, the Principal Tutor, to Ireland on a recruitment drive?'

'You don't want to do that — we will fix you up at a good hotel — you will have a lovely time — all expenses paid,' replied the Group Secretary.

'Well if he does not go, then it will have to be someone else, because it certainly is not my job,' the CNO replied firmly.

'Just sit down a minute will you?' she said, as by this time the Group Secretary was about to burst a blood vessel.

' I told you that I had seen these figures almost as soon as I came here, and I would like you now to listen to my plans to alleviate this problem; I have not had time to complete them yet, but here they are so far . . . .'

At this stage the Chief Nursing Officer outlined to the Group Secretary a long-term plan for: a part-time nursing recruitment officer; liaison with local schools; school/hospital links, where school leavers spend part of their last year in the hospital; a cadet scheme; a pre-nursing course; exhibitions; talks . . . and quite a number of other things, ending up by saying, 'And if I get your support for these plans, and they are implemented, I can guarantee you that in THREE TO FIVE YEARS we will not have any recruitment problem at all.'

The lessons from this story are that (1) she was concerned that something was done to solve the immediate recruitment problem, but felt that it was a task that should be delegated to one of her responsible staff, and (2) she felt that her greater responsibility was to ensure that this problem did not recur, and made long-term plans to secure the future of nurse recruitment.

I am pleased to tell you that at the time of writing this, four years after the incident, the CNO's prediction has come true, they have no student or pupil nurse recruitment problem.

MANAGEMENT IS PEOPLE

This far I have tried to show that in the final analysis all management is patient centred; that the patient/nurse/doctor team need help and support to enable them to function effectively; that this help and support is given by a wide variety of professions; that in nursing, more than most other professions, this help and support is most essential; that the enabling process in nursing administration is governed mainly by the degree of immediate

4

or long-term concern for patient care, depending on the level at which management operates.

It becomes very apparent as we explore management in the Health Services that not everyone is able to be directly involved in patient care, even if they want to be. This means that management can only influence patient care through those delivering that care – i.e. 'people'. Without management having concern for 'people', those 'people' caring for the patient will not be able to do their work effectively.

Just as I said earlier, that it is no good giving good patient care if the ward is freezing cold, or the food is inedible, neither can we expect our nurses to give of their best unless their basic needs are cared for; i.e. good working conditions, or a helpful, supportive environment, a good back-up service – all of which enable them to get on with their job of nursing their patients with the maximum of satisfaction, and the minimum of concern for those things other than nursing the patient back to good health.

Unfortunately, many of those who are actually involved in nursing patients are not able to nurse all the patients all the time. In nursing, once you get to any position of responsibility, it involves you in directing the work of others in order that all the patient care required is given at the right time and that the highest standards possible are achieved.

This leads us to our first definition of a manager, which is: 'A manager is a person who has so much work to do or is responsible for so much work, that she has to get others to do some of it for her.'

In other words, those who are managers have to do the nursing care which they would want to do – if it were physically possible – through others who do not have this same degree of responsibility.

This of course reinforces the first proposition that management is an enabling process, because if we accept that patient care is our responsibility, but we have so much of it to do that we have to have others to help us, then it is only proper for us to give them all the help and support to give that patient care which we would expect if we were doing it ourselves.

Another definition of a manager which parallels this last one is: 'A manager is a person who decides what has to be done and then gets others to do it.'

These definitions of managers have highlighted two things: the first introduced the concept of responsibility (i.e. being in a position in which you have legal or moral duties for which you are accountable to someone else), and the second pointed towards authority (i.e. the right to give orders and to control the work of others).

MANAGEMENT IS BEST USE OF RESOURCES

This far we have had a very inward look at management from the viewpoint of the 'caring professions', but the management activities of those even in the caring professions include the management of resources other than people. People management, or man management as it is often termed, is undoubtedly our most valuable resource, and remains our most important concern, but our management function would be incomplete unless we had responsibility and control of all the resources available to management.

One list of management resources all begin with the letter 'M', which serves as a good *aide-mémoire* when thinking about our total management responsibility. Here they are: men, money, materials, machinery and methods.

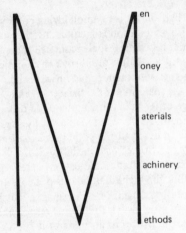

en

oney

aterials

achinery

ethods

Fig. 1.4   Resources at the disposal of management.

The greater part of this book is about the human aspects of management, so I will not dwell on it at this stage. Come to that, I do not plan to treat the remaining resources in great depth, rather introduce you to the wider concept of management by giving you an appreciation of the responsibilities of management for the effective use of these resources.

Money

We often think that our most scarce resource is that of staff, but the fact is that in many cases even if we had the staff we would not have the money available to pay them!

It would be a fairly general truism to state that in the last analysis management decision making hinges on the availability of finance. This has been formally recognised by the inclusion of a treasurer as a full member of management teams at the District, Area and Regional levels of National Health Service management. All other members of these teams are those who have 24-hour responsibility for patients, therefore the treasurer inclusion is based on a totally different criterion — the recognition of the fact that management and money cannot be divorced.

It could be argued that a person is an incomplete manager unless she has control over the financial aspects of her management responsibility, but for most nurse managers embarking on their management function and management education, this will be a responsibility which they will gladly relinquish.

The first reason most managers give me for their reluctance to actively seek financial management responsibilities is a very valid point. They very rightly say that they have enough on their hands ensuring the effective delivery of health care to their patients and public without having to bother about finance.

The second reason I find more difficult to understand, though I must admit to a certain feeling of sympathy towards their argument. It is simply that they state, 'Oh, I am hopeless where money is concerned.'

If this is indeed true, the reason can only be that nurses have been paid so little in the past that decisions regarding what to do with their money have been so clear cut (i.e. only enough to spend on basic essential needs) that they have not had the practice of juggling with the '£ in the purse'.

Though times have been tough for nurses, I cannot really think that this argument can be generally applicable. What could be validly argued is that nurses have had no experience in having the responsibility for LARGE sums of money, and therefore we rationalise our natural reluctance to take on this responsibility by saying that we are 'no good at it'.

Without wishing to over-simplify money management, the principles of handling large amounts of money are essentially the same as handling our own salaries. Having discovered how much we have in our pay cheque, we analyse our needs for the month, evaluate their relative priorities and use the money we have to meet as many of these needs as we can.

We go through various exercises in order to get the best value for the money we spend. For example, aerosol spray deodorants do not last as long as roll-on deodorants, both of which are equally efficient, but the latter is appreciably cheaper; or we may decide that it is better to buy one good-quality article of clothing, as it will be cheaper in the long run even though the initial outlay is greater.

We make similar decisions in the evaluation of management spending. In my own experience I have seen the disastrous consequences of buying a cheap but awkward to handle piece of equipment rather than a more expensive but more convenient nursing aid. It was a patient hoist that we left standing idle almost from the day it was bought because it was so difficult and time consuming to manipulate.

The trend in modern nursing management is to delegate financial responsibility to the level nearest to patient care as is deemed practical. For example, managers at the first level may well be required to handle a small nursing equipment/budget and should most distinctly be consulted on matters such as ward upgrading and major equipment purchases.

Do not be put off by the jargon of financial management. An ESTIMATE is a statement of the cost of things you would like to have, or the cost of running your particular management responsibility. You should try to make this as accurate and reasonable as you can.

After this has gone through the channels, you will receive a BUDGET (usually much less than what you asked for in your estimate!) This is the amount of money you have actually been allocated.

You will then be expected to exercise BUDGETARY CONTROL, which means that you will be responsible for keeping your expenditure within your financial allocation.

There is little doubt in my mind that the principle of delegating financial responsibility to its most practical level will pay dividends. For example, if we nurses had been involved in buying that dust-collecting hoist, I am sure I would have had a much more positive incident to illustrate my point.

Materials

Nursing is a large user of materials. The selection and supply of materials has become a specialist activity in which nurses are only involved in a consultative capacity in decisions affecting materials relating to the nursing function. Needless to say, economy in the use of materials is one of the main responsibilities of the nurse manager. This does not mean economy at the cost of service to patients. On the contrary, our patients must have the material which their care requires. It means that we must ourselves become cost-conscious, and teach our staff to develop this awareness.

As always, we must use these principles with understanding. Recently I heard of a patient being discharged for daily dressings by the District Nurse, and to return to the hospital in five days for possible removal of sutures. He was discharged with just ONE sterile dressing pack. At home the District Nurse, in order to get dressings for three days, had to get the doctor to write a prescription for comparatively LARGE AMOUNTS of cotton wool and gauze, most of which was never used by the nurse or the patient − at least for the purpose it was intended.

Another point which must be discussed under this heading is the 'flow' of materials. This is best explained by asking you to observe a queue of vehicles at a set of traffic lights. You will notice that when the lights are red there are some cars that are stationary, others moving up to join them, then again some stationary cars, and then some moving up to join the queue.

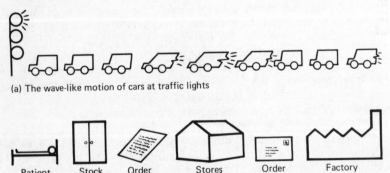

(a) The wave-like motion of cars at traffic lights

Patient   Stock   Order   Stores   Order   Factory

(b) The wave-like movement of materials

Fig. 1.5

8

This same wave-like motion occurs with stores and the use of other materials. There are those you are using on patients (moving), there are those in your store cupboard (stationary), there are those which you have ordered (moving), there are those in the central stores (stationary), there are those which the central stores have ordered (moving), and those in the factory (stationary).

This characteristic movement of materials can be and is calculated quite accurately by those managers who specialise in stores/laundry, etc. They are applying the formula associated with a management technique known as the 'queueing theory'. The point I want to make about this is that just as any 'road up' blockage at the traffic lights causes problems a long way back in the traffic flow, so our 'blockage' in the use of materials causes a great deal of difficulty in the materials queue which other managers in the service are concerned with.

We are probably most guilty of a blockage offence when we hoard materials; this can have disastrous effects on the efficiency of things like topping-up systems. A hospital introduced a laundry topping-up service, having noted the rate of linen usage by all wards over a period of six months, made a few simple calculations and come to a figure for the number of sheets required, including an emergency supply and a Bank Holiday supplement.

It was quite a struggle to persuade the committee to buy the extra sheets required, but finally they agreed, and so they introduced the scheme after a series of staff meetings.

Only four or five weeks after its introduction, the Laundry Supervisor went to the Matron with a complaint that he did not have enough sheets for the topping-up system to work as planned. Needless to say, Matron registered her disbelief, but he soon proved his point and so she investigated. Firstly, she checked his sums – they were correct, so then she visited the wards, and there found her answer . . . a great deal of hoarding by two wards, and just a little by the others.

When asked why they had started to hoard, she found that two of the Charge Nurses were sure the system would not work, so at the first sign that the laundry was having difficulty, the other Charge Nurses started laying aside their little insurance policy. The fact that it was now not working was proof to all that they had been right all along. Matron had a very difficult job to persuade them that their hoarding was the cause.

I am pleased to say that it all worked out well in the end and, except for very abnormal times, has operated well, with only the tiniest amount of hoarding going on!

Machinery

Perhaps we are least of all concerned in the management of machinery. We certainly use machines in the clinical situation, and much of it is very sophisticated.

Theatres, intensive care units and renal dialysis units are probably more intimately concerned with this aspect of management, but it would be true to say that technicians and engineers cope with the management aspects of this asset very well.

We have our part to play by reporting defects or malfunctioning of equipment, and in seeing that the equipment is serviced regularly. With respect to maintenance, many organisations have what is called a planned maintenance programme, which aims to reduce malfunctioning by ensuring that all equipment is serviced regularly, even though it appears to be working well. This is basically a preventative service, rather as we like to prevent people from being ill.

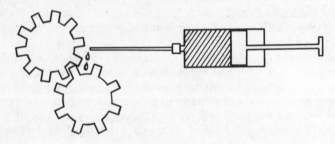

Fig. 1.6   'Immunisation' of machinery (planned preventative maintenance).

Methods

We may not be greatly involved in managing machinery, but we do have a great deal of responsibility over choosing the methods we use in carrying out our patient care. I do not want to dwell on such things as task assignment versus patient assignment versus team nursing, as these are quite well dealt with in books and articles dealing with ward management and patient care management.

There are two things I want to emphasise: the first is the need for continual questioning of our routines and procedures, and the second is the effective use of time, which is the main resource of methods.

Figure 1.7 is a check-list chart which I would like to think that many of you will apply to many aspects of your work, especially those things you have been doing the longest.

Let me give you an incident in my own career which makes one point related to the questioning of routines. When I went into general nursing, I had already completed my RMN, and therefore I was supposed to be competent in basic nursing care. Within a day or so on the ward, I was assigned to take the temperatures of the 24 patients, a task which I happily undertook. ONE AND A HALF HOURS LATER, I reported to Sister that I had completed the task, and received an icy comment, which I, in my innocence, could not understand. Had I not taken each patient's temperature for a full three minutes, and counted his pulse and respirations, and charted them correctly? What more could I do to please her?

It was not long before I realised my mistake — I had done the job

10

Description of Element		Reference _____
		Page _____
		Date _____

The Present Facts		Alternatives	Selection for Development
WHAT is achieved?	WHY?	What ELSE could be achieved?	What SHOULD be achieved?
HOW is it achieved?	WHY that way?	How ELSE could it be achieved?	How SHOULD it be achieved?
WHEN is it achieved?	WHY then? (What determines?)	When ELSE could it be achieved?	When SHOULD it be achieved?
WHERE is it achieved?	WHY there?	Where ELSE could it be achieved?	Where SHOULD it be achieved?
WHO achieves it?	WHY that person?	Who ELSE could achieve it?	Who SHOULD achieve it?

Fig. 1.7   Method study: guide to the use of the critical examination sheet.

properly! Each patient — individually — three minutes! I did not know about a row of thermometers in patients' mouths, effectively silencing them or asphyxiating them. I did not know about 30-second or 10-second pulses or other short cuts. I did not know that patients' respirations are almost invariably 18 per minute!

I soon fell into the ways of the ward, but, significantly, Sister was soon asking why we had to take everyone's temperature twice or four times a day, even though many of them were almost perfectly fit except for the occasional investigation required.

The result of this question was that soon we only took the temperature of those who were ill, and then we had time to take them properly — which was to everyone's benefit.

Time

Now let us look more specifically at time. Parkinson's law states, 'Work expands so as to fill the time available for its completion.' This can be illustrated in certain instances by looking at a person's first day at work. Unless the first few days are carefully planned by her managers, it can appear to the new employee that there is very little work to perform.

Within weeks, however, she becomes inundated with work . . . work has expanded.

Time and methods are very closely linked with each other, but perhaps time is the more important of the two. In a sense, time cannot be wasted, only used unwisely or ineffectively. It has been said that time is scarce, perishable and most elusive. How, then, can time be used for maximum performance?

When I was Nursing Administrator in the community, I had an office in the Health Department which contained all sections of the community service.

A new head of a section was appointed, and was given an office next to mine. As he was not in the nursing service I did not meet him for some time, other than nodding to him in the corridor, but I became fascinated by him.

My reason for this was the frequent appearance on his door of signs which said, 'Back at 3.47 p.m.', or 'In at 10.08 a.m.' or '2.59 p.m.'. One day I could not stem my unquenched curiosity, and made a point of meeting him to see just what kind of a 'nut' this man was.

Fig. 1.8

When I actually met him, I found he was a very nice chap whom I took to immediately, and we became good friends. One day I came right out with it, and asked him what all this '3.33 p.m.' and '2.41 p.m.' tomfoolery was about, and this was his answer:

'Brian,' he said, 'for a long time now I have been aware that time was my greatest resource, and I practise making myself continually aware of time in everything I do. If I sit down to write a report, I say, 'This should take me two hours,' and if it takes me more than that, I question its length or ask myself if I have been too detailed or verbose. If it takes less time, then I ask myself whether it is complete or if it is effective. As to the signs on the door, I estimate how long it will take me to get to my visit, carry out my business and return. I then add my estimate to the time I leave, and that is the figure you see on my door.'

His message was, 'just making yourself aware of time, makes you save time'. Perhaps he applied this rather fanatically, but he did a lot of effective work in the time available. But there are other things we can do to use time effectively, besides just being aware of it.

The awareness of time which my colleague taught me had one very important element in it. That was 'planning'; and to plan the effective use of your time you must be aware of the various time elements which most jobs have. J. Cooper, in his book, *How to Get More Done in Less Time*, suggests four time elements.

1. *Creative Time*

'Creative time' is that portion of time you spend thinking about the task; how you are going to set up the job, and get it done in the shortest time with the minimum of effort. Oh yes, there is no shame involved in getting a job done as easily as possible.

I have always maintained that you can make a job as easy or as hard as you like, and, whatever you choose to make it easy or hard, it is doubtful whether the quality changes very much. I think of the many nurses in our ranks who consider that their effort and dedication can be measured by the number of extra hours they put in. This, in my view, is a doubtful supposition.

Time taken to think creatively about a job is time well spent, and pays a high rate of interest.

2. *Preparatory Time*

This is the time you spend in advance of the job, getting everything ready, doing your home-work, organising your resources; perhaps getting ready for a good start tomorrow in a similar way to what you do prior to going away on your holidays. All the things you do to ensure that all goes well when you actually do the task.

3. *Productive Time*

The task, your job, the hard core of your time — this is premium time. Try to keep unscheduled jobs to a minimum, do your planning well, make a realistic estimate of how much time each job involves, and stick to it. Monitor yourself against your own time standards, which is the very thing my 'back at 3.33 p.m.' colleague was doing.

4. *Overhead Time*

This concerns those things which relate specifically to your work as a whole as well as to your position in the organisation. The time you have to spend in personal relations activities, that extra bit of coaching your subordinate requires, your office housekeeping, dealing with visitors, etc. Something of this has to be built into every task or into every day; they are important to your job, but put them into the right perspective against the other time elements we have discussed.

Using Time

I have said that time could not be wasted, but only used unwisely or ineffectively. Let's now look at the ineffective use of the time resource.

Getting Started

Some people are at their best in the morning . . . others? Well!!! Whether or not the morning is your best time, you can easily be guilty of wasting time getting started. It is so easy and so natural to socialise on your way to your place of work; you just have to have a cup of coffee before you can get started; just the odd personal phone call before you get stuck in; and before you know it, it is time for the official coffee break, and you have hardly done a thing.

Another common occurrence is to do those jobs you like doing first, no matter where they fit into your priorities for the day. I like to look at work as a target: those things I must do (bullseye), those things I should do (inner), and those things which are fun to do (outer).

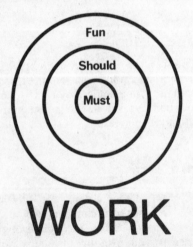

Fig. 1.9   One way of looking at the division of work.

14

If you are anything like me, then your natural inclinations are to do the things you enjoy doing first, then you will probably get a few of the 'should' things later on, and you will no doubt delegate the 'must' things. This is, of course, the great problem, schooling our natural inclinations so that we correctly define our priorities and tackle them in an efficient manner — procrastination is the thief of time. Let's look on the bright side for a moment, for I have frequently found that the 'must' things have turned out to be just as much fun as the 'fun' things were.

Being Disorganised

This is usually most apparent the more a person is under pressure or over-worked. Yet the very reason this condition exists in the first place is because your disorganisation allowed it to happen. Do you handle too many kinds of duties? A classic example of this affecting nursing was the tremendous non-nursing-duties involvement by our profession. We were often so involved with these that we almost allowed THEM to become our priorities instead of PATIENT CARE.

Do you launch into tasks without first thinking them through? Do you accept tasks without evaluating their impact on your work? Are you spending your time on things which contribute to you getting your job done well?

If not, then here is a rule of thumb:
(1)   Assign priorities to your tasks (just what should I as a . . . be spending my time on?).
(2)   Allocate time according to your priorities.
(3)   Schedule the best time for doing tasks.
(4)   Anticipate problems and the methods for handling them.
(5)   Delegate.
(6)   Avail yourself of modern aids to work.

Diversions

It is easy to find yourself going up a diversion and, even though it might turn out to be a more interesting route, it will put a lot of mileage and time on your clock. It is really a question of what you find yourself doing during your premium, hard-core work time. Socialising, personal affairs, spending too much time with people who visit you, making yourself too freely available? Take your choice or even add a few; they all waste time.

Excessive Involvement

This I feel is a trait which nursing harbours: 'It's quicker, easier, better if I do it myself', 'I cannot delegate as I cannot be sure they will do it how I want them to do it'. Perhaps you work too long on a problem so that you obtain diminishing returns from your effort. Sometimes we do not close discussion when it has apparently become fruitless. Stand back and take a cool objective look at your involvement.

Fleeting Contacts

Depending on your job, you could be spending as much as 70–80% of your time in communicating with others in short episodes. I think back to the time when I was Charge Nurse, when someone asked me to keep a record of how often I was contacted by my staff. The end result was staggering, and although it was not possible or desirable to eliminate all of these contacts, I found that by spending time planning the work, I had longer unbroken periods of working time which were very much more fruitful as the result.

Grasshopping

Jumping from one thing to another, one problem, one subject and back again. This again is symptomatic of the need to plan and to arrange your work as sequentially and as logically as you can.

Unfortunately, the nature of our work can be likened to a twisted rope of many fibres; each fibre is a problem, the fibre comes to the top in episodes, some short, some long, but each needs tidying up, or the rope will fray.

While I hope this illustration will temper my optimism with reality, the benefits of work planning will result in the more effective use of time.

Having discussed so far the people aspect of management and the things (resources) aspect of management, I want to deal with the final part of my attempt to define what management is.

MANAGEMENT IS IDEAS

The need for management is created by (1) people, (2) things and (3) ideas. People require leadership that influences them towards accomplishing the desired tasks or objectives.

Things require to be dealt with, those day-to-day elements which require our administrative skills.

Ideas require that the imagination used is channelled towards thinking in terms of not only the task to hand but also the organisation as a whole.

These ideas are often referred to as conceptual skills or cognitive ability. I find it best to describe these skills by stating two things:
(1)   We are all very good at doing what we are told.
(2)   It is very hard to decide what has to be done, and more especially so the more senior the position you hold in management.

Conceptual skills require that we FORMULATE NOTIONS. Where from? How? Why? Yes, indeed, these are difficult questions to answer.

How do you pluck ideas from out of the sky? What gives you that idea? The answer is probably a mixture of many things all contributing to make a viable proposition, but these skills are vital to an organisation which does not want to become stagnant.

It requires an ability to analyse problems; we do that by gathering facts, ascertaining causes, developing solutions and planning their implementation.

The more a manager gains experience, the greater becomes her awareness of these skills and their application.

It requires a manager to pay special attention to the interaction between different parts of the job or different parts of the organisation. She should be able to visualise and interpret the cause and effect of events, some of which apparently have only passing interest to the manager, so that when viewed as a whole, she will recognise a relationship and take action which will either solve or eliminate a problem and lead to greater efficiency.

Fig. 1.10   Conceptual ability is the transferring of ideas gleaned from many sources into appropriate managerial action.

The foregoing discussion on 'What is Management?' can only be a start. As we move into the next chapter we will be continuing this discussion by posing the question 'Is management an ART or a SCIENCE?' and then trace the various approaches to management before discussing how we manage.

REFERENCES AND FURTHER READING

Brown, J. A. C. (1954). *The Social Psychology of Industry: human relations in the factory*. Harmondsworth, Middx., Penguin.

Cooper, J. (1963). *How to Get More Done in Less Time.* Tadworth, Surrey, World's Work Ltd.

Falk, R. (1970). *The Business of Management: art or craft?* Harmondsworth, Middx., Penguin.

Fisk, H. L. (1969). *Principles of Management.* Cincinnati, Ohio, South Western Publishing Co.

Jay, Antony (1967). *Management and Machiavelli.* London, Hodder & Stoughton. (Also published by Pelican Books, 1970.)

Mayston, E. L. (Chairman) (1969). *Report of the Working Party on Management Structure in the Local Authority Nursing Services*; Department of Health and Social Security, and Scottish Home and Health Office. London, HMSO.

Moonman, E. (1961). *The Manager and the Organization.* London, Tavistock Publications. (Also published by Pan Books, 1965.)

Salmon, Brian (Chairman) (1966). *Report of the Committee on Senior Nursing Staff Structure;* Ministry of Health, and Scottish Home and Health Department. London, HMSO.

Stewart, R. (1963). *The Reality of Management.* London, William Heinemann Ltd. (Also published by Pan Books, 1967.)

Webster, Eric (1964). *How to Win the Business Battle.* London, John Murray.

Management–
an Art or Science?

If management is an ART, then we must be looking towards human motives and work; if it is to be a SCIENCE, then we should be examining the elements in the actual work itself.

During our professional training we are taught a great many facts, the rights and wrongs of nursing, and a series of exact procedures for every situation. When, as qualified nurses, we make our first foray into management education, we are faced, perhaps for the first time in our lives, with situations where there are no rights or wrongs, and no set answers to our problems.

When we turn for guidance to management books or management lecturers, we are often overwhelmed by the torrent of conflicting advice to which we are subjected.

At various times managers, writers and researchers have made various pronouncements on 'How to Manage', and each pronouncement has its followers. You will have to make up your own mind, and to help you, I am going to briefly trace the history of management thinking, placing special emphasis on those who have made a particular impact on management, and about whom most management courses will have expected you to have read.

HOW IT BEGAN

Jethro, the father-in-law of Moses, is often quoted as the first management consultant, but for practical management ability we must go back even further to Joseph, who handled Egypt's agricultural policies with the utmost efficiency.

Without much problem we can trace the development of management principles from the Hebrews to the Chinese ... the Greeks ... the Italians, right through to the Industrial Revolution in Britain.

It is somewhat later than this that I want to start the survey in detail, with the commencement of what has become known as the 'Scientific Management Movement' or 'School', whose founder was undoubtedly F. W. Taylor.

FREDERICK WINSLOW TAYLOR (1856–1915)

Taylor is usually described as being born of well-to-do parents. The importance of this is reflected in the excellent educational opportunities which his parents afforded him. His trips to Europe and periods of school in France and Germany gave him a first-class background for a career in law which was to commence in Harvard.

Eye trouble (brought about by long hours of study under a paraffin lamp) made him consider an alternative career, so in 1875 he began an apprenticeship as a machinist and turner.

Though his eye trouble had proved temporary, he enjoyed his work and soon gained promotion on account of his superior education. He did not enjoy the clerical jobs which this promotion gave him, but while he was in one of these posts (in a tool room) he began to formulate his ideas, which were later to form the basis of his approach to management.

It was the thought of standardisation which occupied his mind. How long did a particular job take? Was it always done the same way? Was that method the most efficient? Gradually through a series of experiments he developed the concept of 'time and motion' studies; the total flow of work from entry into the workshop to completion and despatch; the setting of working standards both in quantity and quality of output.

He conducted most of these experiments while he was a foreman. Having come up from the shop floor, he knew the tricks of the trade, and proved to be a hard taskmaster.

He asked the machinists to produce more – that did not work; he operated a lathe himself to prove that his request was reasonable – that did not work. Finally he brought in intelligent labourers, trained them as machinists, and, in return for the opportunity of learning a good trade, they were to do a fair day's work – but that did not work.

What Taylor was experiencing was the tremendous pressure from working associates to do only as much work as would allow them to get by. (We still experience this in industry today – most of you will recall seeing newspaper articles about groups of workers wanting management to get rid of a man who is 'working too hard'!)

Taylor cut their pay by half, and even then it took some time before they finally increased their production . . . but then what happened? The men began to deliberately break their tools or machines by way of protest.

Taylor made them pay for all breakages, accidents or not; what a fight it was – three years of battling before he finally won through. The fault he decided was that of management who did not know how to gauge a 'fair day's work' accurately, so he pioneered the science of measuring each element of a man's work, thus doing away with the rule-of-thumb method.

His principles of scientific management did not stop with time and motion; he had a great deal more to say, but perhaps the three most important areas were:

(1)   Selection of the right man for the job.
(2)   Emphasis on the ONE RIGHT WAY of doing the job.

(3)   Ensure control is in the hands of the supervisors who must decide
the methods, time study and incentives to be used.

It is most notable that for all Taylor's commitment to the scientific
method of management he stated, 'There is another type of scientific
investigation which should receive special attention, namely, the accurate
study of the motives which influence men.' (Urwick and Brech, 1945.)

I think he, too, was questioning whether management was an ART or
SCIENCE'

OTHER WRITERS OF THE SCIENTIFIC SCHOOL

Strangely, Britain did not take up 'Taylorism' for many years, and the
early scientific writers are almost exclusively American.

Frank Gilbreth (1868–1924)

You will hear of people like Frank Gilbreth (incidentally, of *Cheaper by
the Dozen* fame), a bricklayer by trade, promoted to estimator, thence to
supervisor and management. He and his wife, Lillian, took a particular
interest in 'motion study' and developing man to his fullest potential by
training, work methods, improved tools and good working environment.

Henry Gantt (1861–1919)

His development of the 'task and bonus plan' is the basis of many
incentive bonus schemes of today. For all his bonus plans, charts and
production control methods, he always emphasised that, 'In all problems
of management, the human element is the important one'.

The Taylor, Gantt, Gilbreth trio form the basis of the scientific school
of management which has been developed over the years, until now in the
computer age it has become both a sophisticated management tool and a
simple common-sense approach to management efficiency.

THE HUMAN RELATIONS SCHOOL

In 1913, a book was published entitled *Psychology and Industrial
Efficiency*. Its author was Dr Hugo Munsterberg, a Harvard professor who
had studied at the first 'laboratory' for the study of human behaviour in
Leipzig in 1885. This laboratory was set up in 1879 by Wilhelm Wundt.

From this, and the inevitable recognition by our 'scientific trio' that
the individual is central in any working situation, we can trace the origin
of the 'Behavioural School', whose approach to management was to
emphasise individual and group motivation and relationships.

21

We have already established in Chapter 1 that 'managers get things done through people', so for us it is quite easy to understand the necessity to study the workers and their needs, but the late nineteenth century had a different viewpoint.

It was therefore quite revolutionary when a Harvard associate professor conducted some experiments at the Hawthorne plant of the Western Electric Company in Chicago.

Elton Mayo (1880–1949)

(George) Elton Mayo was the man mainly responsible for these experiments, which began in the 1920s. He was born in Australia, and trained as a psychologist. During his academic career, he pursued the study of social and industrial relationships.

His work was characterised by being practical and experimental rather than theoretical, and the 'Hawthorne Experiments' or 'Studies' were to be the first significant milestone of the behavioural school.

The Hawthorne Experiments

Mayo's experiments centred on a five-girl team of telephone assembly girls, whose productivity record had to be clearly defined prior to the experiments.

This group were moved to a separate room, but with all conditions standardised to those previously experienced in the main assembly room. After a period of five weeks, Mayo commenced a series of experiments to investigate fatigue and work output.

First, he introduced a 5-minute rest period at 10 a.m. and 2 p.m. Later these breaks were increased to 10 minutes. Six 5-minute rest periods per day were introduced, then back to two 10-minute breaks per day but with light refreshments given.

They shortened the working day by one hour; they reduced the working week by one day.

These experiments were conducted over many months, and the results were staggering! In every case productivity increased with each innovation (not enough to compensate for the loss of a whole day's work when they stopped Saturday work, but certainly their daily output increased during that period).

Mayo was delighted. But to follow his experimental discipline he had to verify his theory, so he eliminated all the experimental innovations and went back to the normal, pre-experimental working conditions. The result? Productivity further increased!

He did all sorts of things during these experiments. One series tested the effect of various levels of lighting. Output rose when lighting levels were increased, and, to Mayo's consternation, ROSE YET AGAIN when they were decreased to the minimum for working!

It is beyond the scope of this book to describe more of Mayo's 20 years of experimenting; suffice to say that these were the most comprehensive studies ever undertaken, and the results of Mayo's work influenced every human relations manager or writer, ever since.

Mayo's eventual conclusion from his work was that the most powerful factors influencing an employee's behaviour were those emanating from the worker's participation in social groups.

Mayo's girls developed a sense of belonging, the supervision they were subjected to was interesting and sympathetic, rather than authoritarian. If management could manage employees in such a way that they felt that they belonged to a cohesive work group, the sense of belonging was more important to them than anything else.

Mary Parker Follett (1865?–1933)

Mary Follett, a political scientist and philosopher, who studied at Harvard and Cambridge, was to play a very important part in developing the behavioural aspects of management.

Her main area of study was the basic human emotions and forces which underline the process of administration and organisation.

She was a woman of wide interests, an authoress, the founder of neighbourhood schemes in Boston, an educational campaigner, a vocational counsellor, and much more besides.

She frequently visited England to study and to lecture; in fact, she spent the final five years of her life in this country.

Her work did more than anyone else's to reconcile the scientific and behavioural managerial schools.

Her concept of leadership was totally opposite to the widely held concept of power and authority. It was not to be a burden to oppress employees with, but rather a lively stimulating activity for both manager and the managed.

Her concept of management was centred upon coordination . . . by direct contact with the people concerned. She saw coordination as a continuous process found in the initial stages of endeavour, and as a reciprocal relation to all aspects of a situation.

Force was impotent — consent was imperative. The human group has a life that is more than just the sum of the individual lives composing it. It is this plus factor that is so significant to management.

Other Writers of the Behavioural School

Oliver Sheldon emphasised management's social responsibility; Chester I. Barnard applied sociological concepts to management. These are but two of the writers who were both influenced by the behavioural school, and also contributed to it in some way. To these I will add some contemporary writers when dealing with their particular contribution to management.

Right now I must endeavour to answer that question . . . 'Management
– an ART or a SCIENCE?'

THE ANSWER

Should the answer be 'COMPROMISE'? Probably not: it would not be
fair to say that the answer lies in between the two schools, or even with
one school or the other.

Both approaches have amply proved their case – a combination of
both would undoubtedly bring about greater efficiency.

I think that management is both an art AND a science, and, as such, is
evolving and developing as more and more research is carried out on its
activities, and as the industrial society is changing.

There are, no doubt, human motives in work which we have not yet
discovered; there are, no doubt, elements in work which we have not yet
analysed.

Others who have followed Mayo and Taylor are adding to both sides
of the argument – filling in the gaps. Meanwhile, you who are managing
have to 'decide what needs to be done, and then get others to do it'. Be
it an art or a science, we cannot keep arguing about it; we must get on
with the job.

THE MANAGEMENT CYCLE

A large number of studies have been made as to the processes by which
managers manage. What do they do first? What do they do last? What do
they do in between?

And what are their answers? They are as many and varied as there are
researchers. In preparing to write this chapter, I studied many different
writers on the management process, and found between them 12 different
management cycles, and 19 different management functions within these
cycles.

Let us have a look at some of them.

Longenecker (1973): proposes the shortest of those I surveyed:
Decision making → Organising (direction and motivation) → Control.

In contrast to this, Dale and Michelon (1969) have eight functions:
Planning → Organising → Staffing → Directing → Control → Innovation →
Representation → Communication.

The next three, you will notice, have quite a lot in common.
Koontz and O'Donnell (1972):
Planning → Organising → Staffing → Directing → Controlling.

Greenwood (1965):
Planning → Decision making → Organising → Staffing → Directing and
Leadership → Controlling.

Massie (1971):
Decision making → Organising → Staffing → Planning → Controlling → Communicating → Directing.

Gross (1968) heads up the final four theories which I propose to quote, all of which are simple and similar:
Decision making → Communicating → Planning → Activating → Evaluating.

Johnson, Kast and Rosenzweig (1973):
Planning → Organising → Controlling → Communicating.

Newman, Summer and Warren (1972):
Organising → Planning → Leadership → Controlling.

Wren and Voich (1976):
Organising → Planning → Leadership → Controlling.

A combined list of the functions which I have surveyed follows:

Activating	Innovating
Administering	Investigating
Commanding	Leading
Communicating	Motivating
Controlling	Organising
Coordinating	Planning
Decision making	Representing
Directing	Securing efforts
Evaluating	Staffing
Formulating purpose	

I found that this survey amazed me, confused me and delighted me; the latter because no one could prove me wrong whatever cycle I decided to follow!

So . . . from all of these, whom do I choose? Well, I plump for a man named Henri Fayol.

Henri Fayol (1841–1925)

Fayol was a mining engineer, who took over an ailing mining company and turned it into a profitable business.

His book, *General and Industrial Management*, originally published in 1916, contains his analysis of the things he did as a successful practising manager.

His book had a tremendous influence on managers and their thinking. For the first time he made people realise that managers were not 'born', but could be 'made'. He pointed out that successful managers work in a systematic way even though they themselves never perhaps realise it. He provided managers with a framework from which they could clarify their thinking about what it is they have to do.

25

This framework is what we are going to use for a similar purpose, i.e. to help us look systematically and in greater depth at what we as managers have to DO.

Firstly, Fayol said we had to:

(1) Forecast; i.e. 'examine the future'.
(2) Plan; i.e. make plans to suit the forecast.
(3) Organise; i.e. build up the structure of the undertaking.
(4) Motivate; i.e. maintain activity among personnel.
(5) Coordinate; i.e. harmonise activity and effort.
(6) Control; i.e. act on knowledge of results.

The cycle is best illustrated in the following model.

Fig. 2.1

I think that when I drew that cycle I should have put a double line down the middle like this . . .

Fig. 2.2

. . . because the more I study the model the more differences I can see between each side.

On the right I see activities that I can do at my desk; on the left I need to be out of my office most of the time to accomplish those activities.

What differences can you distinguish? What about . . . thinking (right); doing (left); administering (right); managing (left); future (right); present (left).

Write down some of your ideas of the differences.

Fayol used the words 'mechanics' (right) and 'dynamics' (left) to distinguish between the two sets of activities. There is no doubt they are different sets — I wonder if you would venture to say which were the most important, the mechanics or the dynamics?

Think about it for a bit.

While it is hard to apportion degrees of importance to that which should be considered as a whole, I have no doubt in my mind that for you, being introduced to the management function — and for nursing at large — the dynamics are the key to success.

No matter how well the mechanics have gone, unless the plan is implemented and the dynamics are right, there will be undoubted difficulties and problems. In nursing we have a real need on the dynamic side of our management. While our first and middle line managers are involved in the mechanics of management, they spend most of their time and effort on the dynamics of management.

This book is consciously slanted towards the dynamics, behavioural, people-orientated aspect of our work, but it would be wrong of me to ignore the thinking, innovating, cognitive aspects of management; so for the rest of this chapter I will survey Fayol's three mechanical functions: (1) forecasting, (2) planning and (3) organising.

Forecasting

As a definition I would offer that forecasting is 'The analysis of relevant information from the present and the past, in order to assess future developments'. This of course is a formal definition. A candidate at an interview when asked what forecasting was about said that 'The future is the immediate past and the present'.

Perhaps the best example of forecasting that we are all familiar with is weather forecasting, which, despite the subjective scepticism which many of us share, is really rather accurate when studied objectively.

Now I am no meteorologist, but I am given to understand that they work from as up-to-date information as they can on the current weather situation, and from this and their recorded and analysed information of similar situations in the past, they can predict what is probably going to happen in the future.

Similarly in management we endeavour to forecast what the future situation will be. In some situations we can forecast with almost complete certainty. For example, the Charge Nurse who says, 'I must have all my staff on duty on Tuesdays when Mr So and So and Mr Whatsisname both have their operating days'. Experience has enabled her to forecast a situation which demands every hand to be on deck.

In other situations it is less easy to forecast the future. Let us take the example of employing a new nurse. We are trying to find out how this nurse will work in the future — in flowery terms we are trying to 'prophesy' which of the candidates will perform best in our organisation.

Sometimes we make a 'good' appointment, and we have forecasted well; other times we make a 'bad' appointment, and thus emphasise our humanity — after all, if we were good prophets then we would have retired by now, having made a fortune on the football pools, horse racing, stock exchange, or whatever your particular interest may be.

What we have learnt from our experience of employing people is that while we do sometimes make mistakes, there are things which we can do to reduce the mistakes to a minimum.

How do we do this? The details are dealt with in Chapter 5, but for the purpose of illustrating the principles of forecasting, we could say that:
(1) We look into the past via the application form;
(2) We look at the present via references and the interview; then with all this information to hand;
(3) We predict the future and back our judgement by appointing the person.

So far we have looked at relatively simple forecasting techniques, but there are some very sophisticated methods of forecasting available to managers. One technique which I have frequently demonstrated is a simple 'simulation' exercise. From actual information on the numbers of emergency admissions to surgical wards over a six-month period, in a particular hospital, we set students the task of running 'wards' (on paper), admitting and discharging patients. I must emphasise that while these were 'paper' wards, every patient (and the information on that patient) had been a REAL patient during the survey. So it is a very realistic simulation.

From this simulation exercise we were able to demonstrate that the course participants were soon able to forecast very accurately the number of emergency admissions they would have in any one day! Yes — they were able to forecast such an apparent uncertainty as 'emergency admissions'. How? Because of a detailed analysis of the past, and the lessons learnt applied to the future.

Another way we were able to use that same exercise was to show them how to economise on bed movements when zoning of patients was done on a patient dependency basis.

At first almost every 'bed' was moved every day as the patient went from high to low dependency, but soon they were able to forecast accurately the dependency progression of each patient, and thus make the number of 'moves' minimal.

Forecasting is done by managers at all levels, and, as I explained in Chapter 1, the longer the time span you are forecasting over, the higher the degree of uncertainty, and the higher the risk or the less certain you can be.

Senior management, when they forecast, have to take into account many external factors — apparently unrelated to nursing — but none the less important to the outcome of the forecast.

As an example of this, at the time of writing this chapter, Britain is in the midst of an economic recession, with high unemployment and job uncertainties in the commercial companies. This has made the secure (even though lower paid) Health Service an attractive employment proposition. The result of this is that we have more staff than we have ever had; in some cases, more staff than we can afford to employ.

So in long-term forecasting we have to look at the conditions SURROUNDING our situation, as well as within our situation.

To sum up then: forecasting is a study of the past and the present, in order that we might make an educated guess at the future, and the reason we want to make this educated guess is so that we can PLAN.

Planning

A definition of planning is: 'Determining a course of action that enables the organisation to meet its stated objectives'.

It is essential to the formation of the plan that the forecasting exercise be completed first, for having an idea of the future enables you to make realistic objectives or goals which you desire to achieve. Knowing what you want to achieve is an essential step to making the plan, i.e. outlining the course of action you need to take in order to achieve your aims.

It is only since the reorganisation of the National Health Service that the term 'planning' when used within the NHS, has meant something other than capital planning (i.e. new buildings and suchlike). Now we have other kinds of planning, e.g. service planning (planning to ensure a good service and a continuing service to our patients and public) and also health care planning (planning to meet the health care needs and demands of our patients and public).

In the management context, however, there are other terms used. Examples are given below.

FUNCTIONAL plans are those made by each functional department, such as the personnel department's plans, the finance department's plans, the nursing service plans.

ORGANISATIONAL plans are those made at various levels within the organisation. These are:
(1) Corporate: top level multidisciplinary plans; say, Regional.
(2) Divisional: still multidisciplinary, but for a smaller section of the organisation; say, Area.
(3) Functional: back to the individual functions of the service; say, Divisional.
(4) Departmental: plans made at, say, Unit level.
(5) Subdepartmental: Ward level plans.

Some textbooks used the terms 'corporate', 'strategic' and 'tactical' to describe the various organisational planning processes.

Planning is also often decided according to time span, and in these cases the terms 'long range', 'medium range' and 'short term' are used; planning described according to the breadth and scope of the plans, uses the terms 'policy', 'procedures' and 'methods'.

Figure 2.3 tries to sort out these different types for you.

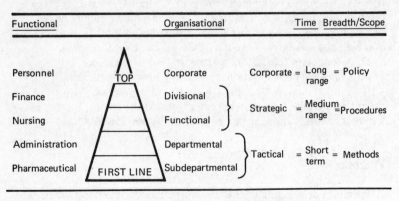

Fig. 2.3   Types of planning.

Planning Cycle

We are looking at planning as part of a management cycle, but planning itself has its own cycle.

Firstly, we outline our plan.

Secondly, we review it against the resources we have, and modify it as necessary.

Thirdly, we put the plan into operation.

Fourthly, we compare the results against our objective, and re-plan to correct any difficulties we have identified (Fig. 2.4).

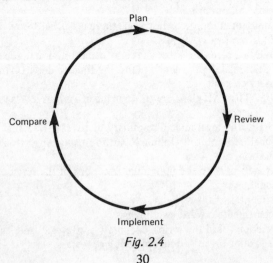

Fig. 2.4

30

Without much difficulty I could quote you many planning cycles, all of which have something to commend to you. Rather than quote a selection of these, I would prefer to draw your attention to the characteristics of a good plan.

I would say that plans should be:

(1) Clear.
(2) Simple in concept.
(3) Objective.
(4) Easily implemented.
(5) Easily controlled.
(6) Flexible.
(7) Complete.

The United States Navy has a slogan which we can apply to many of our management functions, but to planning in particular; it is KISS: KEEP IT SIMPLE — STUPID!

I rather like that typically American piece of advice. There are just a few more hints which might help you in your planning function.

(1) Do not start from where you are and project forward — this can be a very depressing exercise and it seems to emphasise the difficulties. Rather start with your end objective and think positively of what you need to do in order to reach that objective.

(2) Remember the time factor. The longer ahead you are planning for, the more time you need to spend doing your homework in order to reduce the element of risk to a minimum (good forecasting means good plans).

(3) Draw conclusions from ALL the data you have collected, not just isolated parts of it.

(4) Use the model in Fig. 2.5 to help you to remember the continuing planning process — always matching results against objectives.

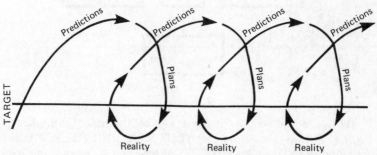

Fig. 2.5   Planning as a continuous rolling process.

(5) Finally, let me emphasise the closeness of forecasting to planning, by running our two definitions into one. I am sure you will agree that this makes the picture complete.

31

'The analysis of relevant information from the present and the past in order to assess future developments, so that a course of action may be determined to enable the organisation to meet its objectives.'

Organising

One of the important skills a manager must have, is that of determining appropriate relationships among the various parts of his organisation. In other words, ensuring that everybody is contributing effectively to the overall objectives of the organisation.

Traditionally − and in textbook treatment of the subject − our thoughts are turned to the organisational chart. This is the 'family tree' of the organisation, which I have already dealt with in Chapter 1, and which the Salmon and Mayston Reports, and now reorganisation, have made us all familiar with.

It aims to present, in a graphic form, the major functions and the lines of authority in an organisation.

The rules for constructing such a chart are quite simple. Usually we draw it vertically, as this is the most straightforward (but we may draw it horizontally − when it is read from left to right − or even circular − but this does become more complex).

The main relationships in an organisation are illustrated in Fig. 2.6.

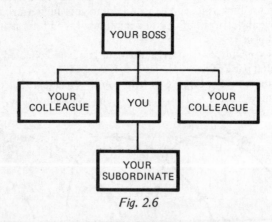

Fig. 2.6

The lines drawn between the boxes indicate the lines of authority. In Fig. 2.6, YOU have authority over YOUR SUBORDINATE; YOU have no authority over YOUR COLLEAGUES because you are on the same level as they are. YOU and YOUR COLLEAGUES are all responsible to YOUR BOSS through the line of authority drawn from your boxes to her.

To indicate the major functions you simply label the boxes with the job title and function performed.

A more complete and formal diagram is shown in Fig. 2.7.

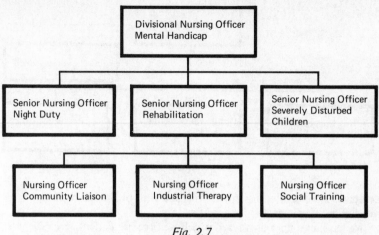

Fig. 2.7

As you can see in the rehabilitation sector which I have detailed, this has been organised under three units — though each one is different, when put together they form a complete rehabilitation programme for the residents.

I do not know that this approach to 'organising' is important enough to continue with — however, I will enumerate the ground rules for drawing a vertical chart, so that you can, if you wish, draw one yourself.

(1) Use rectangular boxes to identify people or jobs.
(2) The vertical placement of boxes indicates the relative positions of seniority (the highest box, the most senior).
(3) Boxes in a horizontal row should be of the same size.
(4) The vertical and horizontal lines show the flow of authority.
(5) The title and function should be shown in the box, and if possible include the name of the person.

A final rule, number 6, relates to staff positions, i.e. those members of staff who have advisory positions rather than actually managing subordinates. The best example would be the Area Nurse (Personnel), who advises the Area Nursing Officer on personnel matters, and does not manage subordinates herself.

The rule is that this type of position occupies a box just below the box of the person she reports to, but is joined to it by a dotted line, as shown in Fig. 2.8.

Incidentally, the term 'line manager' must now be clear to you, i.e. the manager who is in line authority in the organisation.

Having followed the traditional approach to the term 'organising', I want to apply these principles to your working situation.

You will not need to draw an organisational chart — it has probably been done. You are more interested in organising the work you have to do.

The principles are the same. You aim to ensure that all your sub-

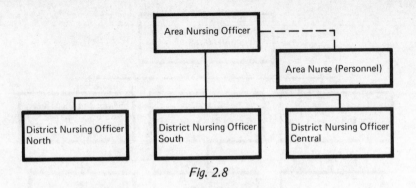

Fig. 2.8

ordinates are contributing to achieving the aims of the job, with the maximum of efficiency.

We have a number of ways in which we organise patient care. There is functional organisation: 'You do the dressings', 'You do the medicines', 'You do the injections'. Then there is team nursing: 'You four nurses are in charge of the total care of these eight patients'.

Perhaps you have to have a mixture of the two, as one Charge Nurse discovered when she introduced team nursing. Everything went fine until 10 a.m., when three teams descended on the medicine trolley all at the same time!

It was a simple matter to rectify by allocating that task on a functional basis.

In the second half of this book I hope to become more practical, and give you a plan to help you approach your work in an organised and systematic way, but for now I will leave you with the principles:
(1) Identify the tasks to be done.
(2) Allocate them to appropriately qualified and experienced persons.
(3) Ensure there is a minimum of overlap between tasks.
(4) Time tasks, and support for these tasks, so that resources are available at the right time and in the right place.
(5) Check on progress in an acceptable manner.

Well, so much for the mechanics of our management cycle. In the next chapter we will be dealing with the very important dynamics of management.

REFERENCES AND FURTHER READING

Dale, E. and Michelon, L. C. (1966). *Modern Management Methods.* Cleveland, Ohio, World Publishing Co. (Also published by Penguin, 1969.)

Drucker, P. F. (1955). *The Practice of Management.* London, William Heinemann. (Also published by Pan, 1968.)

Fayol, Henri (1949). *General and Industrial Administration.* Translated by Constance Storrs. London, Pitman.

Garnett, J. (1973). *The Work Challenge.* London, Industrial Society.

Greenwood, W. T. (1965). *Management and Organizational Behavior Theories – an interdisciplinary approach.* Cincinnati, Ohio, South Western Publishing Co.

Gross, B. M. (1968). *Organizations and Their Managing.* New York, Free Press; London, Collier-Macmillan.

Johnson, R. A., Kast, F. E. and Rosenzweig, J. E. (1973). *The Theory and Management of Systems,* 3rd edn. New York and Maidenhead, McGraw-Hill.

Koontz, H. and O'Donnell, C. (1972). *Principles of Management – an analysis of management functions,* 5th edn. New York and Maidenhead, McGraw-Hill.

Longenecker, J. G. (1973). *Principles of Management and Organizational Behavior,* 3rd edn. Columbus, Ohio, and Wembley, Middx., Charles E. Merrill.

Massie, J. L. (1971). *Essentials of Management,* 2nd edn. Englewood Cliffs, NJ, and Hemel Hempstead, Herts., Prentice-Hall.

Mayston, E. L. (Chairman) (1969). *Report of the Working Party on Management Structure in the Local Authority Nursing Services;* Department of Health and Social Security, and Scottish Home and Health Office. London, HMSO.

Munsterberg, H. (1913). *Psychology and Industrial Efficiency.* Reprinted 1973, by Hive, Easton, Pa. and Arno Press, New York.

Newman, W. H., Summer, C. E. and Warren, E. K. (1972). *The Process of Management,* 3rd edn. Englewood Cliffs, NJ, and Hemel Hempstead, Herts., Prentice-Hall.

Peters, D. (1967). *Principles of Supervision,* Supervisory Series 1. Harlow, Essex, Longman.

Salmon, Brian (Chairman) (1966). *Report of the Committee on Senior Nursing Staff Structure;* Ministry of Health, and Scottish Home and Health Department. London, HMSO.

Urwick, L. F. and Brech, E. F. L. (1945). *The Making of Scientific Management. Vol. 1, Thirteen Pioneers.* London, Management Publications Trust.

Wren, D. A. and Voich, D. Jr. (1976). *Principles of Management: Resources and Systems,* 2nd edn. New York, Ronald Press.

Chapter 3

People and Management

Now as we move on to the dynamics of management, we leave the mechanical administrative functions and come face to face with the realities of management . . . PEOPLE.

We can beaver away at forecasting, planning and organising but with people we must stop, look and listen:

STOP having preconceived ideas that you know what's good for them;

LOOK and see exactly what your subordinates are doing;

LISTEN to what they have to say about their jobs.

We leave behind the comparative certainty of the mechanical functions and enter the world of individuals, groups and communities, all with as many ideas and problems as there are people who comprise these groups.

We dive headlong into psychology; not just ordinary psychology but the psychology of the industrial society, i.e. the society of people at work.

To refresh you visually I will repeat the cycle of management we are examining and this time using the words Henri Fayol used (Fig. 3.1).

Fig. 3.1

I wonder if you can spot the difference without referring back? A hint? There is just one word different . . . Got it! The word is 'commanding'. That is not a word which is acceptable today — we don't seem to find that commanding people to work is correct.

When I ask some groups for an alternative word for 'commanding' I am frequently offered the word 'requesting' but, as nice as that word is, it is only half the story.

The word we should substitute is 'motivation'.

This is creating an interesting and rewarding job in a good environment so that people WANT TO WORK.

MOTIVATION

Motivation is an enormous subject. I suppose there must have been hundreds of books and articles written on this subject alone; but strangely enough one name stands out whenever anyone begins to study or talk about motivation. That name is Frederick Herzberg.

Frederick Herzberg

Born in 1923 in Lynn, Mass., he studied most of his undergraduate programme in New York. His initial subject was history but World War II interrupted his studies.

His experiences during World War II (including an indelible sight of the horrors of Dachau) encouraged him to link psychology with his history studies.

He completed his Master's degree and PhD at the University of Pittsburgh and began his career by researching for the US Public Health Service.

He followed this with a short period as a clinical psychologist before becoming Research Director of a large non-profit-making psychological consulting firm. It was here that he began his research into motivation and developed a theory that has swept the world.

He and his team interviewed 200 engineers and accountants on their attitudes to work; he asked them to recall times when they actually felt good about their work and when they felt bad about their work. The result of this study was to show that people felt good about the job content itself, which Herzberg called 'satisfiers', and felt bad about environmental factors, which he named 'dissatisfiers'.

Here follow two lists of factors, both of which I have re-named. The 'satisfiers' are labelled Motivation factors and the 'dissatisfiers' are labelled Hygiene factors.

Motivation factors	Hygiene factors
Achievement	Company policy and Administration
Recognition	Supervision
The work itself	Working conditions
Responsibility	Relationship with superiors
Growth	Relationship with subordinates
	Relationship with peers
	Salary
	Status
	Job security
	Personal life

37

In summary, Herzberg said that the hygiene factors are important only inasmuch as they must be provided for at a satisfactory level. If they do not reach this level then they will become actual dissatisfiers. But more or better hygiene factors are not true motivational forces at all. At best their motivation value is short lived. Look at your own experience. How nice it is to receive a rise in salary, but very soon the glow of that rise will have been forgotten as it just becomes part of your living requirements.

If you really want to motivate people, to create for them an industrial climate in which they will want to work, then you must concentrate on the motivational factors.

(1) Give your subordinates opportunity to experience a sense of achievement.
(2) Give them recognition for the work they do.
(3) Make the work itself more interesting.
(4) Give them more responsibility.
(5) Create opportunities for advancement and growth in their jobs.

Job Enrichment

A programme on these lines is often called a job enrichment programme. A simple example often quoted is that of a company which had a section of girl typists who typed out mainly standard letters in response to customers' complaints. It was a dull, negative job by its very nature and the turnover rate of these girls was very high. The Job Enrichment Team who studied their work suggested the following:

(1) The girls should be called 'Consumer Consultants'.
(2) They should themselves follow up the complaints.
(3) They should compose their own letter to the customer.
(4) They should sign the letter personally and be responsible for their 'case'.

These few simple changes to a dull job changed it overnight into a worthwhile and satisfying job. The morale of the girls rose and the turnover rate dropped.

They at last had a worthwhile job with intrinsic interest, responsibility and recognition.

OTHER WORKERS IN MOTIVATION

While Herzberg's work dominates the study of motivation, it would be wrong of me not to mention other workers in this field. One whom I must mention, as his work is closely allied to that of Herzberg, is A. H. Maslow.

A. H. Maslow (1908–1970)

Maslow died in June 1970 aged 62 years. Born in Brooklyn, New York, he studied for his degrees at the University of Wisconsin. His career was almost exclusively as an academic; his friends labelled him 'a thinker', 'a searcher after truth' and as 'a man who constantly questioned his own theories'.

Within the context of management, his most valued contribution was his 'hierarchy of needs' which he first published in 1943. The theory he presented then remains essentially the same today, though he developed it in the intervening years.

The basis of his proposal is that man usually behaves as an integrated whole requiring certain basic needs to be satisfied in a progressive upward path.

Maslow said that initially man required his basic physiological needs to be met — that is, he must have air, food, water, shelter, etc.

Once these are met, then man desires safety and security; in other words, protection against danger, threat or deprivation.

The next step requires that his social needs be satisfied — the need for belonging, association, acceptance, giving and receiving affection and love.

Maslow subdivides the next step in the hierarchy — esteem needs — into two:

(1) The desire for self-esteem; i.e. confidence, independence.
(2) The desire for the esteem of others; i.e. reputation, prestige, status.

Finally, the pinnacle of the hierarchy is that of self-fulfilment when man realises his own potential and continuing self-development.

Let us now look at Fig. 3.2 to see this visually and from a more specific management viewpoint.

One of the most important things to remember in interpreting Maslow's theories is that every need does not have to be met at the 100% level before a person moves on to the next level of need. A second point is that we move up and down the hierarchy according to our experience of life and our personalities.

During the comparatively recent upheavals of nursing staff as the result of the Salmon and Mayston Reports and, more particularly, the National Health Service reorganisation, you will have had the opportunity of seeing some of our nurse managers who were operating at a self-fulfilment level in very senior and responsible jobs, exhibiting behaviour appropriate to 'safety needs' as the result of the threat of losing their jobs in the reshuffle, despite the guarantee that they would not lose financially.

Our basic physiological needs alter in relation to our financial situation and indeed to the level at which we require to meet other hierarchical needs. The example I cite is the matter of housing where we start off with the nurses' home and go through the stages of a flat, a terraced house, a semi-detached and then a detached house (if we are motivated enough).

What this is emphasising is that our needs will continually be required to be met either at an ever-increasing stage of the hierarchy or at a higher

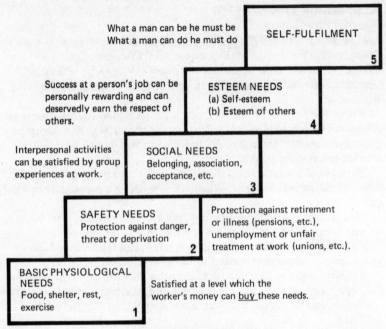

Fig. 3.2 *Maslow's hierarchy of needs.*

percentage of satisfaction. I am reminded of a phrase I once read, commenting on Maslow's hierarchy of needs. It said something like 'Employees' grumbles will never end, they just become higher level grumbles!'

Having outlined the two main influences on the application of the motivation dynamic to our work, I would like to spend a little more time being somewhat more practical and interpretive of these two theories. Before doing so I must quickly add a note of reassurance to those of you who were expecting the name of Douglas McGregor to be dealt with under the heading of Motivation. Believe me, I have not forgotten him and I will have quite a lot to say about him when we come to the section on Control.

How then can we apply what these two men are saying to our working situation?

First let us look at Maslow . . . he has shown us the needs of normal people if they are to lead a normal, satisfying life.

Basic Needs

The basic needs of life which Maslow said must be met can be achieved by even the lowest-paid workers in the Health Service and, although most of us feel we would like more money, the fact is that pay is less of a motivating force than we imagine it to be. When salaries were below subsistence level, then they assumed very large proportions in the eyes of the employee, but now things have changed and employees have 'higher order' needs.

Security

Next in the hierarchy come security needs. If security does not exist or is threatened, then it becomes a real motivator. In 1977 the Health Service finds itself in the extraordinary position of not being able to offer secure employment to many people. Students and pupils who qualify cannot be sure of jobs; those hoping to work a few years over their normal retirement age cannot look forward to that; promotion has slowed down. The effect of this has led to increased union activity, more people joining unions and unions fighting cuts in staff expenditure. In one instance it was alleged that students were deliberately failing their finals in order to remain in employment.

Social Needs

The social needs can be clearly recognised by looking at the different people or groups of people in your unit.

Undoubtedly you will find some who are not at all motivated to work by the need of COMPANIONSHIP. These are the 'loners', those who like to be given a job and be allowed to get on with it without interference from or contact with others. This is certainly a minority of employees.

The larger group is composed of those who gain tremendous satisfaction from work. In nursing, we have particularly the group of 'older' women who come back to nursing when they have brought their families up to a stage of independence. What a breath of fresh air work brings to them after being somewhat cut off from satisfactory social life by the demands of domestic routine.

My experience has been that these women are an asset to any organisation and the delight of managers in that they tend to be mature, confident and reliable workers. This is an important group of workers in the Health Service so let us recognise their motivation force and, as managers, foster a friendly social spirit amongst these nurses.

The third group to look at are those who gain their companionship needs not from work but from the outside. They are the group of people who have their friends from the golf club, church, sports club, politics, etc. They prefer to keep their work life and social life distinct, so clearly they are not motivated in their work by a desire for companionship; this need is met elsewhere.

Self-esteem and Self-fulfilment

The two remaining needs of self-esteem and self-fulfilment are classed as

41

'higher needs'. Fortunately, nursing as a career offers employment at levels which can satisfy these needs, but from time to time we have had to deal with crises which have given some of these jobs quite a jolt.

The Salmon and Mayston Reports did a lot of damage from this point of view as the reorganisation of the Matron/Sister relationship by the introduction of an intermediate grade of Nursing Officer and superior grades of Principal Nursing Officer and Chief Nursing Officer caused great difficulties in connection with STATUS, SELF-ESTEEM and RECOGNITION (Fig. 3.3).

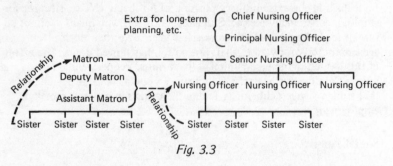

Fig. 3.3

Matron who, being in charge of the hospital completely and working at a self-fulfilment level, suddenly found herself called a Senior Nursing Officer and having two superiors over her! Sister, who had a good relationship with Matron, suddenly found herself having to relate to a Nursing Officer who, in Sister's opinion, had taken many of the interesting and 'status supplying' jobs from her. No wonder the Salmon Report was disliked so much!

Of course if these needs are not met by work then they will be met in different ways outside the organisation, as are the social needs we have just discussed. It is to elicit just these factors that I frequently ask candidates for jobs about their outside interests and activities. One can learn a lot about a person this way if they give positive motivation information, though you must be careful of jumping to conclusions about negative information revealed.

Herzberg's satisfiers and non-satisfiers have a distinct relationship to Maslow's motivation theories in that those graded as satisfiers or motivators contain many of the elements of Maslow's higher hierarchical needs. Let us look at these first.

Motivators

The first group are motivators, i.e. those experiences which create a positive attitude to work. Herzberg discovered that they arise from the work itself. They were feelings of long duration and resulted in greater productivity.

Achievement

Both Maslow and Herzberg ranked this highest. Unfortunately, people tend to look upon this as being 'top of the tree', but to be top of your profession is not the only way to feel a sense of achievement.

A person in any level of work can experience this sense of achievement provided the work she is doing taxes her intellectual and physical abilities to their limit. I have often noticed how satisfied many nurses are in 'humble' but necessary jobs and how frustrated are many senior managers despite their 'lofty' positions. Could it be that some senior managers are in jobs which are beyond their intellectual capacities and even their physical stamina? Possibly so but I think it far more probable that they are frustrated because they cannot see any real achievement despite all their efforts.

Between the frustrated and the achieved are a vast army of workers in the National Health Service. What can we do to help them? There is no easy answer, but efforts made to help employees in two areas have been found useful.

(1) Make every effort to let people see WHY they are doing what they are doing. You can do this in many ways, but giving people the necessary background to their job and training them so that they can do their job well are fruitful areas of approach. For example, a Secretary/typist was promoted to a higher clerical grade and appointed Secretary to the Area Nursing Officer. The first thing the ANO did was to arrange for the new girl to have a 'Cook's Tour' of the Area, seeing both patients and staff. The result was a tremendous commitment to the job and a real understanding of why she was doing it . . . for the benefit of patients and staff.

(2) Examine everyone's job in order to ascertain that it contains the elements of involvement and participation in the activities of the service provided. See that it stimulates them without giving them so much responsibility that the strain proves to be too great.

Recognition

This is another of Herzberg's motivators, and Maslow's too. Everybody needs to be given recognition of merit from time to time but how often do we get it — or give it? A style of management prevalent in the Health Service is to blame frequently, praise rarely.

Do take time to get to know your staff and note those who need frequent encouragement and help. This does not mean that you must never criticise but, when you do so, be kind and firm and also positive and helpful; and don't be so free with your praise that you become effusive — people can get used to it and it diminishes the motivating effect.

As to Herzberg's 'nature of the work' and 'responsibility', we have already touched on this in so many ways that I think I will leave this discussion with only a reminder that the job itself is much more important to the person than many other things.

Prospects

The last of the motivators is prospects. While it is fair to say that to many a young nurse, prospects of promotion are almost immaterial as she is only planning to stay until she is married, to others it is important that they can see a clear career pattern to which they can direct their efforts. This does not mean automatic promotion by putting in the number of years required but the opportunity for a person with the right qualifications and experience to be offered a job suitable to her abilities.

Dissatisfiers

Let us now move on to Herzberg's hygiene factors. We have learnt already that these are not motivators but the important thing about them is that, if they are not met at a satisfactory level, they become dissatisfiers and do not allow the motivators to function.

Quite some time before Health Visitors were attached to General Practitioners, one local health authority moved all their Health Visitors out of their smaller offices, each accommodating four or six people, into one ex-typing pool room, half the size of a football pitch. Naturally to them their working conditions had dropped below what they considered a reasonable level and they grumbled and complained about it. The interesting thing about this was that they did not complain only about their room; they also expressed dissatisfaction about many other things — about their work, which they had never previously mentioned or complained of and which was not affected in any way by the room change.

So . . . we must meet these hygiene needs of Herzberg's at a satisfactory level. Let us look at them again:

Policies
Supervision
All areas of interpersonal relationship
Work conditions
Salary
Status
Security
Personal life

Most of these are within our sphere of ability to control; some, of course, are not. I have already mentioned conditions of work but many of you will be surprised to see SALARY on the list. Pay, at the most, would be a short-term motivator. Earlier I asked if you noticed how soon your annual increment lost its impact. Two or three pay packets and you were waiting for next year's increment! Let our pay fall seriously out of line with other comparable employment and it assumes very great importance — great enough to get nurses out on street demonstrations with placards just a few years ago. Recently we had the benefits of the Halsbury Report — but how soon will it be before we go out on the streets again?

To sum this up we can say that mankind needs:

TO HAVE (his physiological needs and those things which our society says are essential);

TO BE (the kind of person he wants to be and be seen by others to be);

TO DO (that 'something' in their life — if it is their job then they will be motivated);

TO BELONG (we need to be wanted and be befriended — many get this from their job);

TO GROW (to change and enlarge our knowledge, skill and experience).

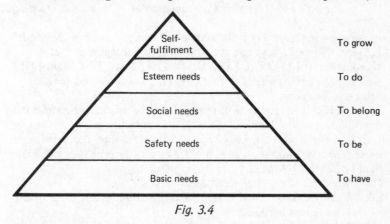

Fig. 3.4

Remember — Man always wants more.

COORDINATION

This managerial function does not always use special techniques; success is usually achieved through the active skill of the manager herself. Definitions of coordination, as with other managerial functions, are many and varied.

I am going to present two definitions to you and no doubt, when you have read them both, you will decide that your own concept of the word 'coordination' is more meaningful than the definitions! And why not? After all it is a word which we in the caring professions use frequently with a fairly precise application. However, managerially speaking, these are the definitions.

(1) 'The process of timing activities and reuniting subdivided work; of combining activities in a consistent and harmonious action.'

(2) 'Maintaining a balanced team by ensuring a suitable allocation of working activities to various members, and seeing that these are performed with due harmony among the workers themselves.'

45

There is no doubt that the central function of the management of any organisation lies in the coordination of its many component parts. In fact it would be fair to say that Mary Parker Follet defined management as COORDINATION — and coordination is management.

What, then, are the special features in management which require coordination? Basically, there are three:

(1)   When a number of decisions are dependent on each other in such a way that the success of one decision depends on the actions of the others (INTERDEPENDENCE).

(2)   If coordination is wanted by some or all of the members of an organisation in order to attain one or more goals (OPTIMISATION).

(3)   When the alternatives (i.e. bundles of actions) which are coordinated together lead to a higher degree of goal attainment than would be achieved by lesser levels of coordination or by independent action.

Now, having looked at definitions and theory, what do we conclude? I suggest that we have progressed to the stage of recognising that coordination is a SPECIAL KIND OF DECISION MAKING, namely the kind by which it is possible to find ways and means of synchronising actions to be taken.

It is difficult for me to be of practical help to you in this coordination function for, as I said in the beginning, the individual flair of the manager and the use of a wide number of appropriate techniques borrowed from other functions indicate success; but if you are searching for guidelines then I offer the following.

(1)   Any form of planning scheme is helpful.

(2)   A manager should define her own responsibilities and those of her immediate subordinates.

(3)   She should have daily individual contact with each of her subordinates.

(4)   She should encourage her subordinates to do likewise.

(5)   She should have regular progress meetings with her subordinates.

(6)   Appropriate committees or meetings should be set up where all representatives involved in a given function meet to discuss the future, make decisions and agree on a coordinated course of action.

As an example of the last, I would suggest that the procedure committee is the most widely experienced coordinating group in nursing.

As for the other techniques which coordination uses, I would suggest that working parties and joint consultation committees are just two examples of coordination techniques.

Coordination and Personality

As always, management involves people, and I would like to help you identify some of the difficult types of people whom you can find involved actively in the coordination process, for these people can cause problems if their activities go undiagnosed and therefore uncorrected.

Firstly, there is the person who believes that nobody else but she can carry out a given task to her satisfaction. This person thinks that delegation is impossible and tends to get involved everywhere. She doubts descriptions of the coordination function and denies the existence of a successful solution to a problem via coordination.

Secondly, there is the person who starts from the point where the interests of the various people involved in coordination are in serious conflict. She openly tries to dominate the others and is not afraid of being hostile.

Thirdly, there is the person who, though acting fully in the interests of the organisation, does so only in relation to what SHE sees to be the general aim of the organisation regardless of others with whom she is supposedly coordinating.

There is no SIMPLE action which you can take to cope with these individuals. Rather it is a matter of time . . . time which you – the manager – spend in coaching, counselling and leading by example. It has been said that the only way to practical coordination is to learn the content of your colleagues' jobs and approach your problems from their point of view.

CONTROL

This now is the last function in our management cycle and it is undoubtedly the most complex. The very word 'control' itself seems to conjure up pictures of coercion – harsh, unbending management – and this is not at all helpful.

In its most simple form, control is purely 'knowledge of results'. I can dress it up in a definition for you if you like: 'An information feedback system designed to enable the recipient to take any corrective action necessary to assure fulfilment of personal or organisational objectives'. You can have that or simply 'knowledge of results' – just as you please.

The control I have just defined is what I like to call 'mechanical' control but there is another side to control which I label 'sociological' control. Here again a definition is called for: 'Any process where a person (OR group of persons OR an organisation) sets out to intentionally affect the behaviour of another person (OR group of persons, etc.)'.

Both types of control require separate consideration if we are going to fully understand the control function.

'Mechanical' Control

When I first went to a university lecture on the subject of 'Control in Management' I was amazed to hear the lecturer spend fully one-third of the lecture time talking about 'cybernetics'. At first I wriggled with embarrassment thinking I had gone into the wrong lecture theatre; then I became interested and finally I saw the point he was making. I will try to reproduce for you some of the points he made.

Firstly, he told us what cybernetics is. It is, he said, 'the study of how things maintain their equilibrium even though they are subject to a changing environment'. As examples of this, he told us how many different kinds of machines worked; the only one I remember is the room thermostat for central heating. It is a machine which keeps the room at a steady temperature regardless of day or night, sunshine or snow. Perhaps for us who have a medical background, the best example of cybernetics is our body. In it are many cybernetic systems; for example, body temperature — we keep at our 'normal' temperature in winter and summer, clothes on or clothes off. Other examples could be chemical balance, pulse rate and many others.

The features of the cybernetic principle which these examples illustrate are:

(1) There is a predetermined state to be maintained; pulse rate 72, body temperature $37°C$, room temperature $21°C$.

(2) The environment is constantly changing, therefore adjustments have to be made continually to keep the body functioning; e.g. whether we are standing or lying down, the pulse rate remains steady.

(3) Information of this changing environment has to be transferred from outside to inside the cybernetic device; e.g. a signal that the air around you is getting colder has to be sent to your central nervous system.

Having told us this, the lecturer summed cybernetics up as being 'the maintenance of a steady state through the interpretation of information and subsequent corrective action' . . . and this is just what managerial control is all about.

First of all, we decide what we want to achieve (i.e. we predetermine the state to be maintained).

Secondly, we measure our current performance in relation to that which we want to achieve (i.e. we monitor the changing environment).

Finally, we take corrective action to ensure that we meet our objectives (the information is converted into appropriate action).

How, then, do we turn this knowledge of cybernetic principles into managerial reality? By examining the three stages of (1) predetermined state, (2) measurement of performance, and (3) taking corrective action.

The Predetermined State

What we are saying here is that we must have standards to serve as a yardstick for our measures of quality or quantity. But what is a standard?

Is it an average? No — for our purpose the average of anything always tends to be on the low side.

Is it perfection? Clearly this would not be acceptable.

Just what is it? I must return to the university lecturer, for he gave us an example which I think is an excellent illustration of what a standard is.

In the game of golf 'par' is the accepted standard by which all golfers measure themselves. It is the number of shots a first-class player normally takes to sink the ball in the 18 holes of a golf course. Let us look at this and try to isolate the components of this standard, using 72 as par.

(1) It is a RECOGNISED STANDARD set by authority of the ruling body for golf.

(2) It is clear that the standard is NOT PERFECTION, for I frequently hear on the radio and TV that 'so and so' has gone around in 'four under par' (i.e. 68 strokes).

(3) It is clear that it is NOT AN AVERAGE, for my own efforts at golf are enough to bring the average down to about 85 strokes!

(4) It does serve as a criterion for comparing efficiency.

Almost the first thing golfers talk about when they get together is their handicap. If they say it is 10, then that means the golfer regularly goes around in about 82 strokes and if it is 1, then she regularly goes around in 73.

From this example we can deduce that a standard is 'a difficult but attainable level of performance'.

Standards in nursing are notoriously difficult to set. We say we know what 'good' nursing is but we have a very hard time defining it. If we want to set about setting standards then we can explore the use of three methods.

1. *Statistical.* This involves the collection of numerical data from which we can establish the present situation and set targets or standards which we want to achieve.

For example, if we say we want to reduce the incidence of pressure sores in our ward, first we must know the frequency at which they are occurring so we begin to collect the facts and figures relating to their incidence on our ward. When you have collected them over a fair period of time, you will then have enough statistics to enable you to set realistic standards to achieve (i.e. a difficult but achievable reduction in the incidence of pressure sores).

I did say 'collect statistics over a fair period of time'. The reason I said this is that the shorter the period of time over which we collect our figures, the less accurate they are likely to be. If, for example, we counted the pressure sores over one week, it could be a very bad week or a very good week; but if we collected the figures over, say, three months, then the good weeks would cancel out the bad weeks and we would have a pretty accurate picture of the true incidence of our pressure sores.

2. *Standards Set by Appraisal.* This is not staff appraisal but rather one based on the notion that an experienced manager knows, say, what a good day's work is.

This is a very unscientific method of establishing standards but in many cases it is the only way a standard can be set and it is quite a valid method of doing so in the absence of factual data.

3. *Engineering Standards.* Under this heading would come Work Study and Organisation and Methods. These involve actual measurement of work in quality, quantity and time or looking at the systems and working methods used; from the data thus collected, we can set desirable standards.

It need not be all scientific, for under this heading I would put what I call 'Time-span Control'. For example, give a person a job to do and indicate the time in which you require her to complete it. By doing this you are setting a standard, e.g. you want a complex task done in a short time then you are indicating a LOW standard; if you want the job done to a HIGH standard then naturally you need to give more (adequate) time for the task in hand. Generally this is a very acceptable control method which we are all happy to work under. I believe we should be using it more consciously and as a specific control technique.

So far, then, we have looked at the first step in the control process — that of establishing standards of performance; now let us move on to the second stage.

Measuring Current Performance against Standards

This, if you remember, is the gathering of information which will then be used to take the necessary corrective action.

Information used for the control process should have four characteristics:

(1) It should be TIMELY: it should be presented at a time when action can be taken. Information produced too early is likely to be inaccurate, as we do not have enough of a 'run' or 'background' to know how we are going. Information — accurate though it may be — which is produced too late to take corrective action is equally useless; we must have information at the right time.

(2) It should be produced in APPROPRIATE UNITS. That is to say, it should measure what we really want to measure. For example, the average occupancy of the beds in a hospital is a measure used as part of the National Health Service control information data. As a measure it tells exactly what it says — the average bed occupancy; but this does not tell you how hard your staff have to work (patient dependency) or the number of different patients nursed in a ward during a period of time (patient throughput).

(3) It should be RELIABLE. Information, to be useful, must be accurate. To produce accurate information, data must be collected over a long period of time. The longer the period studied or analysed, the more accurate the information.

(4) It should be channelled to the appropriate person. This speaks for itself — information must go to the person who can take the action.

In characteristic (1) (timely) and characteristic (3) (reliability) we have

50

a fundamental dichotomy which users and providers of control data are constantly grappling with.

If you are to have information in time to do something about it, then it is likely to be unreliable or at the least contain false pointers from time to time. If you are to have accurate information then the chances are that it has arrived too late for you to do anything about it.

To see the way the necessary compromise is reached, let us look at staff appraisal.

Our current scheme recommends appraisal on an annual basis and that appraisal forms be kept for five years.

Here we see the TIMELY information, i.e. the annual appraisal, at which time you can take the required corrective action, and the ACCURATE or RELIABLE information, which is the bank of five years' appraisals from which can be gleaned a very accurate picture of the person's progress and development. This is just the sort of information you want when writing a reference, which is of course one of the reasons for keeping this bank of forms.

To summarise control information characteristics is very easy. Control information must be . . .

The right information
At the right time
In the right place

Having examined the first two stages of the control process, i.e. establishing standards and the measurement of performance, we now move on to the last part of the cycle — taking corrective action.

Taking Corrective Action

It is here that we must turn to the sociological approach to control for, having got the right information at the right time in the right place, we may well find that we have to take corrective action or, to paraphrase the definition of sociological control, 'We as individuals set out to intentionally change the behaviour of other individuals or groups of individuals'.

And is this not what management is all about? If I had to choose the one most important management function it would be Control, and the taking of corrective action in particular.

For this is the heart of supervision — the implementation of change, the standards of morale, the dynamism of the organisation; all these and many other factors depend on how we manage this function.

Of all the management writers to whom I have introduced you in this book, there is one who has influenced my thinking (and I hope my actions!) more than any other. His name is Douglas McGregor.

51

Douglas McGregor (1906–1964)

McGregor inherited from both his father and his grandfather a strong sense of concern for people. His early life was undoubtedly influenced by his contact with a mission set up by his grandfather for transient labourers in Detroit, of which his father, a lay preacher, became the director in 1915.

We are given to understand that this was very much a family concern with all members of it being responsible for the feeding, housing and religious needs of some 700 men, and Douglas McGregor did his part until he was 26.

His academic career was framed at Harvard where he studied psychology and, later, social psychology. He was at one time president of Antioch College but for the greater part of his life he was Professor of Industrial Management at the Massachusetts Institute of Technology (MIT).

The Human Side of Enterprise, published in 1960, outlined his theories, the most famous of which must be his Theory X and Theory Y. Theory X, he said, was that employees generally disliked work and would avoid it whenever possible; thus most people must be coerced, controlled, directed and threatened with punishment to get them to work towards organisational objectives. Also the theory states that the average person prefers to be directed, does not want responsibility, has little ambition and desires security above all.

Theory Y, on the other hand, says that it is natural for a person to use physical and mental effort in work as well as play and that people at work have the capacity to use imagination, ingenuity and creativity in solving organisational problems, learning not only to accept but to seek responsibility.

In relation to control, McGregor hoped to see the predetermined state and the employee's own aims integrated and control procedures so devised that the employee would be able to exercise control over his own performance.

This principle of self-control he saw as the means of enabling the individual to grow through setting her own objectives and then, with the help of her manager, evaluating her own progress towards achieving them.

McGregor challenged the traditional attitudes most successfully and the impact of his work on managerial attitudes is probably greater than any other behavioural scientist, but changing attitudes is a long, long job. He once said 'Concentration on the human side of enterprise will bring us one step nearer to the good society.' Management is people and concern for them will always pay off.

My treatment of this aspect of control is heavily influenced by Douglas McGregor, as will be apparent in the last section of this chapter.

ORGANISATIONAL CONTROL

All of us have spent and will continue to spend a very large proportion of our lives in various organisations — schools, clubs, associations — places we work and play in. We receive a great deal of benefit from membership of these organisations. Many of the social organisations we belong to extract a payment from us to be able to enjoy their amenities; the organisations we work for pay US to belong to them and work for them.

These work and social organisational memberships are in most ways as alike as chalk and cheese but in one respect they are very similar — they exert control over their members. Control is implicit in an organisation.

To define organisation is a difficult task. E. H. Schein (1970) says, 'An organisation is the rational coordination of the ACTIVITIES of a number of people for the achievement of some common explicit purpose or goal through division of labour and function, and through hierarchy of authority and responsibility.'

A. S. Tannenbaum (1968) says it is an 'ordered arrangement of INDIVIDUAL human relationships'.

In the two ideas presented above we see the conflict which exists in organisational thought. The first talks of the 'activities' of people; the second talks of the 'individual'. I like to think of these two different approaches as inorganic (activities, material, costs, quality, etc.) and organic (people, behaviour, emotions, etc.)

As already stated, control is an inevitable correlate of organisation. It is necessary to help circumscribe idiosyncrasies of behaviour, to help members conform, to give members the requirements to meet the objectives of the organisation.

Organic controls are as difficult to define as the organisations of which they are a part. Some writers use words such as 'power', 'authority' and 'influence' but they differ among themselves as to what these terms mean. To help us overcome some of these difficulties, the term 'process of controlling' will help us visualise what is involved in getting things done in an organisation.

The process of control is best demonstrated by the model shown in Fig. 3.5.

In managerial terms this control loop can be described thus: the manager formulates his intention, then as a manager he exercises another of his functions, i.e. he gets someone else to do the job, which usually produces action in that person. Finally the loop is completed by the manager receiving the information that his instruction has been fulfilled.

This seems a very simple and straightforward way of making sure the aims of the organisation are achieved but we all know the facts show the process to be very complicated and, in many cases, very unpredictable.

It is what goes wrong and why it goes wrong which need explaining.

Most managers feel the need to require that subordinates report on the process of their job — thus exercising control. To exercise this control and also to try to eliminate the problems they see in controlling people (i.e. non-compliance, unreliable feedback), they introduce administrative

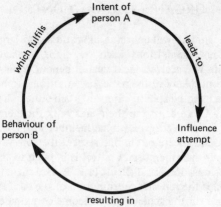

Fig. 3.5   The control process (Tannenbaum, 1968).

procedures. McGregor (1967) argued that it is these very control procedures which produce the problems they are in part designed to overcome.

Unintended Consequences

Control often has unintended consequences.

Non-compliance

This is the root from which all control problems stem. Any control system will bring a measure of compliance, but in addition they yield (McGregor, 1967):
(1)   Widespread antagonism to the controls and those who administer them.
(2)   Successful resistance and non-compliance.
(3)   Unreliable performance information because of (1) and (2).
(4)   Again because of (1) and (2), the necessity for close surveillance.
(5)   High administrative costs.

The above are generalisations but at the end of this chapter I illustrate many of these points, and others, with a case study.

Threat

Controls are often perceived as threat. We should remember that in people 'feelings are facts'. A manager's threat is probably the last thing that we intend when instituting a particular control procedure but do your employees see it in the same way?

54

McGregor submitted that perceived threat is present when:
(1) Punishment – as opposed to support and help in meeting standards and objectives – is emphasised.
(2) Trust is lacking in the relationships involved.
(3) The required feedback of information is negative.
(4) The individual's self-esteem, his career expectations or his emotional security in the relationship are involved.

As examples of how management induces perceived threat, McGregor cited management's pressure for compliance to externally imposed standards. This is where performance levels are measured and standards or norms of performance are required of employees.

Any control using measures of variance is bound to emphasise mistakes, failures and substandard performance.

The attitudes of the management who impose these controls have their effect also. It is observable that staff groups who administer controls have a poor opinion of the honesty of their subordinates.

Tannenbaum (1968) quotes the work of many authors and brings out the thought that management can induce control by 'exchange of resources' or 'sense of justice'. This works in the way that management will dispense some valuable resource in exchange for compliance. It could be 'approval' that management is dispensing or it could be 'in that the manager has given so much to me', i.e. approval 'information', it is justice that I comply with his wishes.

Power and Authority

How else do organisations impose control? Etzioni (1975) listed organisations according to the types of power mainly exerted.

COERCIVE. They (the managers) can apply pressure or penalise those who do not cooperate; e.g. prisons, war-time military organisations, some trade unions.

UTILITARIAN. (1) He can give special help and benefits to those who cooperate with him (rewards: e.g. business and industry).
(2) He has a legitimate right, considering his position, to expect that his orders are carried out (rational; legal authority).

NORMATIVE (use of membership; status; intrinsic value rewards).
(1) I admire him for his personal qualities and want to act in a way that merits his respect and admiration (referent).
(2) I respect his competence and good judgement about things with which he is more experienced than I (expert: e.g. churches, political organisations, hospitals).

It is difficult exactly to pigeon-hole these types of power and naturally there are shades of use of these types and also mixed types in organisations.

Defence Mechanisms

It is sensible briefly to examine the various defence mechanisms which both managers and subordinates share.

(1) AGGRESSION: trying to hurt the person or group causing the conflict, because you personally have been hurt by the person or group.

(2) GUILT: a block due to the limitation of personality.

(3) CONTINUATION: when the conflict is not resolved, but a second-hand choice is made.

(4) DENIAL: refusal to acknowledge facts which could create conflict.

(5) REPRESSION: an active forgetting, particularly of unpleasant memories.

(6) INHIBITION: a fear of speaking up lest the content of the speech should be wrong or unimportant.

(7) CONVERSION: the transference of incapability to a suggestion of illness.

(8) RATIONALISATION: finding reasons to justify words or actions. May be due to clinging for too long to an idea.

(9) IDENTIFICATION: a desire to be like someone else, sometimes found between top management people and subordinates who try to identify with them.

(10) PROJECTION: ascribing to others our own beliefs and behaviour.

There are many basic properties in human personalities; this applies also to organisations, for they are made up of individuals.

Differences and Control

The following section outlines briefly a technique of management which takes into account the differences between people with whom we work, and offers a possible solution to the problems associated with control. It is the theory put forward by Douglas McGregor in his book, *The Professional Manager*, and is known as 'working through differences'.

Requirements for working through differences are outlined below.

Time

This is the most important requirement. It is needed to build up the necessary relationships in order that the differences between people can be managed. In practice the extra time taken in this technique is more than made up by reducing to a minimum the time-wasting over trivialities during the decision-making process, the elimination of the problems of non-compliance and passive acceptance or the activating of the defence mechanism by the traditional control process.

A High Degree of Mutual Trust

Members of the organisation must be free to be themselves without fear of the consequences, e.g. upsetting the boss.

A High Degree of Mutual Support

Genuine concern for each other must replace the competitive element of every man for himself.

Open and Authentic Communications

No member of the organisation should ride roughshod over any individual's views or feelings, even though they may appear defiant, unclear or even irrational. Each should listen to the other, understand and be understood.

Clear Understanding of Objectives

Not only should every member of the organisation show and understand the objectives of the organisation but they should also be committed to them of their own volition.

Respect for Differences

This must be genuine, not just paid lip-service. The member must be able to remain an individual. Without this the organisation will be exerting control in the form of making a person conform. Conformity dulls innovation and creativity.

Utilisation of Member Resources

The abilities, knowledge and experience within the organisation (no matter how 'lowly' the person's position) must be recognised and utilised.

Supportive Environment

Management must create a free and supportive environment, having respect for individual differences resisting any tendency to being restrictive or exerting pressure toward conformity.

Conclusion

A superior planning to use the technique of management of differences should realise that it is a difficult strategy which, if used, can have many different outcomes. Unanimous decisions will not always be reached and there is the possibility that it might fail; but given the necessary time and a reasonably mature management team committed to participative management, it can offer the following advantages.

(1) Resolution of conflict between individuals and groups.
(2) Changed attitudes and beliefs.
(3) It can lead to genuine innovation.
(4) Produces genuine commitment to decisions reached. (The value of commitment is of inestimable worth to a manager by ensuring that effort is directed towards the achievement of objectives to which the members of the organisation contributed.)
(5) Management is strengthened and enriched, developing into a dynamic creative team.
(6) Together with the above advantages comes the virtual elimination of the unintended consequences of control.

Table 3.1 shows the contrast between the old and the new management (see p. 60).

CASE STUDY
South Timms is a city with a population of almost 200,000. It is mainly devoted to naval and marine servicing but has developed rapidly in the past few years, mostly in the direction of light engineering and other consumer goods.

At the time of this study the Local Health Authority nursing services were divided and administered separately by their own Superintendent. The Medical Officers of Health approached the management services unit to investigate the nursing services with a view to recommending changes for the more efficient use of existing staff, and deciding how much, if any, of the work done by fully qualified nurses could be done by lesser trained staff.

It was decided that nursing staff would be asked to record their work on daily activity analysis sheets. The whole scheme was introduced to the staff by first gaining acceptance of the scheme by individual influential members of staff (key members of staff who turned out to be individuals of strong character who were most likely to influence the vast body of 'don't knows' on the staff). This exercise was followed up by meetings with all the staff to discuss the scheme. The terms of reference were explained, but emphasis placed on certain points won the day. These were as follows.

Management	*(1) The possibility of more cars being provided.*
Overselling	*(2) The possibility of being provided with ancillary and clerical help.*

(3) Help with car-parking problems at the health and welfare departments.

The nursing staff then entered into the data collection process of daily activity analysis. This process in many cases required negative feedback; i.e. some individuals did not come up to the common standards and others found they were doing more than the common standard. In the event, the daily activity analysis became known as the daily 'lie sheet'. It was not realised by those filling in the 'lie sheet' that this information was going to be used as the 'norm' upon which future standards of performance would be based. Therefore they logged extra visits (not actually done); did not log time taken in preparing for health education (as this was not seen to be 'work' which would be acceptable to the Director of nursing services); expanded and contracted actual times so as to be seen to start work at 9 a.m. and finish at 5 p.m. The result of this was that the standard performance or 'goals' set as the result of this study were very false.

The data were analysed and recommendations made. These were broadly that:
(1) Goals or targets set at time per type of visit to be aimed for.
(2) Certain clerical help was to be introduced (mainly in filing, not in the area of greatest concern — the actual writing up of reports).
(3) More casual car user allowances were introduced. These were presented to the staff in a series of meetings coupled with a handbook which explained the system in words of one and two syllables (which annoyed the staff as they felt it insulted their intelligence).

Weekly control sheets were introduced which recorded the number and type of activities engaged in during the week. The office could then calculate the 'score'; the target was 100.

Because of the foregoing problems the nurses found themselves working considerably harder than previously (because of poor original data); they were faced with the problem of negative feedback, i.e. they did not reach the target set. Therefore they once more entered up false data in order to reach the set targets. Those who con-

59

Successful *Non-compliance*	*sistently worked genuinely over the 100 target found that they were not getting any extra help, therefore cut down on their visiting to fit the norm, and there arose the obvious need not only to measure work which was being done but also to measure work not being done because of pressure of work.*
Unreliable *Performance Data*	*The result was:* *(1) An increase in the number of recorded visits.* *(2) More controls imposed (i.e. VERY frequent spot checks on mileage).*
Increased *Surveillance*	*(3) Fall in morale (at least 10% of the staff left in the first year of its operation as a direct result of these controls).*

Table 3.1   Comparison of the traditional and the emerging styles of managers

In traditional style, the manager:	In the emerging style, the manager:
Dictates the goals and the basic methods for achieving them to his subordinates; defines the standards for quality and results (production).	Works with his subordinates to identify and resolve work-related problems; guides and assists them in setting the standards and goals.
Uses forceful leadership and persuasion to move or push his subordinates ahead.	Helps his subordinates set challenging goals for themselves by channelling and moulding their own motivation.
Checks up on his subordinates' performance and evaluates it; judges a performance as an achievement or a failure.	Educates his subordinates to check on their own performance and promotes self-evaluation; encourages their achievements and counsels them on how to capitalise on their failures.
Develops his subordinates' abilities and frees the successful ones for promotion.	Provides opportunities for his subordinates to pursue and move into areas of growth and development.
Disciplines subordinates for infractions of rules and poor performance, setting his own behaviour before them as an example.	Mediates conflict by interpreting rules rationally, explaining their usefulness and the logical consequences of violating them.
Develops and installs new ways of doing things; in short, innovates.	Allows his subordinates to develop and install new methods, and helps them do it; induces their innovation.

THE COMPLETE MANAGEMENT FUNCTION

Though we have now concluded the management cycle, the diagram and indeed the activities of the manager are incomplete. Fayol completed his diagram by adding two other management functions. Firstly, communication, which he quite rightly said bound all the activities together; and secondly, decision making, which he said was the basis of management mechanics and dynamics. In the completed model (Fig. 3.6), these are significantly placed – communication going all around the cycle and decision making being the base of the sphere.

Fig. 3.6

CASE STUDY – THE INDIVIDUAL: TIM
In the following case study I would like you to imagine that you are the Sector Administrator. Ask yourself the following questions:
(1) What would you do to relieve the tension of poor staff relationships arising from Tim's various attitudes?
(2) How would you overcome the problem of Tim's reluctance to change in the light of new developments at the hospital?
(3) To what extent would you effect an organisational change to meet this critical situation?

Tim is the Senior Pharmacist at Glenside DGH. He is 53 years of age and has been in post for the past 8 years. Prior to his present appointment he was hospital Pharmacist at Glenside General Hospital, which post he held for 18 years.

Glenside General Hospital is the main hospital in the district, having 850 beds for all specialities, including the Regional Cardiothoracic unit with attendant intensive care ward. The District Headquarters is located at Glenside General Hospital.

The pharmacy staffing situation within the Group is:

> 1 Group Pharmacist
> 1 Deputy Chief Pharmacist
> 2 Pharmacists
> 4 Trainee Pharmacy Technicians ⎫ located at Glenside Hospital

2 Pharmacists located each at smaller hospitals within the Group.

Although technically competent, Tim runs his department in a laissez-faire manner — very muddled, but with occasional frantic spasms of tidying up. He is particularly good with trainee technicians; he gives them a great deal of his time, even to the extent of keeping them back at nights to give them extra tuition.

He is very uncooperative with Charge Nurses and departmental heads. Unless requisitions reach the Pharmacy at the stated times, no issues are made under any circumstances. Such a situation creates confusion since Charge Nurses borrow from their colleagues when they have been unable to submit a requisition on time and when they eventually submit a requisition it is always for three times the amount required, thus enabling them to repay their colleagues and allowing them to keep up their stocks for a future lapse of memory on their part. The Charge Nurses are constantly complaining to the Divisional Nursing Officer and the Consultants about the poor service from the Pharmacy and also of Tim's abusive manner when they approach him for pharmaceutical items in an emergency. They claim that a much better service is provided by the Deputy when Tim is not in the department.

Tim's staff are frustrated beyond measure. His Deputy considers that he is carrying an excess of the work-load together with an excess of responsibilities and is forever having to pacify irate Charge Nurses and departmental heads. Tim is quite unable to retain his technicians; once trained they seek employment elsewhere in the Region.

The Pharmacy staff find Wednesday of each week a particularly frustrating day. This is the day when they are all engaged in the bottling of distilled water for use in the Maternity wards. Tim insists that it is necessary for every member of the department to assist in this function although it means that the pharmacists are wholly unproductive. While this work goes on, the normal routine of the department is at a standstill and issues are not entertained. The staff feel that the bottling process could be dealt with by a minimum of staff and that there need be no interruption of the normal function of the department.

Not long ago a new Accident and Out-Patient Department opened in new premises outside the main hospital building. Tim complains vigorously about the distance of the new unit from the Pharmacy and the many and varied problems involved in transportation. The Sector Administrator has listened with infinite patience to Tim's diatribe on this situation and has repeatedly asked him to set out his views and his thoughts on providing an improved service to the new unit so that they might have proper discussions with the Divisional Nursing Officer, Chairman of the medical executive committee and others concerning the pharmaceutical service to the new unit. Despite continual reminders, Tim has still to submit a written report; four months have elapsed since the request was first made!

Tim is also opposed to any form of a 'topping-up' system to wards and departments. Whereas the Central Sterile Supplies Department is working extremely efficiently with a 'topping-up' system, Tim is not only suspicious of the CSSD but is reluctant in the extreme to provide a 'topping-up' system since he claims that there would be increased difficulties in his accounting procedures. Nevertheless, he does implement a system of ward rounds and both he and his staff have achieved much success with the system.

REFERENCES AND FURTHER READING

Etzioni, A. (1975). *A Comparative Analysis of Complex Organizations.* New York, Free Press; London, Collier-Macmillan.

Halsbury, Lord (1974). *Report of the Committee of Inquiry into the Pay and Related Conditions of Service of Nurses and Midwives.* London, Department of Health and Social Security.

Herzberg, F. (1968). *Work and the Nature of Man.* London, Staples Press.

McGregor, D. (1953). *Line Managements Responsibility for Human Relations*, Manufacturing Series No. 213. New York, American Management Assoc.

McGregor, D. (1960). *The Human Side of Enterprise.* New York and Maidenhead, McGraw-Hill.

McGregor, D. (1967). *The Professional Manager.* Edited by Caroline McGregor and Warren G. Bennis. New York and Maidenhead, McGraw-Hill.

Maslow, A. H. (1943). A theory of human motivation. *Psychological Review,* 50.

Maslow, A. H. (1970). *Motivation and Personality*, 2nd edn. New York and London, Harper & Row.

Mayo, E. (1945). *The Social Problems of an Industrial Civilization.* Boston, Mass., Harvard University Graduate School of Business.

Mayston, E. L. (Chairman). (1969). *Report of the Working Party on Management Structure in the Local Authority Nursing Services*; Department of Health and Social Security, and Scottish Home and Health Office. London, HMSO.

Salmon, Brian (Chairman) (1966). *Report of the Committee on Senior Nursing Staff Structure*; Ministry of Health, and Scottish Home and Health Department. London, HMSO.

Schein, E. H. (1970). *Organizational Psychology*, 2nd edn. Englewood Cliffs, NJ, Prentice-Hall.

Tannenbaum, A. S. (1968). *Control in Organizations.* New York and
    Maidenhead, McGraw-Hill.
Williams, M. R. (1967). *Human Relations*, Supervisory Series 4. Harlow,
    Essex, Longman.

Chapter 4

Where We Work

We have already looked at organisation as a process within the management cycle, but the word has yet another definition applicable to our management outlook. It is the concept of organisations as applied to such institutions as schools, churches, clubs, etc., including places of work. This concept does not look at the process of organisation as in the management cycle but rather as an ENTITY in itself having the characteristics that:

(1)   People comprise it.
(2)   It has a reason for its existence.
(3)   It has a structure of some kind.

Of course we in the Health Service are all part of an organisation — in fact a very large one which, in organisational terms, starts from the Secretary of State for Health and Social Security and ends with our patients and public (although I hope by now you will see it commencing with the patient!). That it comprises people is stating the obvious, but it should be recognised that the Health Service is a very labour-intensive service; it has no mass production line (though some people would like to see our patients as such) — it is people caring for people.

It may shock you if I say that the reason for our existence as an organisation is not just for our patients. I hasten to emphasise that they are the most important and most fundamental reason for our existence but, having patients, we have other responsibilities also.

Teaching, for example — we must train doctors, dentists, physiotherapists, nurses, radiographers and so on. Another example is the prevention of ill health, as opposed to the curing of disease, which is yet another reason for our health care organisation. Perhaps you would like to continue thinking about this and try to find another three or four reasons for our existence as an organisation. You will find the exercise quite an easy one and I hope it will begin to broaden your managerial outlook just a shade more.

Now we look at the third characteristic which deals with the structure of an organisation. We must return to our earlier chapters and recap on our definition of management. If you remember, we talked in terms of a manager being a person who has so much work to do (or is responsible for so much work) that she cannot do it herself and has to get others to do some of it for her.

DIVISION OF WORK

It is this division of the total work to be done and giving it to others which creates the structure of an organisation.

The Secretary of State is responsible for the total National Health Service. He cannot do all the work himself, so he keeps some of it and gives the rest of it to his chief officers at the Department of Health ... who in turn keep some and give the remainder to the Regional Health Authorities, who keep some ... and so on ... and so on ... until you get your work and responsibility and have others do some part of it for you.

I think we are ready now for a proposed formal definition of an organisation; it is: 'the division of the total tasks necessary to achieve the purposes, into tasks that can be undertaken by individuals'. Perhaps Fig. 4.1 will help illustrate this.

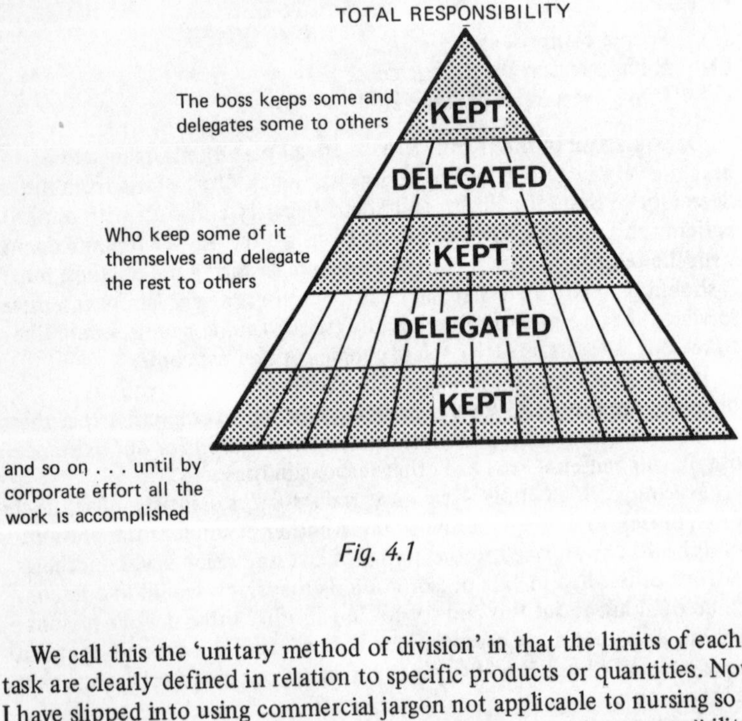

TOTAL RESPONSIBILITY

The boss keeps some and delegates some to others

KEPT

DELEGATED

Who keep some of it themselves and delegate the rest to others

KEPT

DELEGATED

KEPT

and so on ... until by corporate effort all the work is accomplished

Fig. 4.1

We call this the 'unitary method of division' in that the limits of each task are clearly defined in relation to specific products or quantities. Now I have slipped into using commercial jargon not applicable to nursing so let me explain it in nursing terms. If you give one nurse the responsibility for the total patient care of a number of patients — that would be the UNITARY division of tasks. If, on the other hand, you give one nurse the responsibility for medicines, another for injections, another for dressings, etc. — that would be called the SERIAL division of tasks; or, to put it another way, responsibility for a process occurring in a series which, when complete, leads to total patient care.

A third method of dividing work is the FUNCTIONAL method in which the divisions are fixed according to specialised types of work; e.g. personnel management and finance.

In the Health Service we can cite all three of these methods within our organisation, and for you to decide which is best for your patients would be another useful exercise.

This division of tasks throughout the organisation imposes on us a limitation of our function; that is, it defines what we are responsible for and what work we have to do; it gives us rules we have to obey and thus imposes on us a degree of formality which we call STRUCTURE. This leads me to offer yet another definition of an organisation; it is: 'a group of people working together in a formal relationship to achieve the purposes of the organisation'.

Combining the simple managerial definitions of the first chapter, and examples of how management developed with the somewhat more complex ideas I have just outlined, virtually completes the theory of organisations which I feel is required at this stage, though there is much more that I could say and many chapters, and indeed whole books, can be read on the subject if you want to go any further with the subject yourself.

My real concern in this chapter is not the how and why of organisations but how, being part of an organisation, we can make it work as effectively as possible. To do this we are going to examine what has been called the 'ten commandments' of organisation or, to be more accurate, CRITERIA OF GOOD ORGANISATION.

In this section I am presenting the theories of Henri Fayol as interpreted by Col. Lyndon Urwick, a man now well into his eighties and who has probably influenced British thinking and management action more than anyone else. While he was not a particularly original thinker himself, his expertise and contribution to management was to interpret, in the light of his experience, the theories of H. Fayol, W. Taylor and others. I suppose you could say he anglicised them and turned theory into effective practice. His book, *The Elements of Administration,* remains a classic. Evidence of his practical involvement in management is not only found in his writings but also in his name, forming part of the highly successful management consultants, Urwick, Orr and Partners.

Urwick's work on the criteria for good organisation, developed Fayol's seven principles into the ten which now follow. I will state each of them formally and then discuss them. Their purpose is not to lay down a set of perfect rules but rather to say that 'if your organisation does not measure up to any one of these principles, it is not as effective as it could be if it were following them'.

1. THE PRINCIPLE OF THE OBJECTIVE

'All organisations and each part of an organisation must have a purpose, either explicit or implied.'

Objectives are goals or targets set to guide the efforts of an organisation and all its component parts. We have already discussed this to some extent when discussing the characteristics of an organisation. There is very real difficulty in setting overall objectives for the Health Service.

Usually when I ask a class for an overall objective, I get 'good patient care'. Unfortunately, it is just not as simple as that; first of all we have not, as yet, been able to define, or measure, good patient care in a satisfactory way.

Perhaps I can turn to football for a graphic illustration of objectives in action. I have two sons, both of whom go to the same school but one is in the primary section and the other in the junior section. They have separate playgrounds but they both play football during their breaks.

In the primary playground, their idea of football is to kick the ball — never mind where — just kick and rush after it wherever it goes! They have no overall objective.

In the junior playground, things are different; they have deposited piles of coats as goals and divided into teams so at least, even though they still kick and rush, they do have an objective — that of scoring goals.

The stage further is when we analyse club soccer. Now the objectives are much clearer. They have two overall objectives:

(1)   To score as many goals as possible.
(2)   To prevent the other side from scoring.

With these two objectives each member of the team (or we could say 'the organisation') has an individual objective designed to contribute to the achievement of the overall objectives, i.e. the winger's objective is to take the ball upfield quickly and then pass it to the centre-forward whose objective is to score a goal. Then there is the full-back who must mark and tackle the winger to prevent him from doing his task, and thus achieve the second part of the overall objective.

Each member of the team knows exactly what to do and what is expected of each other team member; so together they work effectively to achieve the team's aims. Not so the schoolboys. No objective or limited objectives inevitably brand them as a disorganised rabble rather than an efficient smooth-running team.

But, back to nursing and what about our objectives? Our difficulty in identifying them should not lead us to forsake the principle of objectives. Rather we should direct our efforts towards setting personal objectives or targets for small groups of our staff in specific areas.

Let me give a nursing example of how having a nursing objective can improve our effectiveness.

Little State Enrolled Nurse Jenny is a great girl — a hard worker who really gets 'stuck in' especially when we are short. Many times I have seen her hike 18-stone Annie up the bed and make her comfortable!

Sister Barbara would really like to improve the care her patients get and decides to try to reduce the incidence of pressure sores on her ward; so, having noted how frequently her patients have them, she sets an objective: 'to reduce the incidence of pressure sores in this ward by 10% over the next three months'.

All the nurses have been involved and thoroughly agree that this would be quite an achievement. They all know their place in the plan, from the need for proper nutrition to frequent turning of the immobile.

Once again, staffing is short and SEN Jenny is making patients comfortable by herself. This time when she comes to a heavy patient she remembers the objective. Unfortunately, 18-stone Annie has a pressure sore already, but we must not let this patient get one. So off goes SEN Jenny to get the Auxiliary to help and — hey presto — Australia lift and the patient is up the bed without friction burns. And that is one less potential pressure sore.

I hope this shows that, when staff know clearly what is expected of them and what you want to achieve, their effectiveness improves.

What about other objectives which you could achieve in your part of the profession? District Nurses — what about increasing your specific family health education inputs during your visits? Health Visitors — what about increasing the uptake of the prophylactic programme offered in your practice by a certain percentage? Out-patients staff — can you do something about that old chestnut of 'waiting time'?

Objectives will improve effectiveness just as, when you decide on a Mediterranean cruise for your holiday, you will save more effectively than if you have nothing in mind.

2. THE PRINCIPLE OF SPECIALISATION

'As far as possible the activities in an organised group should be confined to the performance of a single activity.'

In industrial terms, this means that if you train a man to fit wheels on new cars or to solder half a dozen wires in a TV set then they will become very, very efficient at that single task. (Mind you, it does not say anything about the boredom of the job and the low morale associated with efficient drudgery.)

In nursing, we come out quite well on this principle because we specialise. We have:

General Nurses
Midwives
Health Visitors
District Nurses
Nurses for the mentally subnormal
Nurses for the psychiatric side
Children's Nurses
Orthopaedic Nurses
Ophthalmic Nurses

Then within each of these groups we have further specialisation, e.g. the General Nurse specialises in:

Medicine
Surgery
Intensive Care
Theatre
Geriatrics
Casualty
etc., etc.

Then we divide work into yet further specialised tasks by the serial division of tasks; for example:

two of you do the beds;
two of you do the treatments;
one take the temperatures;
and so on . . .

Each stage in the specialisation recognises that the generic nurse cannot be as efficient as the specialist in her field.

Many hospitals have appointed 'Phlebotomists', nurses who specialise in taking blood — which to my mind is much better than all of us having an occasional poke and prod.

Similarly, we specialise in management as Fig. 4.2 illustrates. As we

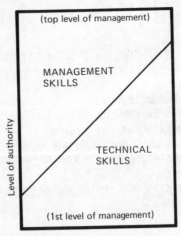

Fig. 4.2

take on increasing management responsibility, so we need less of our technical (nursing) skills and need to specialise more in management skills. And before any of you interpret that diagram literally and deduce that a senior manager in nursing need not be a nurse, let me kill it by saying 'over my dead body'.

3. THE PRINCIPLE OF COORDINATION

'The tasks in an organisation should be grouped so as to facilitate coordination or unity of effort towards the common objective.'

Prior to the unification of the Health Services, a great deal of cooperation existed between the three services and many health care developments were achieved in this way. Coordination, however, is management activity and must not be confused with cooperation.

A manager must coordinate her staff and her activities, and to do this the tasks must be organised so as to facilitate this management function.

Once again, nursing comes out well in this principle, mainly as the result of the Salmon and Mayston Reports. These have brought about the grouping under one manager of similar undertakings in the organisation. For example, the units under a Nursing Officer comprise, say, four or six surgical wards — or medical — or orthopaedic — all grouped together to facilitate management coordination. It is much more effective to manage a group of similar wards than a mixture of specialities.

It can be more economical in that an expensive piece of nursing equipment can be shared by the unit as a whole; I am totally convinced that it would be advantageous to all to have unit allocation of staff rather than ward-by-ward allocation.

One study of a surgical unit's wards showed that, on one day, ward A had a very high dependency while ward B was not at all busy; throughout the week, different wards had their peaks and troughs of work-loads (Fig. 4.3).

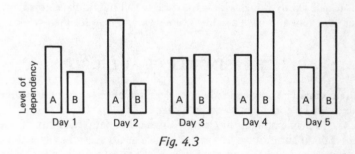

Fig. 4.3

Unit allocation of staff could well have ironed out these differences with advantages to both patients and staff.

The next three principles are inter-related, so first I will state them consecutively and then deal with them separately and finally illustrate their relationship to each other. They are the principles of responsibility (for one's subordinates), of authority (in every undertaking) and of correspondence (between responsibility and authority).

4. THE PRINCIPLE OF RESPONSIBILITY

'The responsibility of a superior for acts of his subordinates is absolute.'

The principle of responsibility can be re-stated in well understood terms, i.e. 'You carry the can for your subordinates!' Certainly you can 'carpet them' and tell them off so that they clearly know you are displeased with them, but when it comes to you answering for events under your management control, you must take the full blame.

This principle is well known in government, and an example which many of you will remember is the Aberfan disaster where a coal slag heap slid and submerged a school, resulting in a tragic loss of life. At that time, the chairman of the Coal Board was Lord Robens and because this event was of such magnitude, he tendered his resignation under the principle of responsibility, even though in real terms he was not personally responsible for this particular slag heap. As it so happens, the government did not accept his resignation but none the less the principle of responsibility was clearly adhered to.

The antithesis of this is the Watergate affair. That a President of the United States of America could remain in office under such conditions continues to amaze me. In Britain, the principle of responsibility would require his resignation before the newspaper ink was dry.

In nursing we are not really used to the consequences of this principle or there would have been a few resignations required over the recent cases of maltreatment by nurses of patients in certain long-stay hospitals. Clearly senior management and some of the medical profession were not blameless in some of these incidents and should have resigned.

As staff are only doing work which we would do if it were physically possible, we naturally remain responsible for them. On the other hand, this responsibility brings with it the need for all subordinates to accept that their superiors have a right to supervise and monitor their work.

5. THE PRINCIPLE OF AUTHORITY

'There should be one, and only one, clear line of direct authority from the top to the bottom of every undertaking.'

The principle of authority is sometimes called the 'scalar principle'. A definition of authority is 'the right to make decisions and to issue instructions to cover the work of others'. To put it another way, a person having authority has the RIGHT to act and the POWER to reward or punish.

From where does the source of authority spring?

Ownership is one obvious source but, as far as the Health Service is concerned, there is no ownership involved so the law is the obvious source of our authority.

Sheer expertise and technical ability is yet another source. When a person really knows what she is talking about, people accept her authoritative viewpoint.

Which leads us to yet another source which is much more complex. It is subordinate acceptance. If a subordinate refuses to accept a manager's authority, then the manager has no authority. If a group of nurses decide to walk off the ward despite the commands of that manager, then the manager has lost her authority.

Management writers differ in their approach to these sources of authority. Some say that it is the laws of the organisation which denote authority; others say it is the acceptance of the authority by the recipient of the order which is the source. What do you think?

In either case there are limitations to the effectiveness of authority, and this principle corrects one of the main limitations: that of overlapping authority.

The principle is saying that if two people exercise authority over the same group of people, you have problems. It says that every person must know who her boss is and who her boss's boss is, so that she can, if need be, go right up the line to the top. This is what is called 'line management'. It is the clear line of management authority which runs from the top to the bottom of every organisation – or, if you like, 'the chain of command' (Fig. 4.4).

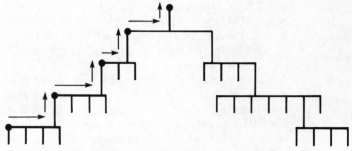

Fig. 4.4   A line, or chain, of command.

6. THE PRINCIPLE OF CORRESPONDENCE

'Responsibility and authority must coincide.'

The final principle of this group ties together the two principles of responsibility and authority. The principle of correspondence states that the two must go hand in hand.

Clearly if you make a person responsible for a job she must also be given the authority to go with it.

It was a common experience prior to the Salmon and Mayston Reports for the following type of incident to occur. The organisational structure was like that shown in Fig. 4.5.

73

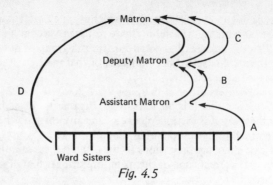

Fig. 4.5

Stage A	Sister has a good idea (or a question . . . or something) and goes with it to her immediate superior, the Assistant Matron.
Stage B	'Yes,' says the Assistant Matron. 'It is a good idea but really I cannot act on it. I think we had better go and discuss it with Miss Bloggs, the Deputy Matron.' So off the two of them go to see Miss Bloggs.
Stage C	Miss Bloggs agrees with both her visitors but says 'Of course, if Matron had been off on holiday or even on a day off, I could have given you an answer but as she is in today I think we ought to go up and see her.' So off the three of them go!
Stage D	Of course Matron makes the decision (exactly the same one that the Assistant and the Deputy Matron would have made) and to all intents and purposes the incident is over — EXCEPT that this kind of thing was repeated so often that in the end Sister ignored her Assistant and Deputy Matrons and went straight to the top.

Stage D had a manifold effect on all concerned. The Deputy and Assistant Matrons felt left out, their morale dropped, their jobs lost a lot of interest and stimulation — yet let anything go wrong and Matron was on to them like a ton of bricks! Matron became more and more busy and the queues outside her office became longer and longer as the Sisters developed this nice status relationship with Matron.

The diagnosis of this problem is easy. The Deputy and the Assistant had responsibility without authority, with disastrous results for the organisation.

Having given responsibility and authority, it must be defined in scope. This has two benefits. Firstly, it publicises the authority and responsibility a person has (and it is important for authority and responsibility to be 'seen' and made known to others), and secondly it prevents the overlap of these principles between members of staff. Overlapping of either responsibility or authority is distinctly a factor limiting the effectiveness of a manager.

What this principle is recommending is that every person should have a Job Description so that her position in the organisation is clearly prescribed in writing.

The preparation of Job Descriptions calls for careful examination of every job from the top to the bottom of the organisation, each level of authority being clearly defined and delineated between the staff at every level, ensuring (1) that no two jobs overlap, (2) that no-one has two bosses, and (3) that all jobs dovetail to realise the total objectives of the organisation.

Most of us have Job Descriptions or variants of Job Descriptions such as role specification, and these are very useful guides, not only to the job holder but to other branches of the Health Service. Many an administrator and professional and technical worker has voiced the opinion that now nursing has followed the principle of definition, they at last know whom to go to for what they want. My reply to them has invariably been — 'When are you going to adopt the same principle?'

Before leaving the subject of Job Descriptions, I should comment on the need for them to be frequently updated, as jobs are continually changing. I do not think they need to be reviewed more than once a year but leaving them much longer than that would not be recommended.

It is an interesting phenomenon to note that in the main, jobs move in an upward direction. What seems to happen is that people absorb some of their boss's job into their own job. Perhaps I can illustrate this for you with Fig. 4.6.

The diagram poses the very real question about what happens to the work your subordinate discards in order to reach upwards herself. If she

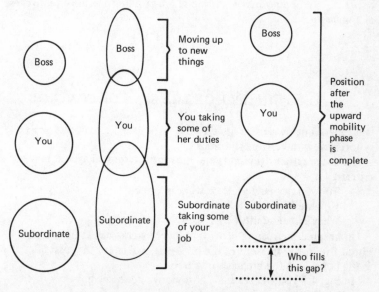

Fig. 4.6

75

has a subordinate the answer is obvious, but if not — then what?

What seems to have happened in nursing is that we have created new grades.

Let us examine nursing from this point of view. Sadly, we as nurses have been only too willing to do doctors' work. As they discard some of their functions we eagerly take them up. (This is very natural and only proves what Abe Maslow said — see Chapter 3.) As a result of this, nursing has become more and more technical and less and less of what I know as 'nursing'. So who does the nursing? Why the State Enrolled Nurses, of course . . . and have you noticed their professional development? It is progressing all the time, and who is doing increasingly more nursing? The Nursing Auxiliaries! They, too, are agitating for the designation of Nurse. And what will happen then is that we will create yet another grade! Perhaps I'm too sceptical.

7. THE PRINCIPLE OF DEFINITION

'The task, the responsibility and the authority must be clearly defined so that all concerned are aware of the scope and completeness of the delegation.'

Having given responsibility and authority, it must be defined in scope. This has two benefits. Firstly it publishes the authority and responsibility that a person has (and it is important for authority and responsibility to be 'seen' and made known to others), and secondly it prevents the overlap of these principles between members of staff. Overlapping of either responsibility or authority is distinctly a factor limiting the effectiveness of a manager.

8. THE PRINCIPLE OF THE SPAN OF CONTROL

'No superior can supervise directly the work of more than five or six subordinates whose work interlocks.'

These are rather rigid limits and must be interpreted against many criteria:

      To what degree does their work interlock?

      How well trained are they?

      What is their ability?

In hospital the span of control probably works out at the level of about five or six. In terms of the organisational chart, the span of control is the bough and the branches of a tree.

In Fig. 4.7 you will see that 'A' directly supervises the work of six people — this, then, is her span of control.

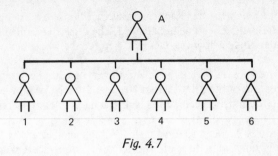

Fig. 4.7

Check your own organisational chart and see how you match up to this principle.

If you are working in the community then I doubt if you come out very well, as it is quite common for a community manager to have a span of control of 20 or even more! This is because the work of District Nurses and Health Visitors does not interlock very much at all; they are all specially trained and are virtually independent practitioners of their specialty.

Having a large span of control brings its special problems to the managers concerned. Communication is more difficult; so, too, are supervision and control, and the possibility of the manager becoming remote from her work and subordinates is a very real danger.

9. THE PRINCIPLE OF BALANCE

'An organisation shall be so structured as to ensure the best balance for the purpose of the organisation.'

Managers must always be aware of the balance of their organisation, as change can easily alter situations.

Perhaps the best nursing example that I can think of involves district nursing. For many years the State Registered Nurse qualification was a prerequisite for district nurse training, and quite justifiably so as there was a great deal of skilled nursing and treatment to be given at home.

However, for a few years before I came to be a District Nurse (1961) things had been changing. Almost imperceptibly in some cases . . . rather dramatically in others. The incidence of tuberculosis had declined considerably, antibiotics had become well established and were very successful when given orally. People were living longer as the result of good medicine and improved living standards. These are but a few of the things I could mention which had changed in district nursing.

We were giving fewer injections and more time-consuming visits to the elderly and infirm. We seemed purely to be bathing a large number of patients, and, while any service offered to the needy is rewarding to a nurse, I could not help feeling that I did not need to be an SRN to carry out much of my work.

Of course I was not alone in this feeling; it was shared by many people in the profession. What had happened was that things had changed and the organisation had become unbalanced. The organisation had become staffed with people who were over-qualified for the work they were required to do.

The remedy is now well in hand and the balance has been restored by the introduction of the SEN District Nurse and the Nursing Auxiliary to the community nursing team. The result is a more effective service, a happier staff and a reduction in expenditure.

Now perhaps we need to look again. With planned early discharge and considerably reduced periods of hospitalisation, more acute work is being done in the community. One interesting piece of research has suggested that the coronary occlusion patient nursed at home does just as well as the same case nursed in the Intensive Therapy Unit! Who knows – could we be heading for a new imbalance?

I also think the National Health Service reorganisation was a re-balancing exercise. The organisation was supposed to serve the patients and public of our country and it was found that the three separate divisions – the Local Executive, the Local Health Authority and the Regional Hospital Boards – did not form a structure which best suited the aims of the NHS. Hence the unification of the three services to enable a balance of health care to be planned, organised and coordinated.

10. THE PRINCIPLE OF CONTINUITY

'Continuous reorganisation must accompany changing conditions.'

There is a clear link between the previous principle and this one, but this should be interpreted in a more dynamic and creative way. Here we have the concept of continual review by management. Management asking questions, delving, enquiring; applying the who, what, where, when and why to every situation. This is the way to make progress – getting out of the rut, asking 'why' rather than stating 'We have always done it'.

Simple examples can be cited, such as my experience as a post-registration SRN student, taking the temperatures of the 24 patients in my first ward (page 10).

Perhaps this example is more appropriate to a discussion on standards but I am using it to illustrate the fact that someone said 'Why are we taking everybody's temperature – even when they are up and about doing teas and everything else?' Why not just take the temperatures of those who really need it AND TAKE THEM PROPERLY! They were good questions which led to better professional care.

Let me ask another question. Why do we make all the beds by 10 a.m.? Answer: doctor does his rounds then and he likes to see all the beds nice and neat and tidy. Someone once asked the doctors to note which beds had been stripped and made and which had been just pulled up. They couldn't tell the difference! Surprise, surprise! In this case I think we are the victims of social pressures. The facts are that unless your beds at home are made by 10 a.m. you are considered a pretty hopeless housewife — at least by your neighbour who has dropped in for coffee!

At one Charge Nurses' meeting they decided that each ward would keep its own supply of shrouds instead of them all being kept in the female medical ward. 'What shall I do with the shroud book?' asked the Charge Nurse on that ward. 'What shroud book?' asked the Nursing Officer. I will not bother you with the hilarious conversation and incredulity which followed but the end result was that the Charge Nurses revealed that between them they were keeping more than 12 separate books! Why? Because it had always been done. I am pleased to report that the number of books kept now is down to half the original total.

These are simple examples to demonstrate the need for management to have an enquiring mind; it is a continuous ongoing process; it must be dynamic, never standing still. It must change to meet the ONCOMING situation rather than the crises revealed day by day.

TYPES OF ORGANISATIONS

I must reiterate that this chapter is not really attempting to cover organisational theory, but a review of the principles above would be incomplete without some short discussion on the types of organisation in which we may find ourselves working.

Mechanistic

The type of organisation in which the majority of us work is one in which most of the above principles are quite strictly applied. In this type we find that work is being organised according to strict rules and is accomplished by the use of authority.

I call this 'ours is not to reason why, ours is but to do or die'. I think I may be a bit harsh, placing NHS institutions firmly into this category, but certainly none can deny that we are hedged about with rules and regulations and work is seen to be more important than the people doing the work.

Organic

This type of organisation is virtually the opposite of Mechanistic. Here managers' jobs are not clearly defined and the authority of the manager and her relationship with other managers is much more flexible. The sort of organisation which this type suits best is that which is frequently having to cope with change and requires a high degree of innovation.

The characteristic of this is that management is people centred.

Systems

This type of organisation is really a midway point between the Mechanistic and the Organic organisations (though I am sure its proponents would be horrified to hear me say it!).

In this organisation, management take into account six interacting situational factors:

(1) The size of the organisation.
(2) The degree of interaction.
(3) The personality of the staff.
(4) The similarity of goals.
(5) The level of the decision making.
(6) The state of the system.

They aim to 'regulate and organise these six functions into an integrated whole so as to achieve the aims of the organisation as effectively and as economically as possible'. In essence this is yet another definition of the word organisation, i.e. arranging the parts of the organisation.

I think I must leave organisational theory there. It becomes very complex and perhaps you might like to follow it up at your leisure, but I will recap what I have said.

Think of the three types of organisations as an answer to the question 'What is being organised?'

(1) If it is the work that is being organised then the organisation is Mechanistic.
(2) If it is people who are being organised then the organisation is Organic.
(3) If other factors in the organisation are being organised then the organisation is the Systems approach.

As this chapter ends, so does the first part of this book. Up to now I have involved you very much in the theory of management. But theory is theory; it can be challenged, argued about, disproved, exalted; people each have their own pet theories, just as I have. Don't merely accept what I have said — read other books, discuss things amongst yourselves; as long as the end result is a better understanding of the reason behind the practice of management, I will be very happy.

As for me, I'm anxious to become of more practical help to you and from now on I am going to try to give you some practical information and help in dealing with some of the more important management functions which you are or will be facing.

REFERENCES AND FURTHER READING

Cuming, M. W. (1968). *Reducing the Odds.* London, King's Fund Hospital Centre.
Cuming, M. W. (1971). *Hospital Staff Management.* London, William Heinemann.

Dale, E. (1973). *Management: Theory and Practice,* 3rd edn. New York and Maidenhead, McGraw-Hill.

Koontz, H. and O'Donnell, C. (1976). *Management: A Book of Readings,* 4th edn. New York and Maidenhead, McGraw-Hill.

Likert, R. (1967). *The Human Organization: its management and value.* New York and Maidenhead, McGraw-Hill.

McFarland, D. E. (1974). *Management: Principles and Practice,* 4th edn. New York and London, Collier-Macmillan.

Mayston, E. L. (Chairman) (1969). *Report of the Working Party on Management Structure in the Local Authority Nursing Services;* Department of Health and Social Security, and Scottish Home and Health Office. London, HMSO.

Millard, G. (1972). *Personnel Management in Hospitals.* London, Institute of Personnel Management.

Pugh, D. S., Hickson, D. J. and Hinings, C. R. (1964). *Writers on Organisation.* London, Hutchinson. (Also published by Penguin, 1971.)

Salmon, Brian (Chairman) (1966). *Report of the Committee on Senior Nursing Staff Structure;* Ministry of Health, and Scottish Home and Health Department. London, HMSO.

Urwick, L. F. (1974). *The Elements of Administration.* London, Pitman.

Chapter 5

Square Pegs—
Square Holes

Square pegs in round holes? 'Not if I can help it,' say most managers. The fact is that none of us can help making a wrong appointment on occasion — the real problem is when we rarely make the right appointment.

The selection of the right person for the right job is a very complicated business which too often is treated very lightly by those responsible for the appointment. One of the problems is that so many people think they are good judges of character and ability in others; that, on the basis of a 15-minute interview for which they have done no preparation, they will invariably make the right decision!

Of course it is a lot of nonsense. Getting the right person for the right job takes a lot of hard work and considerable thought. Even after we do all we are supposed to do, it is still possible to make a mistake; after all, we are only human and we are considering our fellow humans.

Twice so far in this chapter I have said in different ways that it is easy to make a mistake, so it is time I made my point. The point is that, while no selection process or system is infallible, we are less likely to make a wrong appointment if we approach the subject in a systematic way than if we do it in a haphazard manner.

At work today I had to calculate the average cost of a Nursing Auxiliary in a geriatric hospital and I was staggered to find that each Auxiliary cost the Authority an average of £3,200 per annum (early 1977). Now most of us think very carefully before we spend £5 and even more carefully before we spend £50, and as for buying a house — my, how carefully we go into that transaction!

The appointment of a Nursing Auxiliary is going to cost more than £10 on her first day at work; more than £50 in her first week; in only four years her salary (in current values) would buy most of us a very representative house! If she is 18 when you appoint her, she has 42 more years to work and £130,000 of salary to collect. A mistake can cost us dearly!

While I am concerned about the financial implications of a bad appointment, I am even more concerned about the effects of a bad appointment on our patients. How dreadful to inflict upon them the results of our own inadequacies or our own unwillingness to take the right steps to minimise the incidence of wrong appointments.

FILLING THE VACANCY

In management jargon the steps we take to fill a vacancy are called 'the selection process' and it starts off by asking a very basic but very profound question:

Is there really a vacancy?

The fact that a person has left her job has far too often come to mean that we have a vacancy to be filled, but we must not fall into that trap.

A person leaving gives us a very real opportunity to stop, take a breath and review the situation from every angle. Of course in most cases, a person leaving will make you so desperately short staffed that it is obvious that the vacancy must be filled as soon as possible. On the other hand, you could consider whether you would rather have one and a half State Enrolled Nurses in place of one senior Sister; or whether the ward can work without that person and give the post to another ward with a greater need; or whether you can do without the post altogether and save the money.

Whatever the outcome, it is important to have consciously asked the question and to have considered as objectively as possible all the various alternatives to using that post.

Job Description

Having decided that you have a vacancy to be filled, the next stage is to draw up what is generally known as a Job Description. A Job Description is part of an overall procedure for obtaining pertinent job facts, known as 'job analysis'. Figure 5.1 outlines the complete Job Analysis programme.

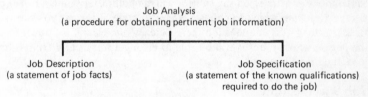

Job Analysis
(a procedure for obtaining pertinent job information)

Job Description	Job Specification
(a statement of job facts)	(a statement of the known qualifications) required to do the job)

Fig. 5.1

But we are considering first the Job Description. How do you go about writing one of these? In some organisations there are people who do very little else than write Job Descriptions, in which case they observe the job, question the job holder and her superior and use all the expertise they have at their disposal to produce a first-class Job Description.

As for you and me, we will have to settle for something less than that, and I suggest that a good start can be made by asking a few questions of yourself.

(1) What is the job?
(2) What specific duties and responsibilities are there in the job?
(3) What general conditions and what special factors may be involved?

83

(4) Where is the job performed?
(5) How are the duties carried out?

Answering these questions will enable you to write down the following:
>Job title
>Location
>Job summary
>Duties and responsibilities
>Supervision given or received
>Working conditions

In case you want further guidance, here are some words which may be useful to you in compiling different aspects of the Job Description.
(1) To describe facets of supervision, what about these words:
     coordinates, controls, monitors, devises, assigns, develops, defines, determines, establishes . . .
(2) To describe the analytical function of a job try:
     investigates, examines, evaluates, appraises, reviews, assesses, interprets, forecasts . . .
(3) To describe relationships:
     liaises, consults, confers, negotiates, cooperates . . .
(4) To help describe the job in general:
     reports, records, specifies, procedures, methods, effective, relevant, studies . . .

The way in which you write the Job Description varies from place to place. There may be a 'house style', i.e. all Job Descriptions are written in the same way within the organisation. Otherwise you may care to look up some books or articles on the subject which could offer you a number of alternatives from which to choose. Whatever style or format you decide to use, as long as it contains job facts logically and clearly set down so that the person whose job it is will be able to distinguish it clearly from other jobs, then it will be useful.

Job Specification

The Job Description forms the basis for the next part of the exercise, which is the Job Specification.

This is a much more subjective document and consists of the value judgements of the compilers as to the qualifications and skills required by the person who is to fill the job we have described in the Job Description.

Ask yourself the following questions about the job:
>What education is required to do the job?
>What qualifications are required to do the job?
>What experience is required to do the job?
>What judgement is required to do the job?
>What training is required to do the job?

Fig. 5.2

What this exercise is making you do is to translate the activities contained in the Job Description into particular skills and abilities that we want the job occupant to have. When we have done this, it is a very short step to describing the very person we are after.

Theoretically it should be a simple matter to form a picture of an ideal candidate for the job — but there are many pitfalls.

The first of these is when the person writing the job specification is over-familiar with the job and states she knows 'just the type of person for the job' and promptly writes the job specification for the job based on personal knowledge of the job (some 15 years ago!), the sort of person she likes (short, quiet and timid — so that she can boss her about!) and the type of person her boss likes (because you must keep in with the boss!).

The point I want to make from that paragraph is that it is essential for the job to be studied objectively from the facts of the analysis and the people currently and directly concerned with the job.

The second pitfall is not describing the requirements of the job in the same terms as the attributes required of the people who are being considered for it; and here we come to the use of 'plans'.

There are two classifications of human attributes in frequent use for selection purposes. These are:
(1)   The Seven-point Plan — originated by Professor Alex Rodger of the National Institute of Industrial Psychology.
(2)   The Five-point Plan — originated by Professor J. Munro Fraser.

Seven-point Plan

First let us consider the Seven-point Plan, which draws attention to the following aspects of the individual.

Job Specification	*Applicant Assessment*
1. PHYSIQUE	
Does the job involve physical strain; is it fatiguing or is it carried out under trying conditions?	*Has she any physical defects or disabilities of occupational importance?*
Does it involve contact with the public?	*Do her appearance, bearing and speech make a suitable first impression?*

85

Job Specification	Applicant Assessment

2. ATTAINMENTS

What standard of general education does the work call for?	What type of education has she had and how well has she done?
Does it require any specialised training?	What occupational training has she had?
Does it require any previous experience?	What occupational experience has she had and how well has she done?

3. GENERAL INTELLIGENCE

Does the work call for someone who is especially 'quick on the uptake' or could it be done by someone who is average or below average in this respect?	What is the level of her general intelligence?

4. SPECIAL APTITUDES

Does the work involve an understanding of mechanical things?	Does she seem to have an aptitude for any of these kinds of activities so that she will be easy to train in one or other of these particular skills?
Manipulative work?	
Easy expression in speech or writing?	
Work with figures?	
Drawing or other artistic expression?	

5. INTERESTS

Does the job provide any outlet for an interest in working with other people?	Does the candidate seem to gain particular satisfaction in social, practical/constructive, physically active, intellectual or artistic activities? What levels of achievement does she set herself and to what extent does she attain them?
For an interest in making or repairing things?	
For an interest in outdoor work or work requiring physical agility or strength?	
For an interest in intellectual matters?	
For any form of artistic expression?	

Job Specification	Applicant Assessment
6. DISPOSITION	
Does the work call for someone who is easily acceptable to other people?	*Does the candidate seem able to stand up to the role which the job involves?*
Is there any element of leadership or influence over others involved?	*Is she sufficiently well organised in disposition to meet these four kinds of demands to the necessary degree?*
Does it call for someone who is particularly steady and reliable?	
Does it require someone who is self-reliant and can carry responsibility?	
7. CIRCUMSTANCES	
Does the job involve travelling or are there any special demands which might interfere with domestic life?	*Are her domestic circumstances likely to conflict with the demands of the job?*
What levels of prestige and remuneration are attached to the job?	*What kind of job has her background and previous life led her to expect?*

In using this plan, it is useful to consider under each heading whether or not the characteristic is:

(1)   Essential, i.e. indispensible if the job is to be done well.
(2)   Desirable, i.e. less essential attributes which may be only preferences.
(3)   A contraindication, i.e. any attributes which could disqualify a candidate.

To illustrate this last point, I have been told about a Matron who had almost a room full of Assistant Matrons (pre-Salmon Report, obviously) when filling one of these Assistant Matron posts which had become vacant; Matron let it be known that anyone who was 'moody' would not get the job. She already had a roomful of moody women and another one would be the last straw!

She clearly had laid down a contraindicating characteristic – if you are moody it will disqualify you! What a character she herself must have been!

Five-point Plan

The next plan sets out to look at the individual from five points of view, from each of which we will see a different aspect of the candidate.

87

Job Specification	*Applicant Assessment*

1. IMPACT ON OTHER PEOPLE

How much of the job involves inter-action with others either in information seeking, instruction giving or normal social intercourse? What are the physical demands of the job? Strength? Endurance?

What reaction does she call from other people? Are her appearance, speech, manner and social sophistication up to the standard required for the job? Is she physically capable to do the job required?

2. ACQUIRED KNOWLEDGE OR QUALIFICATIONS

What general education, specialised training and qualifications are required in order for the job to be performed at a satisfactory level? What work experience is necessary for this job?

Does she reach the minimum qualification standards laid down by the job specification? Is her work experience recent enough and relevant to the job?

3. INNATE ABILITIES OR 'BRAINS'

Does the job need a quick, active mind? Ability to grasp new ideas? What mechanical aptitude/manual dexterity is required?

Does she have the abilities required to carry out the job? Is she capable of using these abilities effectively? Does she have abilities which might show her to have good potential?

4. MOTIVATION

What standard of motivation is required to do the job successfully? High, i.e. leadership, ambition, drive, determination? Medium, i.e. a steady worker, reliable, average initiative, offers reasonable effort? Low, i.e. no initiative, relies on others for guidance, a day's work for a day's pay? Lazy?

What success qualities does she show? At what level is the goal-directed aspect of the individual's make-up; the target she sets herself?

5. ADJUSTMENT

How much pressure/emotional strain does the job involve? At what tempo is the work done? Intricacy? Responsibility? Interaction?

How does she react to pressure? How does she get on with her fellow men? What standards of conduct does she present? Does she show ability to adopt compromise, etc? Does she show ability to adjust to the degree which the job demands?

This plan concentrates more on the dynamic aspect of the individual, though in these five headings you can clearly distinguish the seven points of the previous plan.

Both the plans discussed are helpful if used as presented but they become more effective if adapted to your own specific needs. I myself find these plans invaluable for comparison of candidates both at shortlisting and at interview. At interview they are particularly useful in enabling you to remember each candidate somewhat more effectively.

I invariably use one or the other at interview but now I tend to use the seven-point plan for non-managerial posts and the five-point plan when interviewing for managers. Do try them yourself; I am sure you too will find them useful.

Of necessity, in describing these plans as aids to effective selection, I have had to discuss briefly some of the stages of the selection process before we have completed the subject of the Job Description and Job Specification. I only want to make one final point, which is to emphasise the importance of the exercise resulting in the word picture of an ideal candidate for the job. The reason for this emphasis is that from now on all our efforts will be channelled towards the objective of attracting and employing that ideal person. (Remember the principle of the objective?)

Just in case you have read some other books or one of your lecturers may have mentioned it — the technical name for that ideal person's description is the Man Specification.

ADVERTISING

The next stage is to notify the vacancy and our minds immediately turn to advertising. I learnt from a student I once taught of the phenomenon of 'desperation advertising'. This is the process of dashing off an advert. quickly and phoning it to the press so that when your boss asks you about the vacancy you can say the advertisement has gone to press.

Looking at the quality of press recruitment advertising, I am under the impression that a great deal of desperation advertising is done in the NHS.

Advertising is very expensive and deserves a great deal of your time and consideration in order to get it just right.

Cost of Advertising

It is estimated that current expenditure on recruitment advertising for the hospital service is well in excess of £2,000,000 (£2m). In the main those responsible for inserting these advertisements have little or no knowledge of the principles involved. Consequently money is being wasted (albeit in dribs and drabs locally, but on a national scale it must amount to many thousands of pounds) by hit-and-miss advertising.

Aim of Advertising

The purpose of an advertisement is to attract the person who meets the 'man specification' for the post which is vacant. To achieve this objective we must approach the matter in an intelligent and systematic manner. No amount of interviewing will produce a good person for the job out of a set of unsuitable or mediocre candidates.

Preparation

Job Description

First the Job Description must be prepared. The emphasis is on THE Job Description as this involves a close and objective study of the job as it stands and of how it is envisaged it will develop. 'A' job description is what most people can dash off in 10 or 15 minutes — the two types bear no resemblance.

Man Specification

From the Job Description you can now describe the qualities which the job requires (Job Specification), and from this the profile or specification of the person who will best fit the job can be drawn up.

When you have completed the Job Description and Man Specification you will have most of the information you require to write the advertisement.

Writing the Advertisement

What to include in the advertisement is a very real problem. You will have collected a great deal of information but to use it all would be far too costly. The things you should include will be the points taken from your specification which you can stress in order to influence the right person to apply.

Select from the information you have the key characteristics of the job, the Man Specification, benefits you can offer the candidate and information about your organisation; include this information in a precise word picture which will attract and maintain the interest of the person you want to apply.

In its simplest form the advertisement should be a systematic elimination process activated by giving two categories of information:

(1)   The requirements of the employer.
(2)   The benefits to the employee.

Figure 5.3 is a model demonstrating the inevitable and necessary fall-out or elimination of readers.

90

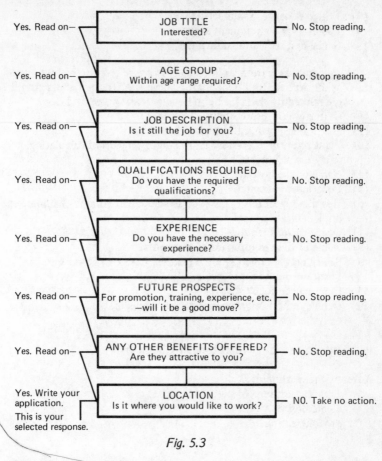

Fig. 5.3

What are the key characteristics you should include in your advertisement? To help you decide here are two lists. The first is from data of Management Selection Ltd (in 1970), giving the order of importance of factors involved in attracting prospective staff.

(1) Definition of responsibility
(2) Location of post
(3) Starting salary
(4) Experience looked for
(5) Qualifications required
(6) Position in organisational structure
(7) Future promotion prospects
(8) Age range required
(9) Name of company
(10) Company's plans for growth
(11) Background details about company
(12) Variety of experience provided

(13)   Fringe benefits, bonus scheme, etc.
(14)   Facilities and equipment available
(15)   Social and recreational facilities

The second list is from a pilot survey exercise given to mainly nursing staff (at the William Rathbone Staff College, 1970); the factors given below were ranked by them in the following order of importance.
(1)   Definition of responsibility.
(2)   Position in organisational structure.
(3)   Point of entry into salary range (that is, means of calculating entry or 'negotiable').
(4)   Name of the hospital.
(5)   Location of hospital.
(6)   Hospital plans for organisation development (that is, Salmon Report implementation).
(7)   Qualifications required.
(8)   Name of the group/board of governors.
(9)   Salary range actually quoted (that is, £xxxx to £xxxxx).
(10) Future promotion prospects.
(11) Experience looked for.
(12) Details of housing/accommodation available.

An Appointment Advertisement Check-list

Advertisements should:
    attract attention
    create desire
    provoke action.

Attract Attention

The advertisement can attract attention by:
(1)   The headline. The job title is usually the main point of attraction, but you might possess another unique selling point which is more attractive — that is, a 'benefit headline'.
(2)   The use of white space, border, illustration, size and type of print.

Create Desire

Create a desire to answer the advertisement by:
(1)   Showing all the benefits your organisation can offer the person who does not want to move.
(2)   Outlining the Job Specification of the person you want.
(3)   Detailing the salary and entry point.
(4)   Describing only the qualification really required.

(5)   Including any other factors which indicate that you can offer job satisfaction.

Provoke Action

Your advertisement must be easy to reply to, with the name and address of the person receiving applications clearly stated.

Where to Place your Advertisement

Local Newspapers

These are suitable for less skilled jobs and entrants into the nursing service; also for part-time staff.

National Newspapers

These are useful for jobs at a very senior level. (If a person is looking for a job then a very modest advertisement will get him to reply; but the power of the press is such that a good advertisement can attract not only the job hunters but also those who are not consciously looking for another job — that is, those who habitually 'scan' the advertising pages just to see what's going on.)

Professional Journals

The professional journals are undoubtedly the most useful medium for most positions.

The National Nursing Staff Committee made the following recommendations (in 1969) which still seem to be most reasonable, though for the reasons given above in connection with national newspapers, I would suggest the use of selected national newspapers for District Nursing Officers and above.

Grade	Advertising Media
5	Local press
	Regional lists
6	Regional lists
7	Nursing journals
	Regional lists
8	Nursing journals
District Nursing Officer	Nursing journals
Area Nursing Officer	Nursing journals
Regional Nursing Officer	Nursing journals

The Ministry of Health (1968) – now the Department of Health and Social Security – have also made recommendations which are most helpful.

Use of Agencies

Agencies are experts in their fields. In placing your advertisement with them you will get a great deal of help and advice free. Only when you require some special services do they make any charge; their income is derived from discounts available to them as an agency. You pay only standard advertising rates. It would seem more than reasonable to use their services.

Basic Principles of Advertising

(1) Advertising is a means to an end and not an end in itself. Since the desired objective is efficient recruitment, advertising must be conceived as an integral part of the recruitment process. It is not a separate activity to be rushed through before the real business of selecting people begins.

(2) The function of an advertisement is to produce action. It is not enough for an advertisement to be seen; it must also work by conveying information which stimulates a positive response.

(3) The foundation of every job advertisement should be a careful analysis of the job itself.

(4) Every advertisement should be aimed as directly and as explicitly as possible at the type of person defined in the Man Specification.

(5) Prospective candidates are most likely to respond to an advertisement when uncertainty and latent doubts have been dispelled from their minds by information telling them what they would like to know.

(6) With these factors in mind, aim to produce a COMPACT list of suitably motivated and qualified candidates and achieve a balance of cost/coverage in reaching these people (Denerley and Plumbley, 1968).

Conclusion

A good advertisement selects the people who are really suited to the job. It cannot create people who do not exist; it can only serve as a spearhead to recruitment.

APPLICATION FORMS

Unfortunately, the National Health Service is stuck with standard application forms for most jobs, but this should not stop us from using them effectively or making suitable additions to them to meet our needs.

The principles of an application form in an ideal situation are fivefold.

(1) It is a means of asking and answering questions by correspondence. This is the most important use. If you ask questions which are worded in such a way as not to be ambiguous, both you as a prospective employer and the candidate can benefit.

You will save applicants' valuable time by not calling them for interview when it is obvious from the application form that they are unsuitable. You will assure yourself that you have a candidate with a good employment record and a great deal of potential to offer the new job . . . all this if you ask the right questions.

To do this you need to follow the next principle.

(2) Design the form around the Man Specification you have developed. Knowing just the person you want will enable you to frame the questions which will clearly identify those closest to the objective you have set. You will be able to match their qualifications, experience and many other factors against those required by the Man Specification.

(3) It should be an aid to comparison at shortlisting.

(4) It should serve as a framework for the interview.

(5) It should be capable of forming the basis of the person's personnel file should she be employed by you.

Clearly there must be a close association between the vacant job, the Man Specification and the application form if the form is to be an effective selection tool.

Even if you are not in a position to design your own application form, there is nothing stopping you from adding to the standard application a supplementary form, containing questions which will elicit the pertinent information enabling you to do the matching process most effectively. Remember, if you don't ask the right questions you won't get the right information; so it's up to you.

Receiving the application forms is a very straightforward exercise except that you should always delegate one person to deal with them so as to avoid overlooking a candidate and avoiding other confusion which often arises when there are 'too many cooks'.

When the closing date is past, you should screen the applicants against the job requirements and sort out those who are obviously unsuitable. Deal with these people quickly and kindly so as to ensure that their hopes are not raised needlessly only to be let down badly in the end.

Remember the whole of this selection procedure is a public relations exercise. You are showing people who don't work within your organisation how efficient and how humane you are. Selection exposes your organisation so make sure you do nothing to mar its image; let those obviously unsuccessful know that they are not being considered any further.

Next choose, say, four or six candidates for interview. If you have done your homework properly, you should have attracted a nucleus of that number, all of whom — on paper — could do the job. This should avoid having to keep a pile of reserves 'in case we don't make an appointment first time around'.

Personally I feel it is better to re-advertise rather than keep a group of 'reserves' on tenterhooks while you interview the first team. If it has been your experience not to appoint the first time around, I would seriously question the effectiveness of your selection process.

It seems to me that when most people apply for jobs, they are serious and it is a very unsettling experience for them to apply and have to wait for the result. However, if you do keep back some reserves, write and let them know something of what is going on and give them a date when they will be notified about your action.

Let me emphasise that speed, consideration and good manners are the keynote in successful human relationships during the selection process.

REFERENCES

References are obviously in disrepute at the moment. Even at the best of times they are of dubious value when you consider that the candidate is hardly likely to nominate a referee who is antagonistic to her.

Approaching her current employer should be somewhat more useful but what is commonly being used is the telephone conversation with the referee; however, be careful to arrange suitable bona fides, as you could find yourself talking to 'anyone' over the telephone.

Make the best use of your referees by again asking them questions which you think are pertinent to the job and appropriate for the referee.

If the person gives her vicar as a referee and the job has a management content, then ask him what events she has organised for the church, how do people work for her, how does she treat her responsibilities to the church?

Don't just ask his opinion whether she is suitable for the job — that is simply a waste of time.

Ask her current employer about sickness and absence, technical ability, managerial flair, her social acceptability by seniors and juniors. Again — ask the right questions of the right people. It will pay dividends.

When should we take up references?

(1) Pre-screening, i.e. when each application form arrives? I can't really see any need for this at all.

(2) Post-screening, i.e. all but those clearly unsuitable? Possibly useful but you should have obtained the candidate's permission to approach her current employer.

(3) After shortlisting? Most certainly; everyone who reaches this stage must expect her employer to be approached.

(4) After interview? A bad practice for many reasons. Here are some of them:

(a) 'Subject to satisfactory references.' If she does get a bad reference then you can find yourself in a difficult position involving your loyalty towards the confidential reference and the referee who gave it.

(b) It is very time consuming for those waiting to hear if they are successful.

An alternative to the referee can be found in the staff reporting systems currently being developed in the National Health Service. In this system there is a very real chance that the references will be more accurate and more factual and, best of all, the candidate will have a shrewd idea of what the reference contains; but more about this in Chapter 10.

TECHNIQUES FOR SELECTION

There are a variety of selection techniques available to prospective employers other than the interview. In fact, the more I read and the more research that is done into interviewing, the more the evidence piles up against the interview as an objective and effective selection tool!

Here are some of the factors I have read about recently — that interviewers fairly consistently choose the second-best candidate and that interviewers make their minds up in the first two or three minutes of the interview — and this decision is based on whether they like the look of the face! Both these points come from very reliable sources, and I could quote a lot more in the same vein.

Why do we continue to interview? The answer seems to me to be quite straightforward. It is that the interview enables us to identify those unquantifiable factors which enable us to decide whether or not we would like to work with the candidate and whether she would fit into the organisation. Other selection techniques cannot do this as well as we can when we meet her face to face.

I will be dealing with interviewing techniques and the different types of interviews in Chapter 11; meanwhile here is a brief survey of alternative methods of selection.

Tests

First and foremost are the various tests. For example, the National Institute of Industrial Psychology publish a battery of tests to cover each part of the seven-point plan; however, to administer and evaluate these tests you will first need to be trained in their use (as indeed is the case for most psychological tests).

Another kind of selection test that you will all be familiar with is the General Nursing Council entrance tests, which have proved to be most useful in predicting the abilities of a nurse to pass the appropriate professional examinations.

Tests can be divided into three main groupings.
(1)   Tests of skill and knowledge.
(2)   Tests of intelligence and special ability.
(3)   Tests of personality, temperament and interests.

In this last group there are a number of odd techniques which I will list
purely for your interest:
(a)   personality questionnaires;
(b)   projective techniques, i.e. the ink blot and sentence completion;
(c)   gesture analysis;
(d)   graphology;
(e)   associaton of temperament with physical build.

All of these have their various proponents but there remains a lot of work
to be done on them before they can be fully validated.
    The tests which groups (1) and (2) above include are well validated,
and very powerful and persuasive arguments can be made for their use
in the selection process. My own feeling about these tests is that I think
we should use them together with a traditional interview, not just the
tests alone.

Performance Tasks

I want to end this chapter with a short discussion on a selection technique
which is being used more frequently in the Health Service; its name is
the 'group situational performance task'.
    In this the candidates are all brought together and presented with a
task which they have to work together to complete. While they are doing
this, observers note behaviour, action, communication, attitudes etc.,
which the candidates exhibit while they are performing the task.
    Some examples of tasks set are as follows.
(1)   Planning a model town. The candidates are presented with a large
        board on which is marked the river, the railway line and the main
        road, and a large number of model buildings (houses, factories,
        schools, shops, churches, etc.), and between them they have to lay
        out this town.
(2)   Designing a ward. Again, with model beds, partitions, office fur-
        niture, toilet furniture, etc., the candidates have to lay out the
        ideal ward.
(3)   Building a model house with Lego bricks.
(4)   Sometimes the task can be a discussion topic, i.e. 'The pen is
        mightier than the sword'.

    The rationale behind this kind of test is that people will exhibit during
the test the same kind of behaviour which they would at their normal place
of work, and therefore the observers will learn a great deal about the
candidates and their suitability for the post.

I believe this rationale is valid as I have proved it time and time again in these situations and in role play exercises. What I must question is the availability of trained observers who are able to record the group activities accurately and who can interpret the behaviour noted in an authoritive manner.

Group observation is a difficult skill which has to be learnt, and I do not believe we have the trained people in our Service to run these kinds of interviews. However, many hospitals have the necessary trained staff to run tests of skills, knowledge, IQ and special abilities — why not ask around and see if you can introduce some of them into your selection procedures?

TYPICAL PLAN — RECRUITMENT AND SELECTION

(1)   Preparation of Job and Man Specifications. It is essential for the personnel responsible for selection to have a detailed knowledge of the job and the type of person needed in it.

(2)   Draw up advertisement.
      Essential features:
      (a) concise job description;
      (b) qualifications, training and experience required.
      Useful features:
      (a) salary level/wage rates;
      (b) fringe benefits;
      (c) prospects.
      The content of the advertisement is clearly subject to the sort of job to be filled. Care should be taken in choosing the most suitable media for the advertisement concerned.

(3)   Sort application forms. Exclude those which now appear to be unsuitable and despatch 'regret' letters.

(4)   Prepare shortlist of suitable candidates. Invite them for interview (and, if considered necessary, for selection tests).

(5)   Use a systematic plan at the interview.

CASE STUDY — WARD HOUSEKEEPER
The following case study comprises the initial stages in appointing a Ward Housekeeper. You will get further stages in later chapters. At this point I would like you to do two things: firstly, see what you can do to improve the job description, which is presented to you in skeleton form; secondly, decide the order of priority in which you will shortlist the candidates.

Background

Bankfoot General Hospital is a new district general hospital which has been functional for two years. It is a multistorey hospital (five floors) and is designed so as to have its services on the centre floor (theatre suite, x-rays, etc.). Wards are established as functional units of 60 beds per ward unit, there being four such wards per floor. Each floor is under the management of a Senior Nursing Officer (grade 8 of the Salmon Report), and each ward is controlled by a Senior Ward Sister/Charge Nurse.

Ward Clerks have been employed on each ward unit, and whereas their employment has left nothing to be desired the management have decided to extend the role and function of the Ward Clerks to the much wider role of Ward Housekeeper. It is intended to employ Ward Housekeepers on the fourth floor wards for a trial period of 12 months. A Job Description for a Ward Housekeeper is attached.

Additional information concerning the working situation on all floors is as follows:

A topping-up system for: linen and laundry; CSSD;
pharmaceutical supplies (excepting dangerous drugs);
cleaning materials; stores issues.

A ward finishing kitchen is located on each ward floor, there being a central preparation kitchen located in the basement.

Job Description

Post: Ward Housekeeper
          60-bedded surgical ward (male) unit.
Duties: 40 hours per 5-day week.
          Responsible to Senior Ward Sister/Charge Nurse
          To be responsible for:

> Daily completion of the admissions and discharge register;
> Reception and documentation of new patients;
> Collection of forms from admission room and their insertion into patients' case notes;
> Completion of pro forma for despatch to General Practitioner and the Public Health Department;
> Compilation of bed returns, diet sheets, menu sheets, (choice of meals to patients);
> Completion of requisitions for pharmacy, general stores, stationery stores, works maintenance, etc.;
> Compilation of forms from the ward treatment book;
> Compilation of forms for x-ray, pathology laboratory, etc.;
> Collection/distribution of patients' mail;
> Collection/distribution of patients' property;
> Transportation arrangements (ambulance, taxis, etc.);
> Issuing laundry and linen;
> Making empty beds and beds of ambulant patients;
> Service of meals to patients;
> Supervision of the work of domestic staff;
> Arranging flowers.

3 Sunnybank Close
Bankfoot

Dear Sir,

The decision by the Seven Seas Company to sell the liner, 'Cruise Queen', has made me redundant at the age of 50. I have served the Seven Seas Company for 25 years working in many of their ships until being promoted to Assistant Head Stewardess (responsible for all domestic arrangements except those for cafeterias and restaurants) on the 'Cruise Queen' which I have held for the past three years. I am interested in the post of Ward Housekeeper at your hospital and should be glad if you would favour me with an interview.

Yours faithfully,

E. L. Day (Mrs.)

15 Chestnut Drive
Bankfoot

Dear Sir,

Further to the notice in the Bankfoot Hospital Chronicle I wish to apply for the post of Ward Housekeeper. I have worked at the hospital since it first opened and I am now the domestic forewoman in charge of 'E' Section of the domestic programme.

Yours faithfully,

M. Terry (Mrs.)

You know this woman. She has worked with you for the past 12 years, the last 8 being full time. She is loyal, a bit short tempered but her work is well above average.

5 Sandy Lane
Bankfoot

Dear Sir,

Further to your advertisement in the Bankfoot Gazette, I wish to apply for the post as Ward Housekeeper at Bankfoot General Hospital.

I qualified as an SRN in 1949 at Brandon General Hospital, was a Staff Nurse for three years and then a Ward Sister for two years on a female medical ward. Since my two children are now teenagers I would like to return to hospital work but do not want to return to full-time nursing. I

101

feel that the post as Ward Housekeeper would be suitable as it entails not only contact with the patients, but also a variety of other work.

Yours faithfully,

Mrs D. Freeman

'Strathspey'
Woolland Crescent
Bankfoot

Dear Sir,
 I gather from a recent edition of the Bankfoot Gazette that you are looking for a lady of tolerance and sympathy to act as a Ward House-keeper. During many years of voluntary social work I have found that the poor people I have visited and helped have seen in me the qualities which I believe you are looking for in the person to fill this appointment. Before the nationalisation of the hospitals I was, as you remember, very prominent in the committee for raising funds for the relief of poor patients in the hospital and I did, for some time, feel some resentment that my experience had been passed over when the committee for managing the hospitals was set up. However, I now feel that I should forget this slight and am willing to offer my services as a way of responding to the plea from our Prime Minister that we should rally round and work to get old England back on its feet. It may be necessary for me to finish early one or two days a week as you know that I do a great deal of voluntary work, and I cannot let the poor people down who rely on my services so much.

Yours sincerely,

Marcia Nelson-ggwynne. (Miss)

This is the second interview you have arranged for her. She telephoned shortly before the first interview to say she would not be attending.

Department of Employment and Productivity — Employment Service
Professional and Executive Register

Dear Sir,
 I enclose particulars of one of our registrants whom you may like to consider for employment.
 Details of candidate for employment as Ward Housekeeper:

| Name: | Miss Jean Smithson | Age: 24 |
| Address: | 15 Bridge Street, Farndon, Cheshire. | |

Particulars of education and training

Timchester High School for Girls

G.C.E. 'O' Levels: English Language, Mathematics, French, History, Domestic Science.

Timchester College of Further Education

Hotel and Catering Institute Intermediate Certificate, R.S.H. Certificate in Hygiene.

Whilst attending Timchester College Miss Smithson spent two summer vacations working as a cook in a local hospital. In her last post Miss Smithson was employed as a Caterer/Housekeeper in a residential training centre belonging to a large industrial organisation in the Midlands. Miss Smithson seeks the opportunity of employment in housekeeping work in hospitals because she feels that this type of work would be very rewarding. She has just completed a comprehensive course in cleaning technology at a technical college near her place of work.

A quiet, well-spoken young lady, she seeks employment in the north-west. Her hobbies are listed as theatricals, youth club leader, tennis and badminton.

The candidate is available for immediate interview.

REFERENCES

Denerley, R. A. and Plumbley, P. R. (1968). *Recruitment and Selection in a Full-employment Economy*. London, Institute of Personnel Management.

Ministry of Health (1968). Letter of 29 February, reference M/A 146/031. London, Department of Health and Social Security.

Chapter Six

Feet Under the Table

Good induction starts at the recruitment stage. But wait a minute; perhaps not all of you have heard this word 'induction' before, so my first job will be to define it.

'Induction aims to help a newcomer to the organisation adjust as quickly as possible to the new job.' In other words, get her 'feet under the table', in the shortest possible time.

John Garnett, Director of the Industrial Society, has said that 'induction is one of the great neglected areas of management policy' (Industrial Society, 1973). He goes on to list some of the problems which are aggravated by the lack of good induction and ends by saying 'Good induction schemes aren't the whole answer to this problem but there is certainly no answer at all without them'. This is the approach I would like to take in this chapter.

The introduction of an induction programme into your organisation is not going to have a revolutionary effect overnight but it will bring with it advantages that we just cannot afford to ignore.

Good induction is vital to the organisation. Too often we are bringing people into the health care environment, be it hospital or community, whose vision of what is involved has been far more influenced by the TV programmes 'General Hospital', 'Emergency Ward 10' and 'The Angels' than by the realities of patient care.

The other extreme of influence is that propounded by parents, grandparents, etc., who, being determined to put off their relatives from entering the Health Service, regale them with stories of blood and gore or excrement.

Then there is the new entrant's own fears and misgivings, natural to anyone entering a new environment. Her mind is full of questions — very often of the most simple to answer type, but so very important to the person concerned.

There is the story of a young school leaver taking up her first job as a shop assistant. She was employed by the John Lewis Partnership, who are proud of the fact that all their employees are partners in the firm. Some two weeks after she started, someone asked her how she was getting on and what she thought of the store. She replied that it was a nice place to work except for the fact that they did not have any toilet facilities in the store for the staff. 'There were plenty for the executives,' she said. 'There are doors marked "Partners only" everywhere'!

The story must be apochryphal as I know that John Lewis' have a good training department which provides for induction to be properly carried out. I hope the story illustrates that the simplest questions are often the most important ones and that we cannot take anything for granted.

BENEFITS OF INDUCTION

What, then, are the benefits of good induction?

Staff wastage always comes high on the list; this is when people leave before they have made any really useful contribution to the organisation. Researchers seem to have proved very conclusively that good induction can reduce the wastage rate.

They seem also to be very sure that the quality of work is higher sooner and that communications in the organisation improve as the direct result of the induction programme.

Good induction helps a new employee to identify with the organisation quicker and this commitment makes her a more motivated and efficient worker. She will get to know and like her job quicker and will, as a result, get a great deal of satisfaction from it.

If we want to gain these benefits then it is essential that we start early. Which brings me back to my opening statement: 'Good induction starts at the recruitment stage'.

To repeat a point from the last chapter seems appropriate here. I said something like 'the selection process is an important public relations exercise'. During selection we expose our organisation and its efficiency (or lack of efficiency) to non-members of the organisation, and whatever they experience leaves an impression. This becomes important from the induction point of view after you have made your choice of employee and let her know.

If she gets good information in a speedy and friendly way she will have a favourable impression of the organisation she is coming to work for. This pre-employment information is not really in your hands — mostly it involves the Personnel Department, but you should have been involved in the interview at some stage and no doubt you have shown the new employee around the department and had a short chat with her. Make no mistake about it — this is part of induction.

While she is working her notice, the Personnel Department will be sending her details of her new contract of employment, hours of work, pay, pension; joining arrangements, date, time, place; travel arrangements, parking place, reimbursement of expenses, etc. Though this is not completely in your hands, do feel free to monitor how efficiently this service is performed for you and give the Personnel Department feedback on the effectiveness of the service they provide.

While this is going on you should be preparing to receive the new employee, making sure everything is ready for her arrival on the first day and thinking about how you are going to arrange her induction. Here are a few points you might like to keep in mind.

She is not likely to remember a great deal on her first day so don't flood her with information you expect her to remember but emphasise the things of most value to her. I think these would be:

(1) Job factors enabling her to do her job safely and in a reasonable manner.

(2) Reassurance – this can be done in a number of ways, but giving the starter a person of first contact for help and advice is one useful technique.

(3) Help to get her accepted by the social groups with which she is working. Introduce her around, pointing out people of similar interests (age, other new starters, etc.).

(4) Try to arrange her programme in sequence with the day's work. Naturally it can't all be done like this but, when it is time for coffee or lunch, let the person of first contact take over. That person might also be an alternative to you when it comes to accompanying the starter on visits to other departments with which she will come in contact whilst doing her work.

(5) Refresh yourself from the starter's application form on some of her interests, especially if she is new to the area. You may have been able to look up the names and addresses of secretaries of local societies in which she has stated an interest; library membership, a few recommended eating places, suitable clubs, discos, etc. We should not forget that there is more to life than just work.

(6) Counselling is not a very well established service in hospitals but if you do have a counsellor, then make sure that your starter is introduced to her.

(7) Then don't forget the simple but important things like getting her on the payroll, telling her when and how she gets paid, any special safety factors and getting her measured for a decent fitting uniform as soon as possible. (You might have been able to arrange the last even before she started.)

Over the next two weeks induction can continue in appropriate sequence to cover in greater depth the needs of the new employee.

Basically, there are four specific areas of information to which you should give your attention besides what may be termed 'general information':

(1) Organisational information.

(2) Departmental information.

(3) Employment conditions.

(4) Health, safety and welfare at work.

How you arrange for the starter to receive this information depends on you, but clearly you, as her immediate superior, have the greatest vested interest in her and as such you should be involved as much as possible. It is a time when you can establish a good working relationship with her which will be of mutual benefit over the years to follow.

Induction courses are run by many health authorities and these can be extremely valuable. Some organise them so that the new employee does not go to her place of work until she has been through the course — which could last as long as a week. Others run them afternoons of the first week; others on a 'day release' basis over about six weeks; and yet others wait until the person has worked for four or six weeks before taking her off the job for an induction programme.

While all have their good points, it seems to me that people come to your organisation to do a job and they should be allowed to get to grips with this job as soon as possible. Provided you give them a sound departmental and job induction, much of the other information can wait and indeed will be more appreciated when they have become more confident in their job.

TYPES OF INDUCTION COURSES

When thinking about induction courses, try to group your ideas around the needs of three categories of new entrants whom you are likely to employ:
(1)   School leavers.
(2)   Mature newcomers to hospital life and work.
(3)   Transferred professional staff.

If any of these are recent immigrants to this country, then they will need a little extra consideration almost in the form of an 'induction to Britain' course.

The following are examples of programmes for these groups which might act as a catalyst to you in developing a course to meet your needs.

The School Leaver

Cadets

Don't keep them away from the wards and departments too long. They will be keen to start in on their work. They have had enough of school so I suggest a series of half-day sessions on the lines of the following.

Day 1	1. Welcome and introduction to the course
9 a.m. to	2. Form filling (getting them on the payroll)
12 noon	3. Residential/catering facilities
	4. Issue of uniforms
	5. Useful information (a)
Day 2	1. 'Your hospital — its past, present, future'
9 a.m. to	2. Tour of hospital, with short talks by heads of departments at each place visited (you need not do it all in
12 noon	one day)

107

Day 3   1. Patients and their relatives
1 to 4 p.m.   2. Personal and community health
              3. Continue tour of hospital

Day 4   1. Education and training opportunities
1 to 4 p.m.   2. Your right to representation (professional organisations, trades unions)
              3. Fire precautions and safety at work
              4. Useful information (c)

Learners

There is no reason why they should not join in with the Cadets and the Education Department give their special induction information at other times during the day.

Newcomers to Hospital Life and Work

Here are examples of two programmes mounted monthly in two types of hospitals. In both cases the courses are completely multidisciplinary, with the supervisor caring for the induction needs at the work place.

Induction/Orientation Course (Psychiatric Hospital)

9.00   Introduction and welcome
9.15   Patient care
9.45   Contracts of employment
10.15   COFFEE
10.30   Pay arrangements
11.00   NHS reorganisation
11.30   Fire precautions
12.00   LUNCH
13.00   Film (psychiatric nursing)
14.00   Health and hygiene
14.30   The hospital and its organisation
15.00   TEA
15.15   'Your hospital — a profile'
15.45   Voluntary help in hospitals
16.15   Final question session
16.45   DISPERSE

9.00	Introduction to the course: the hospital organisation
9.30	Treatment of mentally handicapped in hospital — Psychiatrist
10.00	COFFEE
10.20	Hospital care of the mentally handicapped — Senior Tutor
11.00	VISIT: shopping centre, Children's Home, Engineering Department, Laundry
12.00	Mentally handicapped in the community — Social Worker
12.30	LUNCH
13.30	VISIT: Main hall, Clinical Centre, Department of Industrial Training, Adult Home, Catering Department
15.10	Occupational health service — Nursing Sister
15.40	TEA
16.00	Hospital voluntary services — Voluntary Services Organiser
16.30	Discussion panel or open forum
17.00	DISPERSE

Transferred Professional Staff

I suggest that a morning devoted to a formal induction course should be sufficient. It would concentrate on local specific information.

Phase 1	'The hospital — a profile'
Phase 2	Pay arrangements
Phase 3	Tour of hospital
Phase 4	Panel/discussion with representatives from management and staff organisations.
Phase 5	Lunch — attended by heads of departments and representative of staff organisations — giving opportunities for informal discussion.

Recent Immigrants to Britain

In considering the course content to meet the special needs of new immigrants, I strongly advise that you consult with your local Community Relations Officer, as immigrants of differing ethnic origins have different needs. Usefully from our point of view, these ethnic groups tend to live and work in the same area so our task does not become too complicated in that we normally have to consider just one country of origin in our plans. The United Kingdom Council for Overseas Student Affairs have produced (1976) a most useful document which I recommend to you.

INDUCTION LITERATURE

This is yet another way of giving staff the necessary information, but it cannot take the place of a planned induction suitable for the individual.

It usually takes the form of a staff handbook and has the advantage that it can be read at leisure and be retained for ready reference by the starter. With this in mind, no doubt you can think of certain routines and administrative procedures which lend themselves more readily to the written word than to verbal explanation.

SUMMARY

Before finishing this chapter, let me briefly review the induction process.

Induction aims to:
(1)   introduce the starter to her job, department, hospital (or other part of the NHS) and the NHS as a whole;
(2)   help the employee to quickly feel part of the organisation and become committed to her part in caring for the patients;
(3)   create and maintain a high level of morale;
(4)   give essential information and answer numerous personal questions.

It does this by:
(1)   good pre-employment communications;
(2)   planned induction by the immediate superior;
(3)   formal induction courses;
(4)   staff handbook.

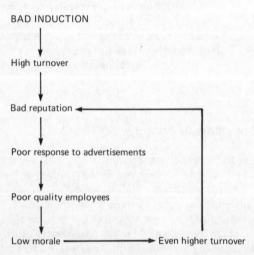

Fig. 6.1   The vicious circle created by bad induction.

By effective induction we hope to:
(1) enhance the reputation of the organisation;
(2) increase job satisfaction;
(3) reduce the turnover rate of staff.

Induction Check-list

Group Information

Name
History
Location
Aim

Organisation Information

Name
Organisation
Names of relevant personnel
Employees

Departmental Information

What are its aims
Where it fits
Jobs
Organisation
Supervision – names
Colleagues – names
Departmental rules
Breaks: tea, meals

Pay and Hours

Rate
Deductions
Queries

Pay

When and how
Loans

Hours

Overtime
Week-ends
Shifts
Checking on and off

Services, Welfare and Amenities

Holidays: bank
   annual
First aid/sickness
Pension scheme
Sickness: notification
   certificate
   pay
Canteen
Cloakrooms and toilets
Uniforms/protective clothing
Social club
Savings club
Telephone calls
Education
Parking

Standards

Efficiency
Quality
Safety
Good housekeeping
Absenteeism/lateness
Smoking, cooperation
Discipline, expectations:
 you, from her
 she, from you

111

Personal Relationships	Miscellaneous
Help and cooperation	Travelling
Requests	Fire precautions
Time off	Trades union
Promotion. Personal details you and her	Friends

Well, so much for getting her feet under the table. In the first few weeks most of the starter's immediate needs will have been met by induction and then she can get on with her job; but we must not leave it there. She will still have job needs which we must meet on a systematic basis. Day-to-day supervision will cope with a lot of it but what most people need is time set aside for a periodic chat about the job with their immediate superior.

After about six months, we should consider the induction period over and start right in on a system of staff development and performance review, but more about that subject in Chapter 10.

CASE STUDY – INTRODUCTION TO PETER'S WARD
What do you think of this induction document? What other ideas for innovative induction do you have? Why not spend some time planning an actual induction course for one of your own staff?

There are 24 beds for male medical patients here and you can expect to have good experience in acute nursing and in cardiac work. As the ward is team-assigned, you will have your own patients and share the work with one other nurse for most of the time you're on duty. This means that you will have more chance of doing senior work: which will be hard if you don't know enough! So find out all you can about your patients – use the reference books in the ward as well as your textbooks. Ask as many questions as you like – we are here to help you. You'll hear about the other patients (as well as your own) every day, too.

Please bring your GNC Schedule soon, so we can keep it up to date. We hope you will enjoy it here, and you'll be able to learn a lot.

Who's Who

Nurses	See duty rota
Orderly	Mrs Janet Gambious
Maid	Miss Peggy James
Houseman	Dr Charles Stornway
Registrar	Dr Henry Slott
Consultants	Dr Arthur Hunter
	Dr William Paget
Cardiac Doctors	D. Jones
	M. Dickson
	H. Elliott

Medical Students	See notice board
Medical Social Worker	Miss Kate Newport
Physiotherapists.	Miss Joan Fleming
	Miss L. Angus
Cardiac Technician.	Miss Tomme
Chaplains	Fr Jarrett (Church of England)
	Mr Browne (Non-conformist)
	Fr Murphy (Roman Catholic)
	Fr Greenbaum (Jewish)

Reference Material Available Here

Ward Manual
Nursing Procedure book
Admin. Procedure book
MIMS
National Formulary
Drug pamphlets
Patients' notes and x-rays
Textbooks
Instructions on: Admissions, discharges, weighing patients, testing urine,
clothes and valuables
USE THESE — THEY ARE FOR YOU

How Much do you Know?

Where is the mitral valve?

How do you prepare for a barium
meal?

When are antacids given?

How do you give breathing
exercises?

Where does a left heart catheter go?

What are the signs of heart failure?

How do you recognise atrial
fibrillation?

Why are anticoagulant drugs used?

Where is the apex beat?

What does digoxin do?

What is Selora?

How is isoprenaline given?

Why are some blood pressures
recorded 'lying and standing'

What is a waterhammer pulse?

To Study a Case

When you have learnt all about a patient you will be able to recite:
name — age — home — work — family and visitors — religion — signs and
symptoms — history — investigations, and the answers — nursing care —
any problems — treatment and medicines — prognosis — aftercare arrangements

Try to learn all this about FIVE patients each week. Keep a notebook —
it will be priceless when you come to your Final Examination.

Doctors' Rounds

'Seeing my doctor' is as important to the medical patient as 'my op.' to the surgical. It requires the same sort of formal setting and preparation:

> Patients in or at bed: comfy, tidy, quiet
> No smoking
> No urinals out
> Windows shut for warmth, quiet
> Doors shut
> Notes and instruments on trolley at bed
> X-rays at viewing box
> Urines in specimen cupboard

All rounds are accompanied: please come too — but listen carefully — you may be asked questions.

Times of Rounds

Mondays:	a.m. House Physician and Registrar
	p.m. Dr Hunter teaches
	Dr Paget consults
Tuesdays:	a.m. Dr Hunter consults
	p.m. Outpatients Department
Wednesdays:	Outpatients Department
Thursdays:	a.m. Registrar round
	p.m. Dr Paget teaches
Fridays:	a.m. Introductory Medics (teaching round)
	p.m. Joint consultation round

Sister's Pet Fads

Blanket bathing: school style only!
               two nurses, usually
Beard, teeth, nails, mouth too
Pyjamas warmed
Handwashing bowl after bedpans
or
Stop-off at handbasin for the chair-bound
Mouth toilet and observation.
Up-to-the minute fluid chart accuracy.
Aftercare of equipment: no procedure is complete until the apparatus has been cleansed, serviced, and is ready for next time.

What's Different Here

For you:	Duty planning: see pin-up board
	Check card for your practical work
In the work:	Low salt diets: red salt cellars (Selora); always give mustard; salt-free vinegar
	Charts: draw dot-to-dot lines: red for 4-hourly, black for daily or bd; count 'hearts' for full minute
	Fluid charts: measure in millilitres; total at midnight only

Pressure areas: turn at times on chart
keep dry
NEVER wash unless soiled

The Patients

1	Arthur Smith	coronary — 2nd week
2	James Milligan	chronic bronchitic
3	Henry Hester	left heart failure
4	Peter Parry	gastric ulcer
5		
6	Chas Farnburgh	virus pneumonia
7	William Petty	for investigation: chest? carcinoma
8	Pedro Sanchos	influenza
9	Lucas Ostrieto	right thrombophleb
10	Paul Berens	duodenal ulcer
11	Albert Edwards	diabetes
12		
13	Alfred Ross	for investigation: hypertension
14	John Borough	coronary — 3rd week
15	Stan Vorskawski	for investigation: angina
16	James Pearson	patent ductus
17	James Penfield	aortic stenosis
18	Thomas Jones	for investigation: abdominal pain
19	Peter Martin	gastric bleeding
20	Morgan Evans	duodenal ulcer
21	James White	mitral stenosis
22	John Roster	coronary — 2nd week

NOW GO AND LOOK IN ALL THE CUPBOARDS AND CORNERS

You can help patients best if you know where to find things.
So explore, and then try this quiz:

Where is (or are):

Keys
Window-opening pole
Ophthalmoscope
Heparin jars
Spare toilet rolls
Spare sugar store
Air rings
Hot water bottles
Arm splints
Paper tissues
Valve rubbers

REFERENCES AND FURTHER READING

Industrial Society (1973). *Induction.* Notes for Managers, No. 21. London, Industrial Society.

United Kingdom Council for Overseas Student Affairs (1976). *Nurses in Training from Overseas*, Guidance Leaflets. London, Department of Health and Social Security/Royal College of Nursing.

This is the first time I have mentioned the Notes for Managers series, but there are a large number of very useful small and inexpensive publications on the whole range of management functions. For a complete list you could write to: The Industrial Society, Robert Hyde House, 48 Bryanston Square, London W1H 8AH.

I have always consulted these small publications widely, in both my lecturing and writing activities.

Chapter Seven

Coach or Driver

Douglas McGregor said in his book, *The Human Side of Enterprise*, 'Every encounter between a superior and a subordinate involves learning of some kind for the subordinate'.

When I examine this statement in the light of many managers I have seen in action, I often wonder just what the subordinate does learn! Certainly not very much which she can use in developing her own skills, except perhaps to reinforce her resolve not to like her boss!

The context in which McGregor made that statement clearly implies that all managers should be teachers of their subordinates. Managers should be vitally interested in developing the abilities of their staff through every avenue open to them.

The origin of the chapter title — Coach or Driver — is derived from two polar approaches of managers towards training. There are those who do no training whatsoever except delegate or order task after task to be completed, usually in the shortest time possible and then are critical of the results. These people I label drivers — i.e. taskmasters who are continually cracking the whip.

Now I don't want you to get the impression that I am against reasonable discipline or against a superior expecting her subordinate to work hard. On the contrary, I am a believer in both; but the manner in which the 'driver' manager implements work is totally non-effective.

This approach engenders resentment, fear and lack of confidence which in turn leads to inefficiency in the individual. She is in a vicious circle.

On the other hand, there is the manager who is a coach. She tries, by giving her staff carefully planned tasks, to systematically increase the ability and experience of her staff. She continually appraises performances, gives praise for good work and positive suggestions when improvement is necessary.

Which are you — Coach or Driver?

Perhaps as yet you are neither, as up till now you have considered training as belonging to the teaching department and as having nothing to do with your job. If this does not fit your approach then I should remind you that your staff are your most important resource in providing good patient care. Their competence, experience and loyalty set the standards of care given to your patients and you determine the level of these qualities in your staff.

That person we appointed in Chapter 5 — are you going to let her sink or swim? or are you going to identify and meet the needs she has in relation to her job?

It is very clear that every manager is responsible for training her staff when we recall from our earlier discussions on 'What is a manager?' that we discovered she was a person who had so much work to do that others had to do some of it for her. These staff, who are doing some of the work you would like to do if it were physically possible, need your help and support to do their job . . . and this includes training.

Not only are you responsible for training your staff but you are also obviously the best person to do the training. You know the job, you know your staff and you want your patients to get the best possible care.

If you need further convincing of the value of training your staff, consider the following:
(1) Training helps staff to learn their jobs quicker.
(2) Existing staff can be helped to improve their performance by training.
(3) You can help them keep up to date by training.
(4) Well trained staff work better and make fewer mistakes.
(5) Labour turnover is reduced and the subsequent retention of staff is of great advantage to the patient.
(6) Your organisation gets a good name and people will want to come and work for you.
(7) Your staff will become loyal and committed members of the organisation.

HOW TO CARRY OUT YOUR TRAINING RESPONSIBILITIES

Usually training is divided into three groups:
(1) Training at the place of work.
(2) Training within the organisation.
(3) External training.

I propose to examine each of these in turn, but the cycle shown in Fig. 7.1 is common to all of them.

TRAINING AT THE PLACE OF WORK

This is often termed 'on-the-job' training. It is, in my opinion, the most effective form of training we have as it is practical, it is relevant and it is most often done in a one-to-one basis (i.e. one teacher to one pupil) which is undoubtedly the best form of teaching.

The first identifiable technique in this category is 'sitting with Nellie'.

118

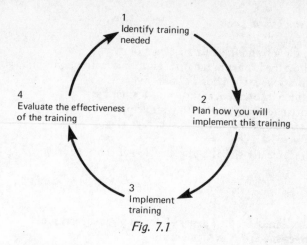

Fig. 7.1

Sitting with Nellie

This is when you assign a new member of staff to work with an experienced member of your team. This exposure to work under guidance can be very effective provided you choose your 'Nellie' correctly.

Make sure she herself is up to date and knowledgeable about her job and that she has the talent required to do this sort of work. Be sure she does not pass on any of her bad habits to her trainee and be sure to give her time to do the job properly.

Job Instruction

This is usually done in a systematic way by following a basic four-step process after having analysed the job you are going to teach and broken it down into easy stages.

1. *Prepare the Learner*

Put her at ease — perhaps by stressing the informality of the instruction.

Create interest in learning — give reasons why the job is done and its benefits to the patient when done properly.

Establish two-way communication — that is, make sure the learner is talking and will ask you questions, etc.

Check existing knowledge — find out how much she may already know about the job.

Make sure she can see and hear what you are going to teach her.

119

2. *Give the Instruction*

Outline the job and the separate stages of it.

Instruct the learner in the first stage; thus instruction can be given by demonstration, explanation or both.

Continue instruction, ensuring the learner has:

(a) mastered each stage with your help;

(b) is aware of the 'key points' in each stage;

Instruct clearly and at a pace the learner can cope with.

3. *Practice*

Have the learner do the job herself under your supervision.

Correct any errors as they occur.

Check understanding — i.e. why she is doing each part of the task.

Encourage questions.

4. *Follow Up Instruction*

Put the learner to work.

Indicate sources of help.

Visit as appropriate to check as necessary.

Job Rotation

Here we are aiming to give the trainee a great deal of experience in the working situation in a short space of time by moving her to new jobs for short periods.

There are five principles to take into account when mounting such a programme.

(1) The individual must be briefed as to what she is expected to learn at each change of job (i.e. the objective).

(2) The person supervising the trainee must also be aware of the objective of placing the trainee with her.

(3) Jobs should be selected for the learning they offer not as a means of supplying an extra pair of hands.

(4) Progress should be checked to ensure the objectives are being attained.

(5) Do not give the trainee more responsibility than her previous placements and experience will allow. (Too much can make learning a burden rather than a pleasure.)

Whenever you want someone to acquire practical skills of a varying nature in as short a period of time as possible, this can be a most useful training method.

Projects

A great deal of project work has been done in the Health Service over recent years, mainly as the result of the increase in management training. This training tool has been used to give participants practical experience in applying the knowledge and skills learned via previous training or education. Of course, projects are used in nurse training as well as in the management field and they are a most useful technique.

Undoubtedly project work is somewhat more of an 'intellectual' exercise but this does not mean the project is not relevant to work, as I will emphasise later.

If you are given a project to do then your tutors will be looking at your abilities:

(1) To plan an original investigation appropriate to the requirements of the particular problem situation you are investigating.

(2) To find, select and arrange the material needed for an investigation to the depth required by the nature of the project.

(3) To analyse the information gathered, draw appropriate conclusions and make practical recommendations.

(4) To present information in a precise and logical manner.

None of these things can be achieved in an enjoyable and motivated manner unless the choice of project is really suitable.

I once read a golden rule for choosing a project. If I remember it rightly, it was 'Make it vivid, make it movable, make it relevant'.

Each of the three parts of that golden rule is important, but if I have to emphasise one of them it is the matter of making projects relevant to the training required by the student and relevant to the job she is training for. If you can achieve this, then the important matter of a motivated learner is most likely to be the result.

Here are some points for your consideration, whether you are setting the project or being expected to do the project.

(1) The trainee should have the general nature and objectives of project work explained.

(2) She should be totally involved in the choice of the topic.

(3) The topic chosen should be:
   (a) relevant;
   (b) appropriate;
   (c) within the competence of the trainee from the point of view of her ability, the time available and the depth required by the project.

(4) All project work must be adequately directed by the teacher or supervisor. ('Adequately' should be interpreted as meaning sufficient to see that the project develops along the lines towards the objective of the exercise, but not so much as to dampen the exercise of original thought and individual effort.)

TRAINING WITHIN THE ORGANISATION

In-service Courses

Whenever a group of trainees have common training needs, then training within the organisation can be considered. Basically they are courses of instruction organised and conducted by the members of the trainees' organisation.

Internal courses always have the advantage of being tailor-made for the trainees. There is no need for participants to have to go through the process of interpreting principles of other industries to make them applicable to their own industry, as the course directors and lecturers speak in terms of the policies and procedures of the participants' own organisation.

The lecturers are all experts in the practical aspects of the subject they are teaching, so they are less likely to theorise. They are aware of the real problems within their field and can pass on their knowledge and experience to the trainees.

A further advantage is the opportunity these courses give for the supervisors teaching on the courses to obtain invaluable feedback regarding some of the methods, procedures and equipment that their staff are working with.

It is quite easy to list other advantages of in-service training; e.g. the time and place can be arranged conveniently, the costs are less (i.e. no lecturer's fees, travel, subsistence, etc.), the value of the mix of trainees from different parts of the organisation. Whilst I do not want to exclude other forms of training, I must say that a well designed and well executed in-service course will take a lot of beating.

There are a few points to bear in mind for in-service training courses.

(1)   Identify common training needs. The staff appraisal forms might well be one fruitful source, but otherwise identify these needs by frequent contact with those with potential training needs and their managers.

(2)   Set your course objectives.

(3)   Organise the course in close consultation with the organisation's 'experts' on the topics concerned.

(4)   Brief both course participants and those giving the lectures.

(5)   Monitor progress during the course.

(6)   Evaluate the effectiveness of the course and the teachers you have used (this will be useful when you are designing the next programme).

Just one more piece of advice before we leave in-service courses: while I am obviously an enthusiast for in-service courses, do take care to ensure that you do not become too inbred or insular. You can best do this by including some sessions by 'outsiders' or by some persons who can inject new ideas into the organisation.

Programmed Learning

Most of you will be familiar with this term but may not have detailed experience of it. The technique is based on a simple concept of presenting information, asking questions on this information and letting the respondent know immediately the result of her answer.

The material is presented in a series of logical steps and correct answers must be given before the learner can move on to the next step.

A wide range of programmes is available, either in book form or for use on a special machine. I have found either of these methods very effective for individual learning at the learner's own convenience and her own pace.

The availability of any programmes and facilities for programmed learning should be brought to the attention of all your staff and they should be encouraged to spend time either learning or refreshing their knowledge by this most convenient teaching method.

I would emphasise that these techniques are useful for the learning of facts, procedures, etc., and not for any topic requiring attitude changes, opinions or behavioural changes.

Training Packages

These are commercially available training 'kits'. They comprise all the necessary components for an organisation to run their own courses. There is usually a training manual containing lectures, discussion topics, tips for teachers, etc., audio-visual aids, and case studies and exercises.

While some of these package deals require the instructor to be 'trained' first, many do not need even this. It has been my experience that these packages can be rather expensive but multiple use of a package can quite quickly pay for itself.

An example of a useful package which does not quite fit into this particular category but none the less should be mentioned at this time, can be found in those marvellous tape/slide features offered by the Royal College of General Practitioners. These can be used for individual learning in much the same way as the programmed learning technique or as a group lecture followed by led discussion.

Wherever an organisation does not have the time or personnel to do all the necessary preparation for courses (i.e. the collecting of information, designing the programme and producing audio-visual aids) then these packages are a good idea.

EXTERNAL TRAINING

External Courses

This term needs no explanation. Sending people off on courses has been almost a preoccupation for nursing since the Salmon Report. People collected courses rather like indians collected scalps on their belts (the more scalps, the better warrior) — the more courses you had attended, the better manager (or whatever) you were!

Even though for many years I earned my bread and butter by running external courses, my scepticism as to who and why people were selected for attendance at these courses, remains.

They have a valuable contribution to make to training but attendance on a course because it is the 'done thing' is useless; furthermore, because *we* can't do anything with that person, let's see what *they* can do' is similarly an invalid reason for sending people off on courses.

What, then, do external training courses offer and how should we use them?

(1) They provide opportunities to obtain qualifications of an academic, professional or technical nature.

(2) They provide your organisation with the opportunity to send people for training in subjects of which the organisation has little or no knowledge or expertise.

(3) They can meet individual needs of members of staff where the numbers are insufficient to merit an in-service course, or where you are unable to release all those with this training need at the same time.

If your staff are to gain the most benefit from their course then it is absolutely essential that you and they get together before they leave and when they return. This is labelled 'pre- and post-course briefing' and is a poorly practised procedure. Though the subordinate is attending the course, without your encouragement and commitment the full benefit will not be available to the participant.

This means that you will have to go to a lot of trouble to find out which course will best suit your particular member of staff. These are some of the things you ought to find out before you select a nurse for a particular course.

General Information

(1) The type, reputation and number of organisations offering apparently suitable courses.

(2) Location, timing, frequency, duration, etc., of the courses available.

(3) Costs — direct and indirect.

Educational Information

(1) Aims and objectives of the course — overall.

(2) Aims and objectives of the various component parts of the course (i.e. topics and what participants are expected to achieve/gain from these sessions).

(3) Training techniques employed.
(4) Qualifications and reputation of staff and lecturers used by the organisation.
(5) Facilities and amenities available; i.e. library, information services, etc.
(6) The student 'mix' aimed for.

Having obtained this information, you should discuss it with your prospective nominee so that together you can decide which course best meets her needs and the needs of your organisation.

On receipt of the course programme and papers you should then arrange the pre-course briefing (and if they have not arrived two weeks before the course, you should do the briefing without them).

The following are guidelines for you — as usual, offered not as a comprehensive check-list but as a starting point for what will best meet your individual needs.

Who Does the Briefing?

(1) The person's immediate superior or the departmental/divisional head. Preferably the immediate superior.
(2) The Personnel Department will no doubt be willing to offer help should you think you need it.

Course Aims and Objectives

(1) Explain why she has been selected for the course and what is expected of her.
(2) Explain the course aims and objectives to her.
(3) Ensure you both have a copy of the programme.
(4) Go through the course programme in detail with her.
(5) Explain the need for her to be continually relating academic (and sometimes abstract) concepts to her own working environment. Offer your help to do this with her.
(6) Try to arrange for her to meet with a previous course participant so that they can have an informal chat about both the academic and domestic arrangements.

Course Methods

(1) Outline the benefits of external courses — especially the opportunity it will afford her to discuss work problems with people of similar interest.
(2) Explain the importance of active participation — especially during informal lectures, discussions, etc.
(3) Offer help and advice on 'how to study' and on note taking.

(4)   Brief her on project work if appropriate; if possible, offer her typing and copying facilities.

(5)   Help her to identify possible project topics, i.e. problems in her part of the organisation which she might usefully study and, all being well, be able to implement on her return to work.

(6)   Check on the reading list and be able to offer her whatever books are available within the organisation.

(7)   Explain that there will be a post-course follow-up and that she will be expected to write a report on the course, talk about the course at the next Unit meeting or any other 'feedback' arrangements you may have.

Domestic Arrangements

Make sure she is aware of the domestic arrangements of the organisation.

Expenses

Explain what expenses she is entitled to claim and how she should claim them.

Post-course Follow-up

(1)   How well were the stated aims and objectives of the course met?
(2)   Was the course relevant to her training needs?
(3)   What were the strong points of the course?
(4)   What did she consider was lacking in the course?
(5)   Can she now, and will she in future, constructively criticise you and the organisation as the result of her new knowledge and skills?

To be Followed Up Later

(1)   Has her performance improved as the result of the course? (Possibly maintained via staff appraisal.)
(2)   What changes has she introduced to her workplace as a result of the course?

Summary

External courses are ready made, easy to arrange and generally offer a wider range of skills and expertise than you can from within the organisation, but be sure you send your staff member on the right course for her and it is not too general for her needs. If you do encounter this problem then consider approaching your local college/polytechnic and see if they will mount something for your specific needs — you will usually find them most helpful.

TRAINING TECHNIQUES

The following are some useful training techniques you may want to use yourself or your staff may come across on their course.

Group Discussion

This technique is used either to complement or punctuate a lecture or a demonstration; to give an opportunity to 'digest' and deepen knowledge gained in other ways; to reinforce and/or correct knowledge.

Dependence by the trainee entirely on her own powers of learning is not something we want to encourage, particularly when so much of the teaching we give is related more to concepts than to straight facts. The problems of learning in isolation are those of differing abilities:

(1)   To concentrate.
(2)   To select appropriate material.
(3)   To appraise the material being presented.

In group discussion, the members support each other as their abilities and deficiencies do not coincide. Interaction takes place between students and teachers and between students and students, which not only allows educational objectives to be achieved but also offers an excellent environment for attitude change and the development of interpersonal skills and relationships.

Size of Group

It is hard to give a ruling on this. Three would be fine at the bedside but not so good in a classroom. Groups of ten or more rarely allow all to participate fully and give opportunity for small splinter groups to have a chat together while the main group is concentrating on the task in hand.

It is possible, with a great deal of skill and practice, to manage quite large groups reasonably well but never in an entirely satisfactory manner.

Much depends on the arrangement of the group. Sprawled out in easy chairs with a large central space gives a great deal of opportunity for some of the group discussion pitfalls (which I will mention later), while a group of seven seated around a round table seems an ideal arrangement to me, both numerically and in the environment.

No doubt you will find a number you can handle and enjoy and will try to keep to that.

Some Hints on Group Discussion

(1) Know what you want to achieve during the session (i.e. set your objectives); do not allow discussion for its own sake.

(2) The discussion should be on a topic or knowledge or experience which is common to the group. (This is not a time to teach new knowledge except where gross ignorance is discovered.)

(3) Preferably set the students some preparation for the group discussion (i.e. prescribed reading or describe a case).

(4) Keep introductory remarks to a minimum required to get the discussion going.

(5) Aim to get the discussion going between all members of the group rather than back and forth between you and them. Try to act as a referee — just come in to correct facts and to keep the discussion to the point.

One way of checking how the discussion is going is to draw a chart and plot each communication with a line. Examples are shown in Figs. 7.2–7.5 (the teacher is 'A'). From these rough diagrams you can begin to diagnose how things are going in your group.

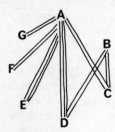

Fig. 7.2   There is very little group discussion; rather teacher/student discussion.

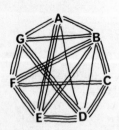

Fig. 7.3   Here things are going pretty well.

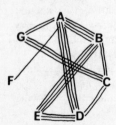

Fig. 7.4   Here someone is being left out.

128

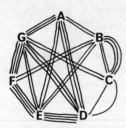

Fig. 7.5 Here a splinter group has been started by B and C, and C has just involved D in it also.

Problems in Group Discussion

(1) Slackness in preparation (this can be levelled at the teachers, too).
(2) Sleepiness.
(3) General failure to participate.
(4) Splinter groups.

Any of these should be dealt with gently but firmly RIGHT FROM THE START — don't let bad habits start.

Hints to Enable Discussion

(1) Be provocative (but not ridiculous).
(2) Try direct questioning which will lead to discussion areas.
(3) Avoid evaluating students' remarks yourself — let the group do it.
(4) The silence! Perhaps the topic is genuinely exhausted; if not, inject fresh questions perhaps to a particular member of the group.
(5) Don't make any member of the group appear foolish.
I shall be dealing with various types of group member in Chapter 11.

Closing Discussion

(1) Preferably when it is in full flight and you have achieved your objectives.
(2) When it has dried up — then end by giving a briefing for the next discussion.
(3) Do not drag it on and on.

Case Studies

These are factual or fictional occurrences presented, usually in written form, and the participants are asked specific questions at the end of it.

Thinly veiled factual occurrences are usually the most effective; otherwise carefully compose a case study to suit your educational aims.

When preparing a case study and/or briefing participants, give only enough background material to enable reasonable discussion to take place. If you give too much background, students often latch on to a comparatively unimportant detail rather than the general objectives presented.

Students will frequently criticise you for lack of background — but in real life situations I frequently find it difficult to obtain all the facts. This could be the basis for your retort to them.

Feedback is essential. Control it; for timekeeping and objectivity and keep it sharp and to the point. The rules of group discussion should be followed during feedback.

Management Exercises

These are 'games' designed to enable participants to appreciate certain aspects of the management function.

The group is divided into teams, usually to run certain parts of the organisation, and various ingenious methods are used to simulate real life conditions from throwing a dice and moving around a board to a computer terminal for each team.

The latter is very sophisticated and I have found the more simple games the more effective. One you may have already come across involves the simulation of three groups within the organisation — (1) senior management, (2) middle management, and (3) the workers. Their task is purely to sort cards! But what fun and what learning!

Don't look upon them as just playing games. Enjoy them certainly, but remember there is a serious side to them.

Formal Teaching

Despite all the techniques of teaching which we have at our disposal (and there are a lot more than I have reviewed in this chapter), the formal teaching method is still the most widely used. When you try to analyse the reasons why, it usually boils down to being able to put a lot of information over in a short time.

Whether or not the recipients remember all they have been taught is very doubtful but at least the teacher feels satisfied!

Learning and training are basically concerned with changing or introducing new behaviour. This is an integral part of life, for we all have to adapt to the behaviour of other people or to adopt new patterns of action for ourselves. In life we learn by experience but unfortunately we cannot experience everything; we have to learn at work, therefore we must frequently resort to teaching in order to reach our training objectives.

Having taught — learning is not guaranteed but the adherence to certain principles can enhance the chances of effective teaching of your staff.

Fact. The greater the passage of time from teaching the subject, the less your learners are going to remember (Fig. 7.6).

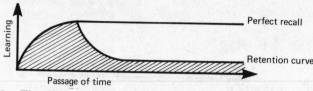

Fig. 7.6   The shaded portion is the retention curve and shows how the passage of time erodes the amount of recall. If recall were perfect then it would remain at the same level as when teaching finished.

R_x. *Overlearning.* We need to teach a subject at a level beyond the needs of the practice. We do this by repetition and teaching at a higher level.

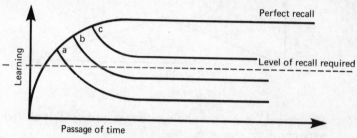

Fig. 7.7   The level of overlearning required so that the retention curves (a, b, c) eventually meet the level of recall required.

Fact. It is impossible to learn the whole curriculum in one 'read'.
R_x. Divide up your objective and teach it piece by piece.

Fact. Students cannot easily absorb material which is new to them.
R_x. It will be remembered more easily if you can relate it to something which the learner already knows, e.g. via analogy or by anecdotes.

Fact. All learning needs reinforcing.
R_x. The most effective reinforcement is 'praise'.
    A study done on the effectiveness of praise as a reinforcing agent gave the following results.

(1)   The control group (they were taught just as they usually were). They improved at first then the improvement wore off.

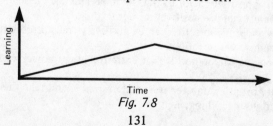

Fig. 7.8

131

(2) Ignored (they were just taught, then ignored!) Their learning increased but fell away quite soon.

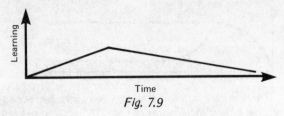

Fig. 7.9

(3) Criticised (i.e. negative reinforcement). They learnt more quickly at first but then really went downhill.

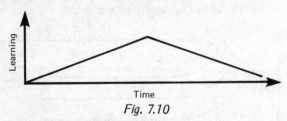

Fig. 7.10

(4) Encouraged (i.e. positive reinforcement or praise). This group showed a continual, progressive increase in learning.

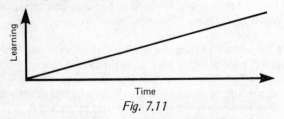

Fig. 7.11

Therefore give encouragement and praise whenever it is deserved (and sometimes when it is perhaps not fully justified). You may use criticism as it is also quite effective PROVIDED it is constructive and you follow criticism with encouragement.

Fact. Some things which are learnt for one purpose can be transferred to other purposes.
R_x. Identify positive (helpful) transfer areas and use them, e.g.:
(1) A pianist can use positive transfer to the organ.
(2) A hypodermic injection can be positively transferred into an intramuscular injection.
(3) An enema can be positively transferred into a bowel wash-out.

Identify negative transfer areas (interference) and take them into account in your teaching, e.g.:

(1) Economy is a negative transfer area to a nurse who is used to disposables.

(2) Fahrenheit is a negative transfer area to a nurse who is used to Celsius.

(3) Avoirdupois is a negative transfer area to a nurse who is used to metric.

(4) Hospital is a negative transfer area to a nurse who is used to home.

Fact. People's attention span wanes after the first 30 minutes or so.
R_x. Put the most important things first; reduce the length of input; Use other teaching techniques, i.e. involvement, practical work or discussion.

Fact. No matter how much we try, we reach a stage when no more learning takes place for a while. These stages are called the 'learning plateaux'.

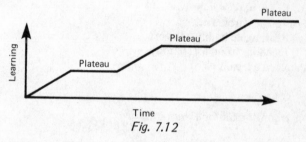

Fig. 7.12

R_x. This is a natural process and when we see this happening then we should leave the subject for perhaps more interesting things. We can then start again.

Fact. People are often confused by what they have been taught.
R_x. Review and check what you have taught shortly after the learning process is completed. It helps sort things out for the student.

I hope these points will be useful to you. It takes a long time to train a teacher and, while these facts won't qualify you for a teacher's certificate, I do hope they will make your teaching more effective.

SUMMARY

For your further interest and help I offer you the following two teaching plans as a guide to you should you embark on anything of this nature.

133

A Plan for Teaching

Prepare and Plan

(1) Take time to prepare and plan.
(2) Consider aims of the lesson — what are you trying to put over?
      (a) How much time do you have?
      (b) What is the prior knowledge of the class?
(3) You must know your subject.
      Subject matter suitably presented
      (a) according to size of class;
      (b) in logical order (beginning, middle, end).
(4) Visual aids.
      (a) Are they available?
      (b) Are they suitable?
      (c) Know how to improvise.
(5) Learning environment.
      (a) Reasonable bodily comfort.
      (b) Freedom from distractions.
(6) Prepared a lesson plan?

Promote and Maintain the Desire to Learn

(1) The enthusiasm of the teacher infects the class.
(2) Create interests via
            incentive
            curiosity
            competition
            realism
            variety
(3) Use as many of the senses as possible (sight, hearing, smell, taste, touch).
(4) Encourage maximum activity and class participation.
(5) Be simple.
(6) Human factor:
      (a) Be firm.
      (b) Be honest.
      (c) Be fair.
      (d) Be approachable.

Confirm that Teaching has been Assimilated

(1) Summarise at the end of sections and of class.
(2) Check by questions — verbal and written.

How to Instruct

Prepare to Instruct

(1) Prepare a teaching plan.
(2) Collect all the equipment necessary to do the job as it should be done under normal conditions.

Prepare the Learner

(1) Put the learner at ease.
(2) Establish two-way communication.
(3) State the job and find out *what she already knows about it.*
(4) Arouse interest in learning the job.
(5) Ensure that she is in the best position for observing the work of the instructor.

Give the Instruction

(1) Outline all sections of the job briefly to illustrate scope of the job.
(2) Instruct her in the first section — help her to master it.
(3) Instruct her in the next and subsequent sections — help her to master each in turn.
(4) Then have the learner do the job throughout.
(5) Correct any errors as they occur.
(6) As mastery is gained, encourage the learner to explain what is being done and ask questions as necessary.

Develop the Instruction

(1) Put the learner to work.
(2) Indicate her future responsibilities.
(3) Indicate sources of help.
(4) Encourage final questions.
(5) Visit as appropriate to develop skill.

Avoid jargon   Be patient   A 'picture' is worth a thousand words

CONCLUSION

Training will not solve problems of faulty management, neither will it serve as a substitute for sound selection and careful placement of employees.

If a person is of limited intelligence, training will not increase her learning potential nor will it guarantee increased performance or greater efficiency in every case.

Remember that it is not possible to 'learn' anyone anything and forgetting is easier and quicker than learning.

BUT

When we have properly motivated our staff to learn, given them competent instruction, helped them to transfer their learning to their work and ensured continued practice in the use of newly acquired knowledge, skills and attitudes . . .

THEN

we can reasonably expect:
>Greater cooperation
>Greater employee versatility
>Better communications
>Improved morale
>Fewer grievances
>Increased employee satisfaction
>Lower absenteeism and turnover
>Improved methods and systems
>Increased productivity
>Reduced supervisory problems

Having now recruited, inducted and trained our employee, in the next chapter we will turn to her continued support and development.

CASE STUDY — DOES SHE EXCEED HER DUTY?
The Ward Clerk is a splendid person; she has been with you for a couple of years now and seems to be able to do whatever you ask her, smoothly and pleasantly. She has got the hang of all the slips and forms, and understands where to send things and who should be notified, on all occasions. She has an excellent manner on the 'phone too. But your Staff Nurse does not seem so happy with the situation. In fact, she has complained to you that she is not learning much about ward administration 'because the Clerk does it all'.

What points should you check on to decide whether this feeling is justified?

How can you plan to overcome this attitude of your Staff Nurse? And will it create any difficulties with the Ward Clerk? You cannot bear to think that she might get upset at all — her work is invaluable.

REFERENCES AND FURTHER READING

Hague, H. (1973). *Management Training for Real.* London, Institute of Personnel Management.

McGregor, D. (1960). *The Human Side of Enterprise.* New York and Maidenhead, McGraw-Hill.

Roberts, T. J. (1967). *Developing Effective Managers.* London, Institute of Personnel Management.

Singer, E. J. (1969). *Training in Industry and Commerce.* London, Institute of Personnel Management.

Singer, E. J. (1974). *Effective Management Coaching.* London, Institute of Personnel Management.

The Institute of Personnel Management have a wide range of small, inexpensive publications which are very useful to nursing management. Their address is: Institute of Personnel Management, Central House, Upper Woburn Place, London WC1.

Chapter 8

Getting the Best from Them

So far — we have appointed, inducted and provided training for our new employee. Now we must move on to the next stage, which is to provide an environment in which our staff can work and develop effectively.

While our physical environment is important, we have already learnt from our study of Herzberg's work that it is only a hygiene factor and as such, provided it is kept to a certain acceptable level, it will not figure largely in our employee's morale unless other things also fall short; then our environment can cause some problems.

It would be more appropriate for a book on personnel management to dwell on the environmental aspects of work. Instead, I want to look at the managerial environment or the climate of supervision within the organisation, for without an acceptable climate of supervision people cannot work happily or effectively.

Effective supervision is a combination of many things:

(1)   Knowledge of the organisation.
(2)   Knowledge of the organisation's objectives.
(3)   Effective discipline.
(4)   Good delegation.
(5)   Training ability.
(6)   Knowledge of job.
(7)   Ability to deal with people.
(8)   Effective leadership.
(9)   Ability to communicate.
(10) Record keeping.

The list, though not complete, is rather formidable but fortunately the skills required can be learned.

Returning to our earlier discussion on management, we agreed that a manager was only a manager because she was responsible for more work than she herself could do, and so had to get others to do some of it for her. As you are doing work for which another person is responsible, you must expect to have your work supervised.

LEADERSHIP

As I have said before, there is nothing wrong with the principle that we should all be supervised; the problem is how we are supervised. The same question arises when we consider in this chapter what is perhaps the most singularly important factor in supervision — LEADERSHIP.

In some ways we are following on from our discussion of the Hawthorne experiments and others in the behavioural school of management where it was accepted that management effectiveness was related to the manager's ability to guide, motivate and integrate the work of her subordinates (as opposed to the scientific school who, you may remember, thought that work should be simplified, organised and very closely supervised).

Since their early work, the behavioural school of management have demonstrated both by experiment and in practice that various styles of management have different effects on staff. For example, McGregor's theory X: if management think that their employees are dunderheads, lazy, work-shy and lacking the desire to work, then employees will act in that manner. On the other hand, theory Y management styles demonstrate that management which encourage employees to control themselves, gain the cooperation of their staff and reap the rewards of more efficiency at work.

Knowing this, how can the individual go about developing an effective leadership style?

Finding the answer to this question puts me in something of a dilemma as I am convinced that there is no one 'right way' of doing anything with people; so I have decided to survey a few of the more well known management theories from which you may make your choice to accept, adapt, or reject as you so wish.

Let me start by briefly looking at leadership from three points of view.

1. Leadership by Status

In a society such as ours, we are all very much aware of the role of status. When we perceive that a person has more status than ourselves, it is very natural to adopt a subservient role.

Rightly or wrongly we invariably follow this pattern and thus the roles of leader and led are assumed. Our nurse training makes us very vulnerable to status despite the changing attitudes within nursing. I have mentioned previously the effect of the loss of status on Matrons and Sisters as a result of the Salmon Report. I am also reminded of the oft-repeated story of the patient who asked her District Nurse when she was going to be a 'proper nurse' like the Sister on the ward from which she had recently been discharged! Our district nursing colleague was obviously the 'poor relation' and lacked the status and thus the influence of her Ward Sister/Charge Nurse in hospital.

2. Leadership and Influence

To 'influence' is to lead; to 'have influence' is more on the lines of status.

Here we are concerned with the ability of a person to influence others. The fact that some are able to exercise this ability does not necessarily make them good leaders or acceptable leaders in the managerial sense but they are undoubtedly leaders in the truest sense of the word. Adolf Hitler was a tremendous leader and become such solely on his undoubted ability to influence his people. The sad thing is that he used his influence for evil rather than good. The ability of someone to influence her subordinates, is an enviable trait.

3. Leadership and Esteem

This is a much more valid viewpoint of leadership. It implies that the leader's team follow her leadership voluntarily because they hold her in esteem. Usually it is the esteem which they have for her professional skill and expertise which the team follow. The leader has to demonstrate her abilities and, having thus succeeded, also succeeds to the role of leadership by the esteem in which she is held by her subordinates.

Leadership Characteristics

In looking at leadership from these three viewpoints we have touched on words such as 'abilities', 'traits', 'qualities', etc. While it will soon become quite obvious that I hold no brief for such characteristics, I have to mention that from a psychological point of view there are four characteristics which are associated with effective leadership.

Intelligence

An intelligent person seems able to grasp the decision-making and analysis tasks which are so essential to effective leadership.

Extroversion

There is little doubt that the person with an outgoing personality has a head start over the average person when it comes to establishing relationships so necessary in the leadership role.

Lack of Neuroticism

I think this speaks for itself.

It is this characteristic which separates the ordinary leader from the leader with flair, ideas and breadth of vision. While these people can make mistakes, most of them make three leaps forward while the rest stay still.

Traditionally we divide types of leadership into three types of behaviour patterns:
(1)   Autocratic.
(2)   Democratic.
(3)   Laissez-faire.

These points, together with the concern of a leader for people and/or for tasks, form the basis of the following discussion on various dimensions of leadership behaviour.

DIMENSIONS OF LEADERSHIP BEHAVIOURS

Autocratic/Democratic

The clearest description I know which demonstrates these leadership patterns is contained in Fig. 8.1, which illustrates diagrammatically decision making along a continuum ranging from autocratic behaviour to democratic behaviour.

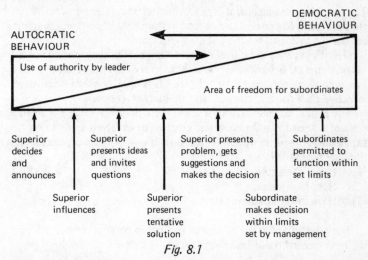

Fig. 8.1

We are certainly working in a time when democratic leadership is to be desired, but before anyone goes overboard on democracy we will do well to look at a few relevant points.
(1)   No matter how democratic you want to be, you cannot relinquish your responsibility by delegating it to someone else. This of course

141

means that the democratic leader is taking fairly high risks whenever she delegates decision making to her subordinates.

(2) Having once delegated decision making, the leader must examine her future role in the decision-making process. Further participation by the leader might inhibit the effectiveness of her team but, conversely, her participation might result in her contribution of good ideas.

(3) Your staff should be aware of the style of leadership you are practising as it makes a great deal of difference when subordinates know how you plan to use your authority.

I once took a new post under a dynamic and somewhat charismatic leader and for six months (or thereabouts) waited for her to give me orders. One day in sheer desperation, I went into her office with a long list of things I wanted to do. This resulted in a superb session between the two of us and my initiative was rewarded as I went on to complete these tasks.

As the result of this I recognised that she was the type who did not order but expected her staff to initiate and implement on their own. Being so conditioned to being told what to do, it took me a long time to diagnose this pattern of leadership. Had she identified it for me I would have got started much quicker.

(4) Democratic leadership is not identifiable by the number of decisions you allow your team to make but rather the significance of decisions you entrust to your staff.

The remaining management styles, while retaining the autocrat/democrat element, tend to concentrate on contrasting the concern which the leader has for the task and for the people in his team.

Over the years a great deal of research has been done following Elton Mayo's original behavioural research. In every case that I am aware of, managers demonstrating a high degree of 'people' concern were more effective than those showing high 'production' concern.

The conclusions invariably reached were that too much management control is harmful and that where employees are given a great deal of support and freedom of action, not only are they more productive but they are more likely to:

(1) Enjoy their jobs.
(2) Have high morale.
(3) Have lower absentee rate.

The question of effectiveness in leadership plays an important part in the next dimension of leadership we will discuss.

Reddin's Three-dimensional Management Style

Often we judge effectiveness by a person being at work on time, answering letters promptly, having a tidy desk, making quick decisions, etc., but Bill Reddin (1970) calls this apparent effectiveness.

Real effectiveness, he says, should be looked at in three ways.
(1)   Leader effectiveness: the extent to which the leader influences her team to achieve the group objectives;
(2)   Managerial effectiveness; the extent to which a manager advises the output requirements of her position;
(3)   Personal effectiveness: the extent to which a manager advises her own private objectives.

Reddin further emphasises the point by contrasting 'efficiency' with 'effectiveness' as follows:

Rather than be efficient	be effective
Rather than do things right	do right things
Rather than solve problems	produce creative alternatives
Rather than safeguard resources	optimise resource utilisation
Rather than follow duties	obtain results
Rather than lower costs	increase profit

To improve effectiveness we should understand the leadership function, and Reddin's approach is a three-dimensional approach based on three planes (Fig. 8.2). The diagram is built up from four basic styles

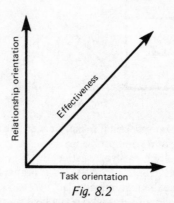

Fig. 8.2

of leadership which, when practised effectively, lead to a further four styles being identified plus a further four styles when produced less effectively.

A brief description of these polar styles follows; to effectively introduce a 3D management style would require you to at least read Reddin's book or, ideally, attend a training course dealing specifically with this.

AUTOCRAT: No confidence in others, unpleasant, concerned only with the immediate task.

BENEVOLENT AUTOCRAT: Knows what she wants and how to get it without creating resentment.

BUREAUCRAT: Dedicated to rules and procedures — controls through their use.

143

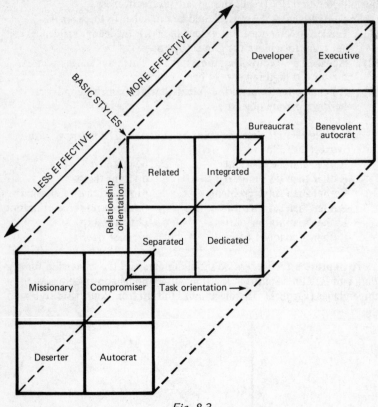

Fig. 8.3

COMPROMISER: A poor decision maker, lets others and things influence
    her, avoids pressures and problems.

DESERTER: Uninvolved, passive, negative.

DEVELOPER: Trusts people implicitly and is primarily concerned
    with developing them as individuals.

EXECUTIVE: A good motivator who sets a high standard, treats everyone
    somewhat differently and likes team management.

MISSIONARY: Primarily interested in harmony.

In presenting his theories, Reddin emphasises the need for flexibility
in styles to suit the situation rather than developing one particular
style.

Blake and Mouton's Managerial Grid

While not exactly three-dimensional in concept, the similarity of the two
axes on which this grid is plotted should be noted. I am not trying to
infer that there might be copying going on, rather emphasising that most

of these visual presentations of leadership involve People and Production;
Relationships and Tasks; or other variables on the subject.

R. R. Blake and J. S. Mouton have divided these two axes into nine-point scales of values and have thus produced an 81-position grid which can describe a manager's style. The five main leadership style descriptions

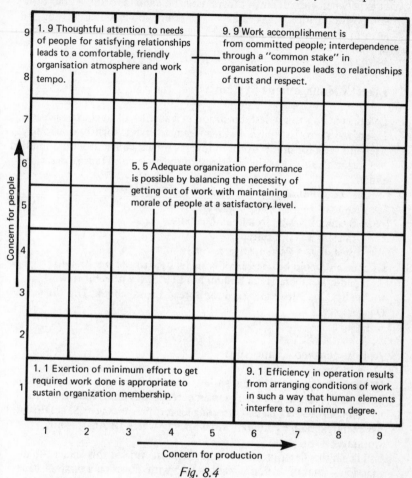

Fig. 8.4

can be seen in the grid of Fig. 8.5. Naturally Blake and Mouton recommend aiming for the 9.9 style but they, too, emphasise the need for flexibility.

Whilst it is not possible for you to diagnose your own grid position without attending a special leadership course, you might be interested in trying to place the grid position for each of the following statements:
(1) I accept the decisions of others.
(2) I place a high value on maintaining good relations.
(3) I search for a workable, even though not perfect, decision.
(4) I place a high value on making decisions that stick.

145

(5)   I place a high value on getting sound creative decisions that result
       in understanding and agreement.

This grid has been widely adopted by many companies and National
Health Service training agencies, so perhaps you may have the opportunity
of experiencing the training programme and coming to know your own
grid position with some accuracy. I can assure you it is a fascinating and
revealing process which should not be missed if the opportunity is offered
to you.

Likert's Management System

Before going on to the last dimension in leadership, I ought to mention
Likert's Systems 1 through 4 of management styles. Rightly or wrongly,
I tend to see a lot of McGregor in Likert's approach and label it 'modified
McGregor'. He also has the similarity of the style continuum I described
earlier.
    Likert's systems are as follows:
        System 1 — Exploitive authoritative
        System 2 — Benevolent authoritative
        System 3 — Consultative
        System 4 — Participative
Of course I would be over-simplifying matters to call it a straight
Autocratic/Democratic continuum but this is how it seems to work out
to me. But don't take my word for it; read Likert's book, *The Human
Organization*.

Action-centred Leadership

Of all the leadership style dimensions of which I am aware, there is none
so simple, practical and easily remembered as this one. It was developed
by John Adair when he was directing leadership training at Sandhurst and
has been taken up by the Industrial Society where Dr Adair is now
working.
    I begin this description in keeping with the title of this leadership di-
mension — that of Action. I want you to write down on a scrap of paper
a long list of words in answer to the question: 'What should a leader be
to lead effectively?'
    Give yourself only, say, 5—7 minutes to produce as many words as
possible. Get cracking and don't read my list until you have finished
yours.
    My list contains only 15 terms; I hope you reached this figure — perhaps
even 20? (When I set a group of trainees this task to do as a team I would
expect them to produce at least 20 but if you're working alone then
12—15 will do.).
    Here, then, is my list — or rather a list derived from a survey of 75 top

executives who were asked the same question:

Ambition	Energy
Cooperation	Fairness
Decisiveness	Foresight
Dedication	Human relationship skills
Dependability	Initiative
Drive	Integrity
Emotional stability	Judgement
	Objectivity

This is a very good list of leadership qualities, as I have no doubt yours is also. The problem comes when you go further and ask your respondents what they really mean when they say 'judgement' or 'foresight'.

I can assure you that that list of 15 can be increased enormously by including the various meanings put to any one of these words. Researchers found 147 different concepts of the word 'dependability' alone!

When you look at that list and try to imagine the leader who has all those qualities, you can come to only one conclusion . . . that the person does not exist who has all these attributes – at least not in human form!

What we have examined here is known as the 'QUALITIES' approach to leadership and, whilst leadership qualities are desirable, it is clearly impractical to arrive at a common agreement about the necessary qualities, to identify them or to teach them if they are found to be deficient in a leader.

Where the qualities approach is relevant is in the sense that the leaders should possess those qualities needed by the group to accomplish their task. If, for example, the group regarded that absolute integrity is vital to them as a group and their leader was lacking in integrity, she would not be acceptable as a leader to that particular group.

The next approach to leadership is based on the oft-quoted maxim that 'every situation will produce a leader'. What this is saying is that the person in a group who at that time possesses the best skill or knowledge to deal with the problems facing the group, will become its leader.

What do you think about this?

It is hard to disagree with that proposal as I have known it to occur on numerous occasions.

It is what is known as the 'SITUATIONAL' approach to leadership and, while I agree with its basic premise, when you analyse it you must come to at least three conclusions which will lead you to discount it as a practical leadership style.

(1)   It is very true of crisis situations but less true in the everyday workplace.

(2)   The nursing hierarchy would find it hard for leadership to pass from one person to another as circumstances change.

(3)   The principles of authority and responsibility cannot function in this situation.

Like the qualities approach, we must not dismiss it out of hand. The person who has the skills and knowledge appropriate to the needs of the task and group will make a better leader.

In order that we do not lose sight of this, we must remember that a leader should use the skills and knowledge of those in her group. Therefore as managers exercising our leadership function, let us use the abilities of our staff in the special situations as they arise.

Let us move on now to examine a third approach to leadership. This time I want you to write down a list of activities in answer to the question: 'What should a leader DO to lead effectively?'

Once again, allow yourself 5–7 minutes and aim for 15–20 activities. Try not to read my list until you have completed yours.

Here is my list of 15 words. I always find this one a bit harder than the qualities list. Did you?

Advise	Discipline
Anticipate	Evaluate
Command	Innovate
Communicate	Organise
Constructively criticise	Praise
Coordinate	Support
Delegate	Sympathise
	Train

Having produced this list what can we do with it? This is a problem which must face every researcher. Having asked her questions and received her answers, she invariably has so much information she does not know what to do with it.

Our researcher, John Adair, studied his list and pondered. If he is like me he may even have tried looking at his data upside down to try to get an original thought on the problem!

As Dr Adair looked at his list, gradually an idea emerged . . . he applied it and thus was born Action-centred Leadership. True, it has grown in stature and been significantly developed over the years but the break-through came when he realised that each one of the activities (i.e. the do's) could be defined as meeting either:

(1) The needs of the task.
(2) The needs of the group.
(3) The needs of the individuals in the group.

Have a look at your list and put beside each activity a 'T' if you think it meets a task need, 'G' a group need and 'I' an individual's need. They could meet all three, two of them or just one.

Here is my list again with my ideas on the needs they meet

Advise	I
Anticipate	T G
Command	G T
Communicate	G T I
Constructively criticise	G I

148

Coordinate	T
Delegate	G I
Discipline	G
Evaluate	T
Innovate	T
Organise	G
Praise	G I
Support	G I
Sympathise	I
Train	I G

You may well disagree with my assessment but it does not matter. What is important is that you recognise that groups have three basic needs: task needs, group needs and individual needs.

Task Needs

This means the task's common purpose and the achievement of its goals. A group needs to successfully complete its task and the leader must provide the physical and psychological needs to enable his team to do this.

Group Needs

This means morale, team spirit, etc., and these are achieved by holding the group together as a team working in harmony to achieve the desired goals.

Individual Needs

Groups are made up of individuals and, just as groups have needs which must be met, so have individuals. The needs of individuals frequently coincide with the needs of the team as a whole but, just as often, individuals fall into conflict with their team for a variety of reasons, which results in a less effective team and therefore poorer results.

Figure 8.5 shows us these concepts in visual form. Each of the three circles represents a single group of needs which, as we have previously indicated, a leader should seek to meet.

You will notice that the circles overlap. This demonstrates that they are not mutually exclusive but that each has a bearing on the other.

The essential leadership function is to provide these needs in an appropriate and therefore balanced way. Any over-concern for one or another of the needs gives rise to less effective execution of leadership needs in the other two functions. Let me give you some examples.

Fig. 8.5

Over-concern for Task Needs

I wonder if you have ever worked with a real 'go getter'; someone who really gets on with the job and gets things done. She does not necessarily do it all herself either; other people in her team get things done — but at what cost?

Individual needs are completely lost to this leader — people are only given 'lip service' acknowledgement and are virtually driven along, not led.

The group is only consulted when it is absolutely necessary in order for the job to be done, and consequently there is little teamwork and a great deal of individual frustration and confusion.

Using Adair's model, the situation can be demonstrated as in Fig. 8.6. Over concentration on task needs reduces the effectiveness of leadership by failing to adequately meet group and individual needs.

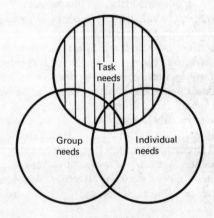

Fig. 8.6

Over-concern for Individual Needs

A Matron of a small hospital earned herself and her hospital an unenviable reputation almost entirely as the result of having many one-to-one relationships. By this I do not mean they were improper except within the leadership context.

Her style involved little cosy chats to individuals — in her office, in the ward kitchen, in a nurse's bedroom, in the corner of the waiting room, in the canteen.

All these chats were 'very confidential' or 'I shouldn't be telling you this but . . .'

She positively avoided seeing more than one person at a time. The result of this was that staff exhibited suspicion, jealousy, rivalry, low morale and disloyalty, which resulted in the hospital being a very unhappy place for staff to work, which consequently had its effect on patient care.

The model in Fig. 8.7 illustrates this.

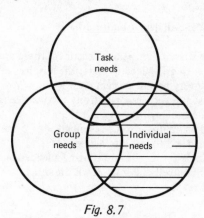

Fig. 8.7

Over-concern for individual needs reduces the leader's ability to adequately meet the team's group and task needs.

Over-concern for Group Needs

Here the manager is 'hail fellow well met'. She gets on well with lots of people. 'Come and work with me,' she is saying, ' and you will really enjoy it'; 'It's fun working here'; 'We are all one big happy family'.

What she does not say is that, while it may be fun, we are not really as efficient as we should be — we don't get the task done as effectively as we could. And she also fails to recognise that while she is relating to groups there are many shy, introverted, reticent individuals whose needs are being entirely overlooked. Their ideas, skills and talents are not being tapped and they feel very badly done by — quite second-rate citizens in their eyes. When group needs are over-emphasised, the task does not get done so well and individuals feel left out (Fig. 8.8).

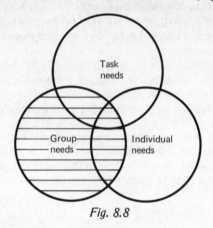

Fig. 8.8

Applying Action-centred Leadership

As with other leadership dimensions described, there are courses available on Action-centred Leadership under the auspices of the Industrial Society. They are very happy to train your leaders or to teach you how to train your leaders, and for a comparatively modest fee (i.e. compared to purely commercial training fees).

Of all the leadership dimensions described, this is the easiest to grasp, to remember and to put into action.

In its most simple form — before starting a leadership task — I would advise you to ask yourself and note down the things you will need to DO in order to meet the:

Task needs
Group needs
Individual needs

Keep these points with you so that you are continually made aware of the need to effectively meet and balance the three needs of your team.

To help you further, let us look at what you need to DO to meet these three types of needs.

Task Needs

(1) Know clearly what you want to achieve (principle of the objective).
(2) Plan how you will accomplish it.
(3) Provide the resources required (men, money, machinery, time and materials).
(4) Give the authority required to complete the task.
(5) Control and coordinate the efforts being made.
(6) Evaluate progress and results.

Group Needs

(1) Set and maintain group objectives and standards required.
(2) Involve the group as a whole in the achievement of objectives.
(3) Minimise any disruptive activity and aim positively to maintain the unity of the group.

Individual Needs

(1) Provide a job which is challenging and demands maximum responsibility to match her capabilities.
(2) Strive to let individuals experience a sense of personal achievement.
(3) Recognise and praise achievements.
(4) Allow self-monitoring and self-control as far as possible.

SUMMARY

We have seen how leadership and management styles revolve around two pairs of concepts; those of (1) Democratic/Autocratic, and (2) Task/People relationships.

Democratic/Autocratic

Research has shown that the more democratic the leadership style used, the more effective is the team. This is not to say that we should always be completely democratic. On the contrary, all leadership demands sensitivity to the situation and the ability to select and implement the most appropriate style. I must say that sometimes it pays to thump the desk a bit and jolly well tell people to get on with it and pull their finger out — most undemocratic but undeniably effective. R_x to be used sparingly as required.

Task/People

Task/People relationships seek to balance the leader's activities and thus make her more effective. In the dimensions within this framework which I have discussed, Action-centred Leadership seems the most suitable approach to us in the National Health Service. It demonstrates that the job of a leader is:
(1) To achieve the required results.
(2) To ensure that the group works well together.
(3) To motivate each individual to play her maximum part.

Action-centred Leadership – Check-list

Task

(1) Do you understand the task?
(2) Have you obtained all available information from your boss?
(3) Have you analysed and defined the problems?
(4) Are you working to a plan?
(5) Are you testing ideas and solutions?
(6) Are you making the best use of resources (time, people, materials, etc.)?

Group

(1) Have you told them enough about the task?
(2) Have you explained why the task is necessary?
(3) Have you got agreement on what the group goals should be?
(4) Have you agreed group standards (time limits, quality, etc.)?
(5) Are you summarising progress (during and at the end)?
(6) Are you criticising the group constructively?
(7) Are you encouraging the group appropriately?
(8) Are you maintaining harmony?
(9) Are you keeping the group to its purpose?
(10) Are you involving them in decision making?
(11) Can you ease the tension with humour?

Individual

(1) Have you given each person an appropriate job to do?
(2) Have you agreed targets with each person?
(3) Have you explained the significance of each person's job to her?
(4) Have you checked understanding?
(5) Have you discovered special skills or knowledge?
(6) Are you consulting, listening and acknowledging her contribution?
(7) Are you telling each person how she is getting on?
(8) Are you disciplining where necessary?
(9) Are you setting a good example?

REFERENCES AND FURTHER READING

Adair, J. (1968). *Training for Leadership.* London, MacDonald.
Blake, R. R. and Mouton, J. S. (1964). *The Managerial Grid: key orientations for achieving production through people.* Houston, Texas, Gulf Publishing Co.

Likert, R. (1967). *The Human Organization: its management and value.* New York and Maidenhead, McGraw-Hill.

Reddin, W. J. (1970). *Managerial Effectiveness.* New York and Maidenhead, McGraw-Hill.

Smith, E. P. (1969). *The Manager as an Action Centred Leader.* Notes for Managers, No. 14. London, Industrial Society.

Tannenbaum, A. S. and Schmidt, W. (1953). *Harvard Business Review,* **36**, No. 2.

Chapter 9

Share Your Burden

INTRODUCTION

I ought to add to the title of this chapter 'and do a lot of good', because it has been said that 80% of learning the skills of management consists of having oneself been well managed.

Delegation — for this is what this chapter is about — is one of the most vital skills of a manager. To delegate is a means of fulfilling your responsibility for developing your subordinates; it is a basic tool of management for achieving results.

In a way, the division of work which I discussed in Chapter 4 is a sophisticated delegation device in that each manager keeps a part of her job and divides up the rest of it. The shared part is, as it were, a delegated function; so in a sense all work is delegated work! (Perhaps when you have finished this chapter you might like to come back to that last statement and spend a bit of time discussing it?)

THE MEANING OF DELEGATION

If you are to discuss delegation then a definition of terms is called for. The first one is from Col. L. Urwick — whose principles of management we discussed in Chapter 4. He says that delegation is 'The allocation and communication of a task, responsibility and authority to a subordinate'.

The second definition I want to present to you is: 'The process of entrusting subordinates with authority to act in a given field, using their own discretion on behalf of their superior'.

The essential difference between these two definitions is the matter of responsibility. One mentions the delegation of responsibility, the other does not; and the question is often asked 'Can responsibility be delegated'?

Urwick states in his principle of responsibility that 'The responsibility of the superior for acts of his subordinates is absolute'. Yet Urwick is the one who seems to be delegating it!

I think the explanation is that delegation establishes responsibility on the part of the subordinate to answer for the way in which he uses the authority which has been vested in him. This authority has been derived from the overall responsibility of his superior, but it is still generally untrue to say that a superior has delegated his responsibilities.

In delegating authority to his subordinate, he has merely established a FURTHER RESPONSIBILITY between himself and his subordinate

156

while remaining entirely responsible for the whole of the work designated by his position.

WHY WE SHOULD DELEGATE

Delegation is not giving out work. Giving out work requires ordering and briefing staff about work which naturally is theirs. When you delegate, you are giving someone a job to do which you would normally do yourself. So why do we do it?

Naturally the first reason would be to 'ease your work-load' . . . a very real reason, as Moses discovered when he was 'Judging all the people'. Fortunately Jethro, his father-in-law, taught him how to delegate very effectively.

Next I would say we delegate in order to develop staff expertise and initiative. Our system in general does nothing to encourage ideas and individuality; rather it serves to stifle individual flair.

Another reason for delegating is to enable decisions to be taken at the lowest practicable level nearest to the patients who are our main concern.

It follows from this that a more senior manager, by delegating some tasks, releases some of her time for those forward-looking tasks such as forecasting and planning.

Delegation does wonders for the morale of your team. Contrast the staff morale when a delegator is heading the team as opposed to an insular, secretive, do-it-herself manager.

Finally — and this might be hard to believe — one of the most rewarding experiences a manager can have is to develop her subordinates for greater things. Certainly you lose them; sometimes they even get promotion to a level higher than you, but even then it is extremely satisfying to know that you have helped them on their way.

WHY YOU DON'T DELEGATE

Maybe it is because there are disadvantages to delegation. In the main, I would narrow these down to six:
(1)   You are certainly initially taking a chance with a subordinate — they may well make mistakes and you will have to weather these.
(2)   There is a lot of work involved in delegating and it could be quicker to do it yourself.
(3)   You can lose out on confidentiality, even secrecy which may be required.
(4)   You will certainly relinquish your command of the detail.
(5)   You could, without great care, stretch your subordinates beyond their abilities.
(6)   It could enable some unscrupulous managers to shirk!

More pointedly, you should look at yourself for reasons why you don't delegate.

Could it be you are too busy — snowed under with work so that you don't have time to fulfil the obligation of examination prior to delegation?

Perhaps you feel insecure about your subordinates so that you are unwilling to take a chance with them?

Sometimes you do not know enough about the work yourself to be able to delegate it or to know what part of it could be delegated?

Fear of losing control once the job has gone from you is yet another possibility.

Perhaps your boss won't let you delegate certain things or perhaps you think you can do the job quicker or better yourself.

Finally, it could be that you simply do not know how to delegate?

HOW TO DELEGATE

By now you will have realised that delegation is more than a communication exercise. In fact, it requires a personal brand of trust between you and your nurses.

When you delegate, the responsibility for working within the limits which you set her is passed to your subordinate . . . which should make you realise the need for you to have done your homework and clearly defined and communicated the limits of discretionary action you are giving to your subordinates.

Delegation is to my mind a less stereotyped form of teaching or lecturing. As such it is important that you have not only prepared yourself adequately but are also ready to make yourself aware of the response you are getting from your staff.

Don't expect a job to be done in exactly the same way as you would do it yourself. There is nothing more frustrating to a subordinate to submit a piece of work which she has completed to a generally acceptable standard and then be directed to correct in order to meet the personal whims of her superior.

Certainly indicate the areas of importance and which are crucial to a successful outcome but, having delegated, you must allow the individual to use her own methods and to imprint the job with her own style.

The second response you should note is the attitude and interest which your subordinate exhibits. The more positive the response the less supervision is likely to be needed, and the converse might indicate that you have not selected the correct person to do the job.

You should also examine yourself and remember that you are trying to arouse the same interest and stimulation which you have yourself. Perhaps you ARE less than enthusiastic, but please don't show it or the results of the delegated task will reflect your lack of commitment. But again, it may be that if this is the case you should do that job yourself and delegate something else of yours which will be delegated and accepted with enthusiasm.

Remember the intellectual demand you are putting on your subordinates. Establish their ability correctly and especially beware of underestimating their ability. This is a common fault of managers who come more or less under the heading of 'no one can do the job as well as I can'.

Be aware that YOU might well need to receive a sense of achievement from what the subordinate does for you. Some managers keep all the glory for themselves and, while our Health Service bureaucracy sometimes demands that the manager takes the praise for her subordinate's work (i.e. the boss often has to put her name at the end of a report prepared by her subordinate), please try to gain your satisfaction by successful delegation and the effective development of your subordinates.

Individuals will always test themselves and this always poses a problem when delegating. What our subordinates frequently do is take the initiative or stand their own ground and not communicate to you what they are doing — in fact, they leave you out altogether!

It is really something that we must expect and even encourage. You see the same behaviour exhibited as a child begins to grow up and flex its wings. It is part of management development and if you want to be consulted/briefed etc., then you should specify what, when and where.

The group in which your subordinate works has a bearing on the job delegated. Her peer group influence is very strong and can affect the outcome greatly. Some people like competition — others do not. It is up to you to decide when it can be used as an effective tool of delegation. Similarly, mild stress is acceptable to those who are confident but many cannot cope with it. Both competition and stress are more apparent in groups, therefore be aware of this when delegating to groups.

Take account of the level of difficulty. Here your time span control can be adjusted as well as your own teaching and supportive role in this piece of delegated work.

Motivation is another consideration. When discussing this in a classroom I have often asked the students to 'stand up'. And invariably they all did. Then we examined why they did it. The answers were many and varied but at the root of it was the uncertainty which people felt at what would happen if they didn't comply and in any case it was easier to do what you were told and be sure. The section on Motivation (in Chapter 3) will give you ideas on why this should be.

Train up your subordinates gradually, increasing the level of difficulty and the degree of responsibility you give them. It will be of help to you also, as you will gain confidence in them as you begin to work closer together. I firmly believe that good subordinates will stand the tests and poor subordinates will wilt away.

WHEN IS A SUBORDINATE READY TO ASSUME DELEGATED TASKS?

An examination of her abilities should enable you to make a valid judgement on your subordinate's readiness for these tasks. I stress abilities rather than shortcomings. We all have shortcomings but, unless your subordinate is demonstrating some definite contraindication to your delegating the tasks to her, evaluate her abilities and then decide on the appropriate task to delegate.

Look for her capacity to absorb additional work-load and her ability to plan and execute a work programme with the minimum of supervision.

Ask yourself questions on the suitability of the person's temperament for the task you have in mind and her acceptability to others with whom she will have to work.

It is of course understood that you always have the right to either withdraw the delegated authority or to limit it as and when it may be appropriate to do so.

Naturally, you do not want to recall any authority you may have delegated unless things are really going wrong. Therefore careful evaluation of your staff and of the tasks you are delegating is important.

The types of tasks you can look at with a view to delegation could be those of a fact-finding nature and the subsequent analysis (prior to YOU making the required decision); the formulation of plans, policies or projects, etc.

Having done the groundwork and your having made the appropriate decisions, who better to implement these tasks than the person who has done most of the groundwork.

There are many other routine tasks which you can delegate but also consider delegating tasks that others can do sooner or better than yourself and tasks which will help ease your work-load such as representing you where your viewpoint can be expressed on your behalf or where you may have over-specialised.

As an example of the latter I can tell you of a member of staff at the William Rathbone Staff College who developed expertise many years ago on a topic which at that time was of very little interest to the National Health Service. Gradually his expertise was called upon more and more until the NHS directed that a great deal of effort was to be made to train all NHS nurses in this management tool.

The demand for this lecturer's services became phenomenal and, though the college had many able lecturers on its staff or available to them, none had done any work in this field as 'X' was the expert! The result was that before the College could expand its programme in the required direction, it had to hold what amounted to an in-service training programme for its own staff on that subject. Needless to say, we never allowed over-specialisation to occur again.

Though this section has been looking at the suitability of tasks and staff for delegation, we should not lose sight of the fact that the manager also needs to have the capacity to communicate the task together with the necessary information and the ability to plan, at least in outline, the course of action required. This of course necessitates a broad knowledge of the work involved.

All of which leads us to the practical application of what I have been discussing. This comes to fruition mainly in the act of delegation.

A PLAN FOR DELEGATION

Notice I have not said 'This is the right way to delegate' but here is 'A' plan for you to consider.

Here I will present it in a discussion style but at the end of the chapter I will repeat it in easy-reference 'hand-out' style.

Define Your Objectives

This is the first stage. Are you delegating to ease your work-load? ... to develop your subordinate? ... to teach? Because I am sure your approach to the job of delegation will be very different if it is for teaching compared with reducing your work-load. The two would require handling in very different ways.

Let us take it further and get it very clear in your mind just what you are delegating. Remember delegation is giving someone a job (or part of a job) which you would normally do yourself. Giving an order or briefing a subordinate are not delegation. So make sure the task is truly a delegated one. Are you going to share the task amongst your team? Keep some yourself? Or have your member of staff do it all but stage by stage?

Next, look at the job itself, the actual work and clearly define it to your own satisfaction. If you are unfamiliar with certain aspects of it, then familiarise yourself briefly so that you can intelligently estimate the amount of work required and the length of time the job might take. This examination of the job will also help you in selecting the right person for the job.

Then concentrate on defining the amount of authority you will be giving and remember that the authority must be 'seen'. When you delegate, your subordinates are frequently communicating and liaising with people with whom they would normally not have very much contact and indeed who may be very superior in rank to them. Unfortunately not everyone is willing to communicate openly and freely with people whom they don't know or who are inferior in rank to them. Therefore it is important that all with whom your subordinate will come into contact while completing the task know that she has the authority to act on your behalf. This is what I mean by letting authority be 'seen'.

Delegate the Work

This is phase two. We are now concentrating on the face-to-face meeting between you and your subordinate when you will actually delegate the task to her.

You will of course know her quite well and will quickly realise whether you first need to put her at her ease. Strangely enough, though you may think that no one could possibly be afraid of you, it could well be that a person being called to your office may well be apprehensive until she knows the reason for the meeting.

161

If you don't already know the extent of her previous knowledge of the task you are planning to give her, you will need to find out from her yourself so that you know the level at which you will pitch your communication. (Remember that the principles of teaching apply to a large extent to delegation and, as we mentioned earlier, to 'find out previous knowledge' is important.)

You should now be ready to tell her (or show her if necessary) the job. Always give reasons, for if a person knows the background to her work she will be able to take intelligent independent action in order to achieve the ultimate success of the job.

You may need to encourage her or inspire confidence in herself; often this can be done by offering her assurance of your support if ever she may need it. This of course must be offered sincerely whether or not it is a tool for inspiring confidence, as you owe this to all your employees regardless.

Feedback

This is the next stage. Check to see if she has fully understood the task. Give her every opportunity to ask questions. Make sure she is aware of the big areas of the task where results are important; then institute some controls to enable both of you to check on progress.

With this, the actual delegation session is finished but you may want me to briefly offer you some help, or control, in relation to delegation.

The word and its function are not new to you any more as it has been a subject of earlier discussion (see Chapter 8). In delegation you must set some kind of control, as a manager who delegates a task and then sits back, taking no further interest, has in effect abdicated not delegated!

Principles of Control in Delegation

(1) Choose appropriate controls in relation to the task set.
(2) You should be able to check progress quickly rather than in a detailed time-consuming check.
(3) Set controls related to the key result areas of the task, e.g. 'When you have done so and so, then we should meet again'.
(4) Set a minimum number of 'feedbacks'.
(5) All concerned must clearly know and understand the controls being used.

Here are some points I have found useful in obtaining feedback on delegated tasks.
(1) Setting up lateral controls is useful. This is merely the tying up of parts of the job with other people or suggesting meetings with others for guidance and review.

(2) A check-list setting out various criteria can be useful in certain situations, especially when the task is being done for the first time. However, it could be misconstrued by an experienced nurse as an insult!

(3) Check on progress at routine meetings, conferences and routine progress reports. These are natural places to talk about a delegated task without appearing to be over-supervising.

(4) Use indirect reminders and chance meetings for quick verbal checks as to how things are going.

(5) Remember always to encourage two-way communication between you from the actual delegation encounter through to the completed task, which means of course that you must always be reasonably accessible to discuss important aspects of the job.

Finally, no discussion on delegation would be complete without a brief mention of the term 'Management by Exception'. Another way of putting this would be to say that 'no news is good news'. Basically the technique requires you, the manager, to assume that everything is going well unless you are told otherwise.

Of course you can't really do that until you and your subordinate have agreed acceptable standards and a progress timetable. Management by exception is a technique which can be used much more widely in all areas of management and management control, but beware of managing entirely by this technique. For a start, all you would be getting is the bad news and that would be demoralising, and secondly I think it would be virtual abdication of your vital supervisory role.

Control by time-span is also a useful technique. When you indicate to a person how much time she has in which to complete a task, you are also telling her the depth to which you want it done and the quality which you require. For example, if you give her one week in which to do a task or six weeks, this is telling her a great deal. It seems that we are quite happy to work under this kind of control.

SUMMARY

Let me summarise by saying that delegation is perhaps the most powerful tool of working through people for the benefit of the organisation and our patients.

It develops individuals' management ability, gives your subordinates the opportunity of using their initiative, and both manager and subordinate strengthen their own working relationship and their own positions in the organisation.

Here is the check-list I promised you.

A Plan for Delegation

Define your Objective

(1) Define what you are delegating.
(2) Define the exact nature of the work.
(3) Define the amount of authority you are giving and let the authority be 'seen'.

Delegate the Work

(1) Put at ease.
(2) Find out (or know) previous knowledge of the work.
(3) Tell and show job if need be.
(4) GIVE REASONS.
(5) Inspire confidence if need be.
(6) Give assurance of support.

Feedback

(1) Check to see if it is understood.
(2) Check on progress.

N.B. The interview must be two-way; therefore encourage questions all the way through.

Definitions (Col. L. Urwick)

DELEGATION: The allocation and communication of a task, responsibility and authority to a subordinate.
AUTHORITY: The right to make decisions and issue instructions to cover the work of others.

NOTE. Whereas subordinates should be made accountable for the work they are given, the superior cannot abdicate her responsibility for work she allocates to her subordinates.

CASE STUDY – THE AGGRIEVED PATHOLOGIST
The 'phone rings and you answer it. But you wish you hadn't, because the pathologist at the other end of the line is really angry! Apparently, a specimen sent from your ward has been wrongly labelled, badly collected and the request form with it is incomplete. He leaves you in no doubt what he thinks of your efficiency!

You apologise and say you'll look into it. When you do, you find that the doctor thought the Staff Nurse would fill in the form for him,

the Staff Nurse thought the third-year student would be able to collect
the specimen and the third-year student thought that the junior (who
was helping her) would have done the labelling properly. The specimen
reached the laboratory unchecked because the Orderly thought it would
be helpful if she took it over with others.

How do you sort out those responsibilities?
How far are you directly responsible?
What authority did you delegate to the Staff Nurse?
What steps can you take to avoid this sort of problem in the future?

FURTHER READING

Allen, L. A. (1958). *Management and Organization.* New York, McGraw-
Hill.
Dale, E. (1952). *Planning and Developing the Company Organization
Structure.* New York, The American Management Associations.
Forrest, Andrew (1972). *Delegation*, rev. edn. Notes for Managers, No. 19.
London, Industrial Society.
Holroyde, G. (1970). *How to Delegate.* Rugby, Warwicks., Mantec
Publications.
Laird, D. and Laird, E. (1957). *The Techniques of Delegating.* New York
and Maidenhead, McGraw-Hill.
Townsend, R. (1970). *Up the Organisation.* London, Michael Joseph. (Also
published by Coronet, London, 1971).

Chapter Ten

Well Done

Though this chapter is about your responsibility to your staff in one particular aspect, I hope that my approach to the subject will result in this responsibility becoming an integral part of your management style.

Certainly we are all concerned with patient care, but, unfortunately, the way nursing is organised a lot of the care which patients receive is not given by you at all, but by your staff. If our patients are to receive the care we think they ought to get, then we have to help our staff to deliver this care at its highest standard, and with the minimum of frustration. If we do not care for our staff in this way then our patients will almost inevitably suffer.

PERSONNEL MANAGEMENT

The function of caring for staff in the organisation is labelled 'personnel management'. It takes many forms and has many various facets. One simple definition of personnel management is that it is 'a service for people . . . by people'. As managers we are both the people receiving the service and those giving the service.

What, then, are the services which personnel management provide?

The list which I like to use to illustrate these services has its origins in some lecture notes of mine. Who the lecturer was I am afraid eludes me, but I am grateful to him for the following logical and most useful list.

Good Personnel Management provides for:

Manpower Planning	A service for looking at work and estimating staffing levels, type of staff and ensuring the succession of jobs.
Selection Procedure	Having planned your manpower needs, unless you go about selecting your staff in a methodical way designed to enable you to make the best choice possible, it will have been a wasted exercise.

Induction	Having selected your person to do the job you cannot just leave her to muddle through. She should be helped by the induction process to settle into her job and into the organisation as quickly and efficiently as possible.
Post-entry Training	Because we have a person working for us we must not forget that she will have further training needs as time goes on; say, a refresher course or help to do the Diploma of Nursing
Recognition of Effort	Everyone thrives on praise and recognition. Every effort must be made to reward work which is well done. Too. often the only time we know how we are going on is when we are being reprimanded.
Environment for Effective Delegation and Supervision	Staff will not work well in an organisation which has a restrictive, negative atmosphere. In such an organisation people become automatons with a dulled sense of responsibility and commitment.
A System of Consultation and Industrial Relations	The more people know of what is going on the less threatened they will feel. The likelihood of poor industrial relations is lessened when there is involvement by all through consultation.
Opportunity for Counselling and Welfare	People need help with their personal needs. A counselling and welfare service is an essential part of every organisation.
Disciplinary and Grievance Procedures	Just as we must recognise effort, so we have to ensure that all know how they can pursue redress for a grievance and the disciplinary procedures which the organisation have if they are required.

Staff Development   We must make sure our staff are prepared and channelled into their most effective areas of service. Flexible, positive measures must be available to enable a person to reach her full potential

This gives us a very broad overview of personnel management, some of which is often provided by a special 'Personnel Management' department, and other parts by the person's manager.

As a manager you have particular responsibility for effective work by your subordinates. They, too, have a responsibility to their employers and themselves.

Edgar Anstey, in his book, *Staff Reporting and Staff Development*, has put this succinctly as follows.

Responsibilities of:

Management	*Staff*
(1) To get the work done as efficiently as possible.	(1) To render good service to the organisation by doing the job to the best of her ability.
(2) To help staff develop their potentialities.	(2) To seek opportunity to develop her potentialities and further her career.

Our ideal as managers of people is to make these responsibilities complementary.

With regard to our responsibility for our subordinates' effective work, John Humble, in his book, *Improving Management Performance*, suggests that if a person is to work effectively, then she has five basic needs:

(1) To be told clearly what is expected of her.
(2) To be allowed to get on with doing her job with the minimum of controls placed on her.
(3) To be told how she is getting on before it is too late.
(4) To be given help and guidance when it is needed.
(5) To be rewarded for her effort.

Here we have a list of things we can give to our subordinates which does not cost money neither do we have to get permission from our superiors in order to give them; following these five points is just good personal practice by a manager.

So far all I have done is tell you what we should be doing for our personnel. Now I want to suggest a means whereby, with a little effort, we can achieve all things.

VALUING YOUR STAFF

I am almost afraid to mention the name of the system whereby we can achieve our personnel management goals, as it causes such a reaction in some people that they switch off immediately. Though why this is so I find it hard to understand, as it is such a positive word.

The word is 'appraisal', but the full title of this management tool varies from 'Staff appraisal' to 'Staff development and performance review'.

Let us look at the word 'appraise' for a moment. Various dictionaries define it as:

To value

To esteem

To set a price with a view to sale

As we are not in the slave trade, I see nothing threatening in these definitions. On the contrary, I am sure we all 'value' and 'esteem' our staff. Let us look just a little deeper at the word itself:

APPRAISE

Remove the first two letters, and we have the root of the word PRAISE.

Perhaps I have spent too long trying to quell doubts which do not exist, so let me define 'staff appraisal' for you.

I think it would be fair to say that staff appraisal is 'to review a nurse's performance, and assess her potential, with the object of identifying any training needed either to improve existing technical/managerial performance, OR to develop her for promotion'.

I must comment on the 'OR' which I have stressed in that definition. The appraisal system offers something for everyone, be they perfectly happy in their job, and totally disinterested in management, or be they anxious to climb the promotion ladder.

It is a system designed FOR nurses BY nurses with only the best interest for individual nurses and the nursing profession in mind. With this system properly used we can do a great deal to improve our professional and managerial development, with a maximum benefit to individual nurse participants in the scheme.

The National Nursing Staff Committee introduced it after wide consultation in 1961, with the following stated aims.

(1) To provide in a systematic way for performance review and to keep senior officers informed of this and of the nurse's potential for advancement.

(2) To provide a specific opportunity for counselling and for the nurse to discuss her progress and to help resolve any difficulties which impede good nursing or management.

(3) To identify any need for further training or broadening of experience.

(4) To enable more reliable and informative references to be provided.

AN OVERVIEW OF APPRAISAL

Putting the definitions, aims and philosophy of staff appraisal together enables us to construct a model of the staff appraisal function.

We have said that it aims to review a nurse's performance and her potential. So the first phase of our model would begin as shown in Fig. 10.1.

Fig. 10.1

It is important that we distinguish between performance and potential. Performance is what we have actually done, and potential is what we are capable of doing.

When we are 'appraising' it is performance that we are concerned with. Potential plays its part, but it must be a separate assessment. We could get very mixed up if we gave a nurse of poor ability a good rating because she worked to her full potential; while giving the nurse of good ability a poor rating because she could have done better.

The objective is PERFORMANCE review, i.e. reviewing what nurse has ACTUALLY DONE. It is not a hunch, not potential, but PROVEN PERFORMANCE.

There is nothing new about reviewing performance. It has been and still is part of every manager's job. We are doing it all the time when we decide who does what and why. We know who needs more experience in doing certain things; who can do such a job quickly and efficiently; who has done a good day's work; and who has not pulled her weight. The only thing that is different in performance review is that we are required to write down our appraisal of their performance and discuss it with them.

Appraisal is essentially a judgement of what someone actually does. It does not concern her personality except when it results in inappropriate behaviour — then you can require a person to do something to correct her behaviour.

I believe we have no right to try to change a person's personality, even if we were able (and I do not think we are skilled enough to do that), but we do have a right to expect a person to change her behaviour, judged by you to be inappropriate, because then it concerns something she has actually done — i.e. performance, not personality.

The judgement process requires us to apply a set of standards. The first part of the appraisal process is for us to fill in the appraisal form; this provides us with a number of areas where we can appraise performance. It is designed to help us judge performance as objectively as possible, and the standard we are using is 'the standard of performance you could reasonably expect FROM AN EXPERIENCED NURSE IN THE GRADE'.

Every time we appraise a person's performance we must use that standard.

This appraisal form, besides providing a general systematic framework to assist us to measure performance, also gives us an opportunity to comment on potential.

Potential is related to performance in certain aspects, but differs in as much as, while we are judging performance, we are also looking at the qualities which our member of staff brings to the job which impresses on us that she is capable of greater things.

Perhaps it is inevitable that when we are looking at potential we think mainly of promotion, but do remember there are more things to our profession than 'management'. Do you have on your staff a potential clinical instructor? . . . Tutor? . . . Health Visitor? . . . Home nurse? . . . Clinical specialist? . . . a nurse who is degree material? We can easily make this list very long. Many people find their niche just by accident and in doing so often waste many years of their professional career. Your judgements can be very valuable to your staff.

When we look at potential from the promotion aspect, we must be careful not to fall into the trap of thinking that promotion means purely an ability to display greater amounts of the skills and qualities needed at lower levels (though there is often some continuing demand for this).

Increasing levels of management responsibility requires DIFFERENT skills and qualities. As a manager moves up the hierarchy, in general terms she is faced with three increasing demands:

(1) An ability to integrate the range of work done by subordinates.
(2) An ability to coordinate the work of her own groups of staff (unit) with those of parallel or complementary units.
(3) An ability to maintain the progress of the organisation towards its objectives while circumstances are changing, many of which are beyond her control. (A good example of the latter is maintaining recruitment levels in nursing despite: a fluctuating birth rate; salary levels offered to school leavers by other professions; higher academic standards required; etc.)

I hope that you recognise from the above factors that performance of relatively routine matters at lower levels can provide only a limited indication of potential for the complex tasks of each successive management level.

Having given performance a minimal role when considering potential, there is a need to provide you with clues as to factors which will help you assess potential for promotion.

The first clue is to look not at the level of performance, but its STYLE or QUALITY.

Secondly, look for qualities that are more closely linked with personal characteristics of the individual's BEHAVIOUR and response to the work at a given management level.

Having discussed performance and potential, let us look at our now expanded model, and add to it our second phase (Fig. 10.2).

171

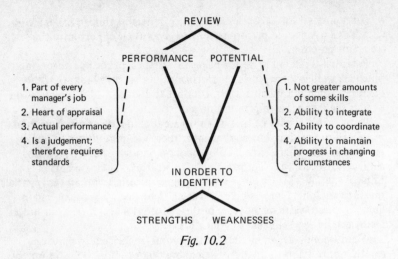

REVIEW

PERFORMANCE   POTENTIAL

1. Part of every
   manager's job
2. Heart of appraisal
3. Actual performance
4. Is a judgement;
   therefore requires
   standards

1. Not greater amounts
   of some skills
2. Ability to integrate
3. Ability to coordinate
4. Ability to maintain
   progress in changing
   circumstances

IN ORDER TO
IDENTIFY

STRENGTHS   WEAKNESSES

Fig. 10.2

STRENGTHS AND WEAKNESSES

Having gone through the process of assessing performance and potential, we will by now have a good idea of the strengths or good points which our staff possess, and it will be very gratifying to them when you mention these, and take the opportunity to give praise and thanks where it is due.

You will find that virtually all of your staff have areas where they perform well, and it is up to you to use these abilities to mutual advantage. Recognition of abilities is good for morale, and if these abilities are called upon and developed it results in job satisfaction for the staff concerned, and of course good service to our patients.

This part of appraisal you will find very pleasant to perform, but the identification of 'weaknesses' or perhaps, to put it more accurately, the discussion which must inevitably result from the identification of these weaknesses is often seen to be traumatic by both the manager and her subordinate.

Yet it is in this very area that real, positive work can be done to the benefit of both the participants in the exercise.

The key to success is in developing a positive, supportive attitude between superior and subordinate; to start with, we will stop using the word WEAKNESSES. This is a very negative and emotive word which conjures up very threatening implications to those on the receiving end of it. Our approach must avoid these perceptions, and I suggest that we begin by substituting the word NEEDS for our previous word – weaknesses.

'Needs' imply a recognition that something will be done about them; that help will be given to those who have needs, either by removing them or by helping them cope with those which we cannot eliminate. Our staff will be much more willing to discuss their needs than to reveal their weaknesses; much more willing to reveal their needs which are going to be dealt with rather than expose themselves to the negative aura surrounding the revelation of their weaknesses.

Needs can fall into three main categories:

(1) Those which the organisation will have to supply (e.g. more staff, better equipment, etc.).

(2) Those which the manager will have to supply (perhaps some of those five needs listed by John Humble on page 168).

(3) Those needs which are within the individual (e.g. help with report writing for management).

In any of these groupings the two-way supportive relationship between you and your subordinate can be developed as together you decide what you can do for her and what she can do for herself and what together you will do that will further help your patients.

Here we come back to restating the main theme of Chapter 1: management should seek to develop a system which enables them to COOPERATE WITH SUBORDINATES RATHER THAN CONTROL THEM; this is the essence of supportive management.

Let us look at Fig. 10.3 and see what our model looks like after this second phase of appraisal.

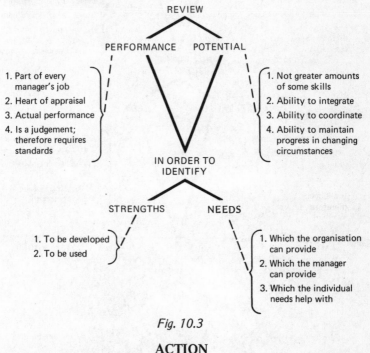

Fig. 10.3

ACTION

The whole of appraisal is quite useless unless something results from the process. Without action, the whole exercise will soon become another administrative chore; the form to be ticked . . . the two-way discussion about the job to be ignored or passed over because it is all a waste of time . . . nothing gets done, so why bother?

We as managers must accept our responsibility to act on the results of our appraisal. We do this in two ways:
(1) By providing development opportunities.
(2) By providing training.

There is no such line between development and training as there is between performance and potential. Sometimes training is development and sometimes development is training, but we can differentiate between the two in broad terms.

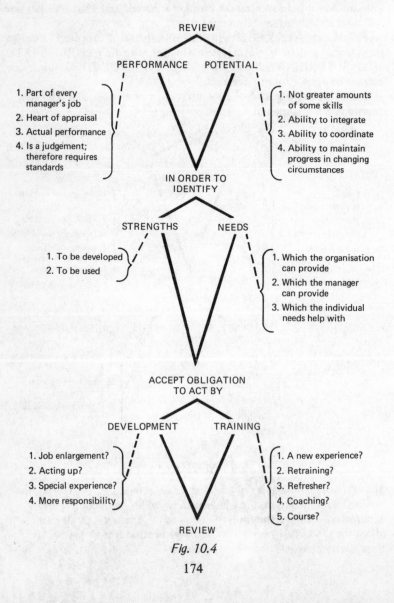

Fig. 10.4

What can we do to develop a subordinate? It will, of course, depend on her strengths or needs, but as catalysts I suggest that we could employ the following:

(a)   Job enlargement.
(b)   Provide for 'acting up'.
(c)   Supply a special experience.
(d)   Give more responsibility.

When we come to training, one thing we must remember is that we cannot send everyone away on courses. The training establishments could not cope, and, even if they could, we would be unable to give a proper service to patients as all the nurses would be on courses. Under this heading I would suggest that we could provide:

(a)   A new experience.
(b)   Retraining.
(c)   Refresher.
(d)   Coaching.
(e)   A specific course.

This then completes our model (Fig. 10.4).

EFFECTIVE APPRAISAL

With this completed model, let us now look at the criteria for effective appraisal.

Assessor

The assessor should have first-hand experience of the job and the employee. Perhaps this is stating the obvious, but acceptance of this principle again brings obligations to the assessor. This criterion usually leads to the employee's immediate superior being the assessor, but in quite a few instances, the subordinate does not see her superior very frequently, or for very long periods, especially if they are working in a small specialised unit away from the main hospital or centre.

In this case it is the clear responsibility of the assessor to get to know her employee and to be aware of standard of performance.

Perhaps the individual who has the most first-hand experience of a person and her job is that person's subordinate! So why not subordinate appraisal? It is a good question, and I will have something more to say about this later in the chapter, but suffice to say at this stage that the temptation to be a 'popular' boss rather than an 'effective' boss is a hard one for most of us to resist.

There is no doubt that the more people who appraise a person, the more accurate a picture we get, so why not colleague appraisal also? Here our problem would be the mutual 'back-scratching' exercise. Both of the above propositions are good, and the objections I have raised are valid, but the over-riding objection is to the enormous amount of time which would have to be spent, each of us appraising the other! It just could not be afforded.

Another stumbling block is the assessor having to have the same expert technical knowledge and experience as the subordinate she is appraising. I really do not think that this is essential to effective appraisal, for two reasons:

(1)   The areas in which we are required to appraise a person are not of a technical nature, they are of a professional and managerial nature.

(2)   I am not encouraging or sanctioning the use of gossip, but the sources of information which you develop are quite amazing.

If a person lacks technical competence and you are that person's manager, then you will certainly be told, or will discover your subordinate's need somehow. It will then be your responsibility to acquaint yourself of this need through discussion and indirect interviewing of your subordinate.

Time

If you are to give a fair appraisal, then you will need to have observed your member of staff over a substantial period of time.

It would be very unfair to judge someone's performance having observed it for less than six months. The longer the period under review the more accurate it is likely to be. The recommended period of an annual review is a good compromise. It allows us to get a good overall picture of the person's performance. The odd mistake can be discounted, and also the odd brilliance; we can then concentrate on her overall performance standard.

Just because an annual review is recommended to us, it does not mean that we can forget all about it until a week or two before the appraisal. On the contrary, the commitment of an annual review brings with it the obligation for frequent, informal, job-orientated discussions between appraiser and appraisee. As we have previously discussed, there are two criteria of information:

(1)   It should be accurate.

(2)   It should be timely, i.e. it should be in time for you to do something about it.

If you waited until the end of the year to tell a subordinate that her performance in, say, 'Report writing for management' was 'bad', she would naturally be very upset if this was the first she had heard of it. Here she would receive an adverse rating and comment on her appraisal form, and even though it might be a correct assessment on your part, it would be very wrong to record it.

On the other hand, if you had been having frequent job-orientated discussions, this need would have been identified by you after the first or second reports she had written. At that time you would have discussed the need, and offered help to her in her next report. You would have given her opportunity and practice in order to enable her to improve this skill.

If, despite your help and support, there was no improvement then you would be justified in giving an adverse rating — but not until you had:
(1)   Identified her need.
(2)   Given her help and guidance to improve her performance.

Having spoken often at lectures about this supportive role, I have been challenged that the outcome of such a course of action would be that it is the superior's fault if she has to make an adverse rating on her subordinate. My answer to that is that it could very well be true if we as managers have failed to carry out our supportive/teaching/coaching role effectively; but also you can take a horse to the water but you cannot make it drink.

Elimination of Prejudice

This is perhaps an impossibility. We are only human after all; we have our own problems, emotions and personality, just as do our subordinates, but any appraisal scheme must have built into it some safeguards to reduce the incidence of prejudice to its minimum.

Many appraisal systems use the assessor's immediate superior as a countersigning officer, with a special responsibility to check for any unfair prejudicial or biased reporting. This, together with the appraisee's normal right of appeal against alleged unfair appraisal via the grievance procedure, is the administrative approach to the problem.

A well designed form also helps to reduce the possibility of this occurring, but what each of us must do, as individuals, is to endeavour to be as objective as possible, mainly by concentrating on actual performance and getting to know ourselves as well as our subordinates.

Uniformity of Reporting

As our Health Service appraisal scheme is national, it is important that, as far as possible, the reporting is done to the same standard in John-o'-Groats as in Lands End. Otherwise, if it became known that a certain district or area gave 'good' reports, then those who were seeking promotion would naturally gravitate to the 'good' rating organisation, get in a couple of years of gratuitous ratings and use this as a stepping-stone to further their career!

As opposed to the free and easy rating standard, the organisation

177

which rated strictly would not attract staff, and would suffer because of its high standards. It could be that I have exaggerated the situation in my examples, but even locally we can find people judging on differing standards, with a result which can be most confusing and unhelpful to our staff.

Again, I must mention the importance of the design of the form used to estimate performance levels. The form can be of positive value if properly designed, and you will see that ours has many good features in it when I discuss it in detail later.

Other than the form, the greatest single contribution to uniformity of standards is the programme of training prior to the introduction of the scheme. Staff must be fully aware of the mechanics of the system, its aims and objectives, the importance of a positive attitude to the scheme and the standards applicable to the performance review. Their introduction to the scheme should give them confidence and ability to perform their role in appraisal effectively.

It Must be Taken Seriously

For the scheme to be taken seriously, it must be *seen* to be taken seriously. This requires us to go through all the procedures conscientiously, setting adequate time for the task and considering carefully the recommendations we make.

If we fail to follow up the action or recommendations which may be contained in our report, then the appraisee will be most disappointed, and let down. As a result, the scheme will fall into disrepute, people will begin to look upon it as yet another administrative chore, and will rapidly and casually put in their ratings and comments knowing that 'no one takes any notice of it anyway'.

Our approach must be to make our recommendations as practical as possible, and within the capabilities of ourselves or the organisation. Our second approach must be to let it be known that we are taking it seriously, and that other people in the organisation are taking it seriously also. All this encourages others to greater efforts and eventually to an acceptance of the scheme.

Added confidence can be given by the senior staff. They should be the first on the scheme, they should be the ones to 'debug' arrangements so that, as more people are introduced to it, the administration will flow more smoothly. I firmly believe that they should also be in on all the training sessions which are arranged for their juniors, so that they can stand up and be counted as being positively for appraisal.

It Must be Human

Our last of the criteria is just as important as the rest, if not more so.

Staff appraisal is a TWO-WAY process between superior and subordinate.
This is what WE have done.
This is what YOU have done.
This is what I would like to achieve in the future.
What do YOU want to do in the future?
What can I do to help YOU?
Will YOU do this to help ME?
What can WE both do to help our patients and public?

Subordinates must be given time to look at their job, to talk about their job, their hopes, their fears. They must be encouraged to develop, to recognise their own constraints and the constraints of the organisation. They must be given an opportunity to experiment, to challenge, to question. All these things and others besides, lead to a job which is always progressing, and to staff who have a high level of satisfaction and motivation.

In the appraisal system, the appraisal interview is probably the most important part of its working.

Staff appraisal was developed by nurses, for nurses — to benefit them as individuals and help the profession as a whole to raise its professional standards and service to the patients. It cannot achieve these aims in a stiff bureaucratic system. It can only be achieved by people recognising the need for them to support and enable other people to do their work well and achieve their ambitions.

THE MECHANICS OF STAFF APPRAISAL

Do not get me wrong when I say 'It is a pity that we have to have staff appraisal'. That statement is born out of the fact that though many good managers and supervisors have been doing staff appraisal all their life, there are just as many who will not face up to their responsibilities to their staff collectively and individually, and who will moan and complain through the informal communication system about their staff rather than DO something about it; that something being to offer help, guidance, development, counselling and all those many other enabling processes of good supervisory practice.

This is dealt with more fully in the Appendix.

RATING SCALES

Earlier, I mentioned design of the form, and its part in helping (1) a uniform standard of reporting to be achieved, and (2) allowing a minimum of bias or prejudice to creep in.

In technical terms, our form is known as a 'six-point, fully descriptive rating scale'.

Six-point means that there are six choices of rating on each scale ranging from 'good' to 'bad' (for the want of better words at this stage of my discourse).

Fully descriptive means that each of the ratings described in a sentence or statement indicating a specific level of performance.

At this stage we should examine this style of rating scale. There are a number of alternatives available, the first being the open continuum (Fig. 10.5). In this you put a mark on the line just where you believe the person's performance falls within the 'good' and 'bad' poles.

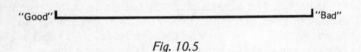

"Good" |⎯⎯⎯⎯⎯⎯⎯⎯⎯⎯⎯⎯⎯⎯⎯⎯⎯| "Bad"

Fig. 10.5

In staff appraisal this gives problems of ready recognition of a definable level of performance. You can use a ruler to measure the position of the mark, but what interpretation you can make for comparative purposes becomes a very individual matter.

In Fig. 10.6 this continuum has been refined so as to locate five positions.

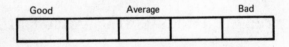

Good   Average   Bad

Fig. 10.6

The two end positions are clearly labelled; the centre becomes 'average' and the two unlabelled points are either above or below 'average'.

Until now in this discussion, I have been using the words 'good' and 'bad', and have now introduced 'average'. Just what do these words mean? Maurice Cuming in his book, *Hospital Staff Management*, has a very good exercise. It is shown in Fig. 10.7a; when you have completed it, turn to Fig. 10.7b on page 184 and compare your answers with mine.

You have just compared your interpretation of these words with mine — I have done this exercise many hundreds of times now, and I can assure you there is no agreement as to what are the top three or bottom three.

The point of this exercise is to demonstrate how we all interpret words differently, and to emphasise that the use of single adjectives to describe levels of performance is quite useless.

In the design of appraisal forms this has been recognised, and short descriptive phrases are used in an attempt to avoid ambiguity.

adequate	
average	
competent	
excellent	
exceptional	
fair	
good	
inadequate	
indifferent	
ordinary	
poor	
reasonable	
satisfactory	
superior	

*Fig. 10.7 (a)   Please number the 14 words above in order of importance —
the highest level of performance of a task being number 1. Fig. 10.7b is on
page 184.*

An example of a 'fully descriptive five-point rating scale' is given in
Fig. 10.8.

Command of English (oral)

Always clear, precise and audible	Generally clear, precise and audible	Sometimes lacks confidence, which inhibits her ability to express herself	Oral instruction sometimes difficult to understand	Inability to communicate due to lack of command of English

Fig. 10.8

There are many things I could say about 'fully descriptive' scales in
general, and also about the example in Fig. 10.8; but I will confine
myself to commenting on the difficulty which many people have in
deciding what rating to give, as their evaluation of performance does not

181

quite match any sentence in any box; very frequently they do not make any rating decision when faced with this problem!

It has been found that describing only the two extremes of the rating scale, and allowing the appraiser to use her judgement as to where she rates the subject in between, gives much more satisfactory results.

Figure 10.9 is an example of a five-point semi-descriptive scale.

Command of English (oral)

Extremely effective				Barely competent

Fig. 10.9

So far in our discussion on rating scales, we have concerned ourselves more with the description of positions on the scale than with the scale itself.

For the first issue on the scale we return to the rating of 'average'. In Chapter 3, in the section on Control, we have seen that average is not a word we want to use in rating scales — it would be too low a standard to use for comparison. What we want is a 'standard' which in our scheme is 'that level of performance which is difficult but achievable'.

In rating scales we also discover from experiments that to give a person the opportunity to rate 'average', or any other middle of the road level, is disastrous, as large numbers of us take refuge in being non-committal and use 'average' all the way down the form (which tells us very little about the person being appraised and a lot about the appraiser!)

When we try to decide how many divisions to have on our rating scale, we again turn to see what experiments have shown us on this matter.

We discover that when we plot the amount and accuracy of information we can extract from rating scales of various lengths that between 5 and 7 points (or gradings) is most advantageous (Fig. 10.10).

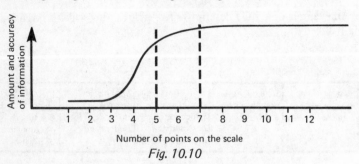

Fig. 10.10

HINTS FOR FILLING IN THE FORM

It is quite possible that our form will be changed in its detail from time to time; therefore, I am not going to comment on the foibles of the current form (and it certainly has some!) but rather direct hints at the filling in of rating forms in general.

(1) Keep both polar descriptions in your mind, weigh them up, balance them and then make your rating.

(2) Fill in the remarks column all the way down before you rate. This will stop you justifying your rating and make you amplify your rating. It will also help your rating decisions.

(3) Fill in your ratings in a random order; say, item 2, 5, 7, 3, 6, 4, etc. The reason for this is that we tend to be influenced by the last rating we made; if this is directly above then it can influence the whole of the form.

(4) All columns are there to be used — remember the standard is that level of performance which you can reasonably expect from an EXPERIENCED nurse in the grade.

(5) From hint number 4 we can see that a low rating need not always be a 'bad' rating. It will probably identify a need for you and your staff member to do something about it; it may be that the person is not too long qualified, therefore she does not yet come up to that standard; it may be that she has low performance in an area of little consequence to the particular job she is doing.

(6) Remember that personal prejudice can be for or against a person; to some extent it is present in all of us. If we know we are prejudiced we can go to the opposite extreme to overcome it — beware; if we do not realise we have it then it will be pointed out to us by someone fairly quickly! This is but one of many personal psychological problems in rating; have a look at the list below and see where you fit in!

Are You . . . ?

A CAREFUL ONE — Do you shy away from an outright evaluation and prefer to rate 'average' because this does not commit you? If so, your reports tell us nothing about your subordinates as they are vague and powerless. Your reports do tell us something about you and that is not too favourable, either!

A BITER — You are at the other end of the scale, you would find something to complain about if you were assessing an angel. Your assessments are predominantly negative, probably caused by human uncertainty which you want to cover up by being aggressive.

BIG HEARTED — You are more pleasant. You appraise pretty well. You will be negative only when your conscience allows you no choice. You try hard but you do have a problem.

PEDANTIC — Are you dedicated to detail? Do you memorise little incidents which are committed against your own strict rules of life? If you are pedantic you will probably remain so until the scales drop from your eyes and you are able to see what is REALLY IMPORTANT and what is not.

183

PREJUDICED — Remember this can be 'for' or 'against' a person. If you are and you know it, you tend to over-compensate. If you are and you do not know it then it will be very noticeable to everyone else.

BIASED — Do you have strong ties of loyalty to your team? If so, you tend to over-rate because everyone in your team is good (i.e. in-group bias).

Do you wear a HALO? If so you also rate individuals highly and with very little spread because you think they are 'good' (as people or workers). They might well be that 'good' but, let's face it, very few people are good at everything; most of us have some weaknesses.

CONCLUSION

I will deal with the very important 'Appraisal Interview' in the next chapter. I conclude this chapter by amplifying the list on Good Personnel Management (page 166) to indicate how staff appraisal fits into virtually all the personnel aspects of both the specialist's personal function and the line manager's personal function.

adequate	9
average	8
competent	4
excellent	3
exceptional	1
fair	11
good	5
inadequate	13
indifferent	12
ordinary	10
poor	14
reasonable	7
satisfactory	6
superior	2

Fig. 10.7 (b)   This is what I think the order should be of the words listed in Fig. 10.7a.

184

Good Personnel Management provides for:		Met in Staff Appraisal by:
Manpower Planning	A service for looking at work and estimating staffing levels, type of staff and ensuring the succession of jobs.	Developing staff and giving sound knowledge of the job and the way it is developing.
Selection Procedure	Having planned your manpower needs, unless you go about selecting your staff in a methodical way designed to enable you to make the best choice possible, it will have been a wasted exercise.	Playing an important part in the writing of references.
Induction	Having selected your person to do the job you cannot just leave her to muddle through. She should be helped by the induction process to settle into her job and into the organisation as quickly and efficiently as possible.	The first appraisal six months after appointment marks the end of the induction period and enables the superiors and subordinates to review the past and plan for the future.
Post-entry Training	Because we have a person working for us we must not forget that she will have further training needs as time goes on; say, a refresher course or help to do the Diploma of Nursing.	Justifying training needs of individuals and of groups.
Recognition of Effort	Everyone thrives on praise and recognition. Every effort must be made to reward work which	Giving opportunity for thanks and praise.

is well done. Too often the only time we know how we are going on is when we are being reprimanded.

Environment for Effective Delegation and Supervision	Staff will not work well in an organisation which has a restrictive, negative atmosphere. In such an organisation people become automatons with a dulled sense of responsibility and commitment.	Improving and cementing working relationships — involving subordinates in decisions which affect them.
A System of Consultation and Industrial Relations	The more people know of what is going on the less threatened they will feel. The likelihood of poor industrial relations is lessened when there is involvement by all through consultation.	The two-way communication process up through the organisation improves both communication and working morale.
Opportunity for Counselling and Welfare	People need help with their personal needs. A counselling and welfare service is an essential part of every organisation.	The appraisal interview provides for both professional and personal counselling.
Disciplinary and Grievance Procedures	Just as we must recognise effort so we have to ensure that all know how they can pursue redress for a grievance and the disciplinary procedures which the organisation	Appraisal must be a positive experience — if you need to discipline or correct a person, do it separately from the appraisal. You may point out a person's needs at an interview, but do not enter into any disciplinary procedure.

	have if they are required.	
Staff Development	We must make sure our staff are prepared and channelled into their most effective areas of service. Flexible, positive measures must be available to enable a person to reach her full potential.	This is implicit in the whole system.

CASE STUDY — BUT IS THE REPORT FAIR?

On your appointment list today, Nurse Brown is to see you about her last two ward reports. She spent 12 weeks in the last ward, and there was a change of Charge Nurse halfway through. Unknown to each other, two reports have been sent in.

First Report

Nurse Brown appeared rather stupid when she came to this ward. But at the end of her first week I learnt that in reality she was very frightened, because her favourite aunt had died in this ward 4 years ago, and she found the memories revived by working here very distressing. We arranged that she be supported by a Staff Nurse whenever she attended a similar case, and she does seem to be a little more confident. Her emotional experiences about caring for such cases have been discussed with her fellow students and she has been able to help them understand a lot. She is still rather slow in her practical work, but, given time, her work is accurate. Her sensitivity to patients suffering from terminal disease allows her to offer them much help, but she should learn to speed up her physical care a little.

Second Report

Nurse Brown shows little interest in the work of the ward, and is often late in carrying out her duties. She resents criticism but frequently needs help from the Staff Nurses to get her work finished. She cannot be relied upon to complete her work, and routine duties are often neglected.

How will you conduct the interview?
What points do you mean to make?
What future aims will you give to Nurse Brown?
Does the second Charge Nurse need help with her reporting? How can you do this, if necessary?

REFERENCES AND FURTHER READING

Anstey, Edgar (1969). *Staff Reporting and Staff Development.* London, Allen & Unwin.

Cuming, M. W. (1971). *Hospital Staff Management.* London, William Heinemann.

Fletcher, J. (1973). *The Interview at Work.* London, Duckworth.

Fraser, J. M. (1966). *Employment Interviewing*, 4th edn. London, Macdonald & Evans.

Harlow, E. and Compton, H. (1967). *Practical Communication*, Supervisory Series 2. Harlow, Essex, Longman.

Humble, John (1969). *Improving Management Performance: a dynamic approach to management by objectives.* British Institute of Management. London, Management Publications.

Randell, G. A., Packard, P. M. A., Shaw, R. L. and Slater, A. J. (1972). *Staff Appraisal.* London, Institute of Personnel Management.

Singer, E. J. (1974). *Effective Management Coaching.* London, Institute of Personnel Management.

Chapter 11

Face to Face

INTRODUCTION

Person-to-person or direct contact is the very essence of management. When We looked at Fayol's management cycle, we recognised two things of particular significance to this topic:
(1) That the dynamics of management involved people a lot more than the mechanics.
(2) That communication linked all the activities, be they on the mechanics side or the dynamics side.

You cannot talk about management without talking about communications; you cannot talk about effective communication without emphasising that the most effective means of communication is by direct contact; and this is what this chapter is about.

Of course, you are in regular face-to-face contact with your subordinates (or should be) and you will frequently talk with them. In fact, without this contact it would be virtually impossible to conduct your work, but how often have you taken the trouble to analyse just what takes place during these meetings?

If you do, you will find a great many purposes for the conversations you have with them; for example:

offering advice,
answering questions,
giving information,
receiving information,
briefing,
giving orders.

Sometimes you might just have a nice conversation with them (and as long as you don't take too long over it, it's a useful exercise).

If we are to make our face-to-face conversations an effective working tool, then we ought to examine these contacts more closely. I am told that an Egyptian Vizier Prah-Hotep, circa 2,500 BC, said, 'A good hearing is soothing to the heart'. Conversation is one of the most universal activities of mankind. From childhood we learn skills of conversation; what is acceptable, unacceptable, humorous and flattering, and so on, but in the work place, conversation is not enough.

Our conversation must work for us and again we return to our principle of the objective. We must first ask ourselves, 'What am I trying to achieve by this conversation?' 'What is its purpose?'

DEFINITIONS

Once we start saying that we are getting out to have a 'conversation with a purpose', I find myself reminded immediately that this phrase is the definition of an interview. Well not exactly, but near enough; judge for yourself . . . 'An interview is the meeting of two or more people to accomplish a known purpose by discussion'.

Here is another definition: 'An interview is a purposeful, directed conversation where one person takes the responsibility for the development of the conversation'.

From these definitions we can extract that not all conversations are interviews, but when the talking has a specific objective in mind and one person leads the conversation, this changes a conversation into an interview.

So I must modify my earlier statement that this chapter was about effective face-to-face communication and exclude conversations. By excluding conversations and incorporating 'conversation with a purpose' I am implicitly talking about interviews.

GENERAL PRINCIPLES OF INTERVIEWING

You must excuse me making the following point but I do advisedly as, in my experience of management teaching, the majority of newcomers to management think of the word 'interview' as having only one connotation — that of the selection interview. But there are as many different types of interview as there are purposes for conversations. The selection interview is only one type of interview and I will be dealing with it specifically later.

Preparation

As we have established that we must have a purpose to our conversations, that purpose will best be accomplished if we plan how we are going to achieve our objective.

(1) Decide what is your objective.
Is it best done in an interview?
Can it be done in the time available?
Are you planning to talk to the right person or should it be someone else?

(2) Gather the necessary information. This is the essence of good planning. If you are well prepared, having all the facts, knowing what are the most important facts which must be communicated and under-

190

stood, then you will be able to lead the interview in a natural and effective manner.

(3)   Plan the actual interview.
What will be your opening statement?
How will you establish rapport?
What questions will you ask?
Can the interview be divided into stages?
What are the key factors you want to impart?
How will you close?

Incidentally, a few headings jotted down are an invaluable help to successful interviews. Have them written clearly where you can see them without making their presence conspicuous, so that the interviewee will not indulge in upside-down reading and anticipate your next move!

Rapport

When we know people well, they are aware of our personal regard for them and this enables us to enter into immediate conversation with them, regardless of the topic. This is not so easy to do with those whom we know less well and who may well be affected by the status problem of the manager/subordinate relationship.

Rapport means 'easy two-way relationships', and the quicker we can establish this, the more productive our interviews will be.

You may attempt to do this in a number of ways. To some of you it will be a natural ability but for those who think they may find it difficult, perhaps I could make the following suggestions.

(1)   Let them know you are interested in them as people, perhaps by revealing your knowledge of, say, their hobbies, their children or other activities.

(2)   Use your knowledge of them to get them talking about their own interests. They will do this more easily than talking about your interests.

(3)   Enlist their help for some small thing or invite them to express an opinion.

(4)   Offer them help and support.

(5)   Discuss (in a positive manner!) mutual friends or places of interest to you both.

Your Acceptability

This follows on from rapport quite naturally in as much as it is important to the success of any interview that what you say should be said in such a way as to have an excellent chance of being taken up and accepted by the interviewee.

If I had to sort out key words for success here, I would use 'modesty', 'respect' and 'politeness'. Here are a few examples to illustrate these approaches.

Modesty

'I am inclined to believe that . . .'
'Though I recognise I am not qualified to speak with authority . . .'
'At the moment I am a bit unsure of where we are heading but I do have a suggestion . . .'
'Could I propose a tentative plan?'

Respect (for the opinions and rights of others)

'Perhaps you would like to consider . . .'
'I think this is something you should decide . . .'
'It seems to me that you might like to choose between the following . . .'

Politeness

'May I come in here?'
'If you would like my opinion . . .'
'I am glad of the opportunity to talk on this topic — thank you.'

These are of course examples of wise, purposeful conversation, and your own skills will lend themselves to your individual method of acceptable approaches; however, there are times when you can quite properly hide behind authority or anonymity.

For example, if you are chairman you may well find yourself saying things like 'It is my duty as chairman . . .' or 'In my position I must endeavour . . .'. Similarly, you may quote the anonymity of, say, the nursing profession by saying, 'We as nurses generally believe . . .' or corporate anonymity by saying 'Together we have to decide . . .'.

All the suggestions I have made are examples of a direct approach, but generally we can expect good results from indirect approaches. 'If I understand you correctly . . .' is a way of imputing your ideas to others which leads them to think your statement is their idea. 'I don't need to tell you that . . .' — here you are assuming that they will be doing what you expected them to do. 'We are all in favour of . . . aren't we?' — here you are attempting to gain their commitment; or the converse 'You don't think . . . do you?'.

As an example of an indirect technique I would like to tell you of a recent interview I attended when the purpose was to tell a subordinate that she was very wrong in conveying confidential information to a trades union before communicating it to her boss.

Boss: 'I was with a number of colleagues from 'X' area when they were discussing how they were having difficulty with senior staff bypassing management and going to the unions with confidential information. I told them that I have absolute trust in my senior managers and I was sure none of them would dream of doing such a thing. Don't you think I was right?'

Subordinate (sheepishly): 'Yes I do indeed.'

And the interview — having started as a conversation, became an interview to achieve its purpose, then reverted to a conversation again. The point was made, taken and accepted in a responsible and acceptable manner.

Thus far we have been looking at the acceptability of your positive approaches, but equally you will need to be sure that you can differ in an acceptable manner also.

To give a gentle hand-off you could say, 'I'd need to think that one over', 'At the moment I'd rather not answer that' or something in a similar vein. As the leader of the interview you might suggest . . . 'There is no need to decide on that now' or 'Perhaps you ought to think that one over'.

More directly but at the same time giving the person a way out, you might say 'I don't seem to have made myself clear' or 'That is a natural point of view' or again 'Many people feel the same as you but . . .'

To concede a point but still disagree try saying 'We seem to be both heading in the right direction but . . .'; 'That is a good point, however . . .'; 'I agree that is a useful suggestion, nevertheless we should consider . . .'; 'That's a good idea; let's think how it may work out in practice'.

Another approach is to praise the individual before dissenting. This is illustrated by the following: 'I hold you in great esteem but . . .' 'I know you are big enough for us to talk frankly about this . . .'

Again these are but a few examples which will no doubt be natural to you to use in appropriate situations. I have presented all these examples as they are useful for us to be aware of how we use words AND HOW THEY ARE USED ON US. A knowledge of what is happening at an interview verbally and non-verbally is an essential characteristic of a good interviewer.

Sensitivity

'To be aware of what is happening in an interview and be able to make the appropriate response' is known as sensitivity.

Things which trigger our sensitivity analysis are known by the psychologist as 'cues'.

Verbal cues are well known to us, for example:
stammering
hesitation
loud speech

rapid speech

These often indicate anxiety:

ers, ahs and ums

beating about the bush

They can indicate a lack of knowledge, lack of preparation or an attempt to 'flannel' your way through.

Some of the cues which people exhibit cause interviewers real problems and I shall deal with these specifically a little further on.

The subject of non-verbal cues or non-verbal communication is quite fascinating and, although I have read quite a lot about it, I am only able to deal with the subject in a most amateur way.

Silences

Don't be afraid of them; don't feel you have to get in quick and say something. They often reveal that you have hit on something which is causing the interviewee some problem and indicates that you could probe that area somewhat deeper with good effect.

Silence could also indicate anger (counting to ten!) or complete incomprehension! In any of these cases, my advice not to do or say anything for a longish period of time still holds good.

Facial Expression

Of all non-verbal communication, the face is the most expressive and the eyes particularly so. To describe the infinite variety of facial gestures is an impossibility and it will have to suffice for me to ask you to be alert and observant of any tell-tale expression and to act appropriate to the message.

Stance or Position

The person sitting on the edge of her chair is nervous; the sprawler, too, may be nervous as this is not an appropriate position when being interviewed. If the sprawler is not nervous, then she is probably blasé if not rude.

A hunched, somewhat apprehensive position is frequently taken by an introvert and the extrovert takes a relaxed open stance.

Friendliness and warmth is shown by closeness, leaning forward, arms and legs apart as well as smiles, smiling eyes and warmth of voice.

Gestures

The hand to the mouth can indicate a dislike of a question or a desire not to answer it. Hands held with fingertips together shows confidence and a decisive and even an inflexible attitude. Hands held tightly together shows nervousness.

Non-verbal cues can communicate a large variety of messages. As an exercise, discuss with your colleagues what non-verbal cues you can identify to express the following:

fear, worry
embarrassment
admiration
dislike
surprise
amusement
awkwardness
aggression

Control

'To cover the topics desired and to achieve your objectives within the time available' — this is control and it is a most difficult skill to master.

It cannot be effectively taught in theory but comes as the result of much experience and practice.

It has been said that in interviews, the interviewer should take one-third of the time and the interviewee two-thirds of the time. If this occurs in practice (and you should make sure that it does) then that means that you have to control yourself (and/or your colleagues) as well as the interviewee.

The first control is that of ensuring the correct balance of talking done by both sides and then making sure the talking is relevant and productive. You will really have to be alert and armed with many subtle phrases to keep the interview tempo up to the appropriate mark.

The most effective control is the questions asked. If you ask what I call a 'Dear Granny' question you will get back a 'Dear Granny' reply — which is a long drawn out, all around the world answer to an open invitation question. For example, 'Tell me what you consider the pros and cons of . . .' The reply depends on the interviewee and, while it is not an illegitimate question, it is not a question to be asked when time is limited. The question could easily be put in a more limiting way; for example, 'Tell me three advantages and three disadvantages of . . .'

Generally questions can be categorised as those designed:

(1)   To encourage rapport.
(2)   To draw out the interviewee's knowledge and experience.
(3)   To amplify and explain statements made.
(4)   To bring the discussion back to its purpose.

If you want to encourage a lot of talking by the interviewee, then prefix your questions with:

Why   How   What

If you want to limit discussion and get information, then the prefixes of course are:

Who   Where   When

Guiding the Interview

Many people spoil an excellent interview by just not knowing when (or how) to stop. As a leader of an interview, it is your responsibility to indicate when it is over. This can best be done by a summing up accompanied by a re-statement of any decisions made and ensuring that everybody understands their part of any agreement.

To know when to do this is up to your sensitivity together with your unobtrusive observation of the clock. Don't do as one of my previous bosses and I did. We got so interested in a description which a candidate was giving of her current job that her time was up before we could ask her any valid questions. Needless to say, she got one of the jobs we were offering! Incidentally, we never regretted the decision to employ her but that event was an object lesson to us which we took to heart.

SPECIAL CONSIDERATIONS

Having discussed the principles which have a general application to all types of interviews, here are a few hints concerning some difficult interviewing problems.

Difficult People

Too talkative

It is hard to say that a person at an interview talks too much as one of our main aims is to get her talking. However, if her answers to questions are so long as to prevent you achieving your objective, then you will have to control her in some way. Before suggesting how you might attempt this, let us conjecture why she is behaving in such a manner.

(1)   She could be very nervous and this is how she reacts to the situation by letting her tongue run away from her.

(2)   She could be a very eager person or possibly a show-off.

(3)   If a person is well informed then she just may be doing it to demonstrate that she is well informed.

(4)   Finally she could be a naturally over-talkative person. Answers to deal effectively with this sort of person are not easy — much will be left to your insight and sensitivity. If you can identify a reason for this behaviour then try to deal with that; i.e. if she is nervous then try to relax her by giving an unhurried impression, perhaps even

suggesting that she slows down or relaxes more.

In general, your questions should more than hint at the need for brevity. For example 'What you have said is most interesting but you have not actually answered the question' or 'You have more than adequately answered the question; can we now pass on to another?' or 'Tell us, as briefly as possible (or in two or three sentences) what do you think of ...' or 'I am sure you will appreciate that we have a lot to cover in the next half hour ...'.

The Rambler

She talks about everything but the question in hand or uses far-fetched analogies and gets lost.

When she stops for breath, jump in quickly and re-state the relevant points on which you asked for clarification. Be nice, smile at her and suggest that she is a bit off the subject. Suggest that time is going on a bit and she should quickly make her point.

The Inarticulate

These people need help. They either lack the ability to put their ideas into words or are so scared/shy that they dry up. Ask questions which are not challenging, e.g. 'What do you like best in your present job?'; 'What are your interests outside work?' Having opened her up on questions like these, you can then proceed to the more probing questions in easy stages.

The Wrong Answer

Occasionally someone answers a question quite wrongly or gives a totally irrelevant answer. Here you must first examine yourself and ask if you put the question in a clear and precise manner or, in the case of a 'wrong' answer, ask yourself if your own answer is the correct one and is the answer you have been given worth considering.

A lead-in question such as 'Perhaps I should re-word the question' or 'That's one way of looking at it' or 'I see what you are getting at but how do you reconcile that with ...'.

It is frequently found to be a mutually embarrassing occasion and has to be handled quite carefully or the interview will collapse without the interviewer having the opportunity, as it were, to redeem herself.

The Interviewee-interviewer

This person manages to get you talking in response to her questions.

197

Whilst there is a time for an interviewee to ask her own questions, she should not be allowed to twist questions which she has been asked in order to make you answer them.

If this happens then I suggest you kindly tell her that she will have the opportunity to ask her questions at the end, so could she just wait a little while. Or 'I am sure you don't really want me to say much more on this point when there is so much more to discuss and very little time allotted to us.'

Questioning Technique

Everybody thinks they can ask the right questions at interviews — that is, until they actually try it. My advice is to write down the questions you are going to ask until you have attended a number of interviews; even then many experienced interviewers still use notes and headings as guidelines.

We always say, 'Don't ask questions which have a YES or NO answer'. This, too, we are all very confident about doing until we ask our first YES/NO question. This is usually immediately followed by two or three more YES/NO questions on the trot — much to our embarrassment!

Asking questions which obtain information, reveal attitudes or motivation, is very difficult. The best hint I can give you is a list of useful prefixes to questions

What do you think about . . .?

Would you enlarge on that please?

Tell me why . . .

How would you react to . . .?

Even with some of these prefixes, the interviewee could still answer 'Yes' or 'No', but that would be revealing in itself.

Then there is the problem some interviewers have of prompting answers to their questions. They often ask a question and then say, 'do you think this or this?'; or else they say, 'You don't think . . . do you?'. In other words they are offering answers and revealing their own preferences when really they should be trying to reveal these things in their interviewee.

Some questions I have found useful are:

'Which of all your jobs have you enjoyed most and why?'

'Tell me something you have done at work which you were particularly pleased about.'

'Tell me what you think you are best at.'

'What do you think you will bring to this job that others might not?'

The answers to these questions can reveal plans, professional growth, insight, confidence and maturity. I am sure your own particular situation will require you to plan your own questioning well in order to elicit the information you require.

Prejudice

It is virtually impossible for someone to be without prejudices of one kind or another. Bias and prejudice result from a combination of your background and culture and the way in which you have reacted to these facets of your life. Generally your attitudes towards life and work reflect these environmental influences.

You will inevitably fail miserably as an interviewer if you allow these prejudices to interfere with your objectivity. They will distort your judgement and make the whole interviewing process a farce. The knack is to 'know your prejudices' and this is easier said than done. People who hold prejudices dearly frequently claim that they are the most objective! It will help if we turn to my opening statement on this topic which said in effect 'Everyone has prejudices'. I cannot spend time proving this to you, but psychologists tell me that it would be reasonably accurate to make this statement. I will tell you about one little experiment I used during a course on industrial relations.

A keen amateur photographer friend of mine supplied me with two identical photos of his father. One I had nicely framed, the other I mounted quite nicely on a photo mount card. As an introduction to prejudice I showed the framed photo to half the class and told them that this man was a manager. The mounted photo I showed to the other half of the class and told them that this man was a shop steward. I then asked both groups to write a pen portrait of this man's character, traits, etc.

Needless to say, the group who thought they were writing about a manager used adjectives such as honest, trustworthy, perceptive, efficient, well groomed; while the group thinking they were writing about the shop steward used words like agitator, rough diamond, shifty, arrogant!

Need I add that the class I was teaching was a group of managers not trade unionists!

To return to the problem of being aware of the nature of your prejudices, you will need to be very self-analytical but preferably ask and listen to what people say in response to your request for help in identifying your prejudices. Neither of these is foolproof but at least they can start you thinking.

When interviewing, endeavour to discount your own likes and dislikes and examine the interviewee's background and attitudes impartially. When you do this remember that you may find that both of you have something in common and this can warp your judgement — so try to be impartial.

Try to discount those personal characteristics about people which annoy you. There is no proof whatsoever that a flabby handshake shows a weak character, that red hair denotes a quick temper, that a low forehead indicates . . . and a receding chin indicates . . . . It is all plain prejudice — so forget it.

The 'Halo Effect'

This is a bias which makes you judge a person (either favourably or unfavourably) as the result of one particular attribute of that person. This one attribute swamps your ability to judge the remaining attributes of the interviewee impartially.

For example — you ascertain that the person has written a number of good articles for the Nursing press; you believe that for a person to do this she must be 'good'. From then on the halo effect makes you evaluate all her other attributes as being 'good', regardless of the facts being presented to you.

These are just a few pointers which I hope will serve as starting points for your evaluation of your prejudices.

INTERVIEWS

Having thus far examined firstly the definitions, secondly some of the general principles and thirdly some special considerations, I will now deal with specific types of interview you may well have to conduct in your management career.

The Selection Interview

Aims

(1) For the employer to obtain further information about the candidate, to enable her to assess whether or not the candidate will be able to do the job being offered and will fit into the team of which she will (if successful) be a part.
(2) To influence suitable candidates to accept the job.
(3) To give the candidate all the relevant information about the job offered and the organisation of which it is a part.
(4) To conduct the interview in such a manner that the candidate feels she has been fairly treated whether she gets the job or not.

In the chapter on selection interviewing, I stoped the process just short of the interview so, in a way, that chapter is completed by reading on from here.

Preparing for the Interview

(1) Ensure that your candidates are clearly expected from the reaction and attention they get from the receptionist, porter or secretary. To arrive and say 'I've come for the interviews' and to be greeted by a

blank look is enough to give an already tense person even more butterflies in her tummy than before. To be treated pleasantly and confidently on arrival helps to relieve some of the candidate's anxiety besides giving a good impression of the place.

(2) Ensure suitable waiting facilities are available: comfortable chairs, something to read, the offer of refreshment . . . and don't wait for her to have to ask you where the toilet is.

I am not going to participate in the question whether or not all the candidates should wait together, but if all the candidates *are* going to wait then it might be less embarrassing for all if candidates who have already been interviewed could wait together separately from those who are waiting to be interviewed.

(3) Reduce waiting time to a minimum. Hanging around at interviews is dreadful so I would suggest staggered appointments and inform the candidates by mail or phone the next day. However, if you do want them to wait to know the results, then make good provision for those having to wait a long time.

(4) Receive the candidate courteously and seat her comfortably, making sure she is at no physical disadvantage. I have come to the conclusion that the physical environment at interviews should be businesslike but not too formal. Certainly use comfortable chairs if they are available but make sure the interviewer has something on which to place her papers. All in all there does not seem to be much wrong in everyone sitting around a table so that you can all see each other without sticking the candidate out on a limb so that she feels isolated and not part of the interviewing group.

Do make sure that the candidate is not seated facing the light of a window or she will soon be effectively blinded, and remove large bowls of flowers which you have to peer around.

If you have to use a room with a phone in, then make proper arrangements for you not to be called or interrupted, not only by the telephone but by people calling in on you.

(5) Make sure you have all the necessary papers and information you and the candidate may require AND that you have had the courtesy to have properly prepared yourself for the interview.

To apply for a post takes considerable courage and to be shortlisted is an achievement. Having asked a candidate to come and talk with you at an interview has placed a good deal of responsibility on you. The outcome of this conversation could affect the candidate's whole life and for an interviewer to treat the whole affair casually — not having done her homework, not having planned her questions, etc. — is not only rude but sheer arrogance. So do your homework; it pays dividends.

Conduct of the Interview

(1) Establish rapport with the candidate as rapidly as possible.

(2)   Have in mind a pattern to follow in the interview which will achieve your objectives. You can use the five-point or seven-point plan as a framework or devise a plan which will enable you to logically explore the candidate's experience, background, attitudes and motivation. Perhaps:
        (a) rapport;
        (b) previous jobs/education;
        (c) the job being offered;
        (d) the candidate's personality/attitudes;
        (e) the candidate's personal situation;
        (f) conclusion.

(3)   Phrase questions in such a way that the candidate is required to do much of the talking.

(4)   Be genuinely interested in the candidate; alert and sensitive to her reactions. I have found that I glean as much (if not more) from the candidate's answers to other panel members' questions as I do from my own. Besides which if you really are alert you can identify and probe areas where the candidate has indicated verbally OR non-verbally that she has a possible weakness.

(5)   Probe in depth points which are crucial or where there may be some doubt as to the candidate's real experience or reasons.

(6)   You must exercise light control over the interview, in order that you cover matters of interest in the time available. Interviews are notorious for running over time. Schedule realistic periods of time for each interview and do your best to keep to it. The least time I would schedule for an interview would be 20 minutes for a simple routine appointment. When somewhat more senior posts are being considered, 45–60 minutes become more realistic.

        The matter of control really lies in the hands of the chairman of the panel but every member can do her part by keeping to the point.

(7)   When you draw your conclusions, do so from the accumulated evidence and not from isolated factors or incidents during the interview.

(8)   Endeavour to keep the balance between formality and informality. Both you and the candidate are aware that this is a working meeting so both familiarity and stand-offishness are out of place.

(9)   If you must take notes during the interview, do so in such a way that you do not break rapport. I would say that it was permissible to take note of facts during the interview but otherwise jot down your points as soon as the candidate leaves the room.

(10) Don't forget to give the candidate ample opportunity to question you. And may I add — don't oversell the job; mention the disadvantages to see how she reacts to them.

To sum up I like the term I read somewhere: 'The three C's — Contact, Content, Control'.

Types of Selection Interview

Panel Interview

This is where a selection panel, ideally consisting of three to five representatives of the employing authority, conducts the interview. Please resist any pressure to have more than five members of a panel and keep it to three or four if possible.

There may be many of you who were once a local authority nurse and who had the experience of being interviewed by the whole of the local health authority; they all sat around the top end of an oblong table with you sitting in splendid isolation at the bottom of it! That situation must be a classic in the series 'How not to conduct an interview'.

While commercial companies do not seem to favour panel interviews, we in the National Health Service practice little else. It is true they are expensive (four or five people's time) and that the control of such a panel can be very difficult, but I believe firmly that 'two heads are better than one' and the mutual support and interpretation of a panel is most valuable in determining who should be offered the job.

The best way of using a panel is for the chairman to act as a coordinator of each panel member's contribution with each panel member exploring a different facet of the job and the candidate.

The chairman will be responsible for establishing rapport, interpreting questions which the candidate might have misunderstood and making sure the candidate has her opportunity to ask questions. Naturally it will be her responsibility to ensure that all the objectives are met within the time available.

It is helpful if each panel member has a large identification plate in front of her so that the candidate knows whom she is addressing for, despite the fact that she will have been introduced all around, her nervous state will undoubtedly affect her memory.

Do try to make sure that those you choose for the panel are not the type to vie with each other as to who asks the best questions. Sadly it has been my experience to see interviews fall apart because of the interviewing immaturity of some of the panel members.

One to One

This is quite common in commerce. It is where the manager interviews the candidates herself and makes the decision alone — and, as she is the manager, 'lives with her mistakes'. I don't see why we don't use this more often for routine, less important positions. It is easier to arrange, cheaper, somewhat easier on the candidate and gives responsibility to the decision-making manager.

This is where each candidate is interviewed in the one-to-one situation by a number of different selectors. As you can see, it is a hybrid of the one-to-one and panel interviews. While I have not personally experienced this technique, it seems to have much to offer in that the compromise between the two methods seems to avoid either's disadvantages.

For a brief synopsis of other selection techniques, refer to Chapter 5, 'Square peg — square hole'.

The Appraisal Interview

This is the interview between the manager and her subordinate to review progress and make plans for the future. It is usually done as an integral part of the appraisal scheme but I would hope that, in the absence of such a scheme, every manager would be appraising her employees regularly as a matter of routine.

Aims

(1)   To review achievements and give recognition for good work.
(2)   To plan future courses of action and to set targets to aim for.

Benefits

(1)   Improves manager/subordinate relationships by emphasising mutual interest in patient care and interest in the work being done by the subordinate.
(2)   Gives opportunity to iron out difficulties the subordinate may have had in working effectively.
(3)   Enables the manager to identify training needs of her subordinates.
(4)   The manager often learns something about herself or the job which is being done.

The Interview

The interview is not an inquisition but an honest, open and frank discussion about the job.

You MUST have some sort of plan for the interview. These interviews cannot be entered into lightly, hoping that everything will go well. I offer the following plan for your consideration and appropriate adaptation.

(1)   Make sure your member of staff clearly understands the purpose of the interview.
(2)   Talk about the job in general — even the Job Description. This is

common ground and will help get the conversation going.

(3) Look at the person's strengths.

(4) Examine her needs and determine to do something about them (i.e. be positive about them).

(5) Discuss targets to be achieved in the coming year.

(6) Discuss hopes/ambitions for the future.

(7) Give opportunity for her to raise any queries she may have.

(8) Summarise main points of the interview. I have found it useful to summarise under three headings:

> 'I have agreed to ... .'
> 'You are going to try to . . .'
> 'Both of us are going to . . .'

(9) Throughout the interview encourage the interviewee to talk – and LISTEN!

(10) *Follow up the interview.* You must initiate your agreed action or the system will be weakened and any suspicion on the part of your staff will be aggravated.

Of course the success of the interview is dependent on many things – for example, a difference in age, skill and experience between interviewer and interviewee; the person's attitude towards appraisal; the moods of the people involved; health; domestic pressures; and so on.

Whilst we must accept that these adverse influences do exist, they should not be grasped as a list of excuses for poor preparation, lack of tact or other bad interviewing practices.

Appraisal should be a constructive, participative exercise centred around the job and gaining the commitment of the person doing that job.

The Counselling Interview

Lately there has been an increase of interest in the role of the nurse as a counsellor. Counselling in this sense is not specifically related to careers but rather to the private, individual problems facing the nurse as a member of the human race.

We, the human race, are alike but different. We are alike in that we want to be recognised as individuals; in needing love and response; in wanting success; in needing security.

We differ in what makes us afraid; anxious; angry; sad; and how we react to life's stresses.

Whether or not we ever set up a counselling service within our organisation, there is a very real need for managers to be ready and willing to take on this role which extends the normal working relationship between manager and subordinate.

Whilst I am convinced that there is a real need for special training in the skills of counselling, I recognise the reality that many of you are doing this or have found yourselves in the position of being a counsellor without having any choice. With this in mind I offer the following brief guidelines and advice, and suggest that if you want to know more, seek out some counselling training for yourself.

Aim

The aim of counselling is to help a subordinate cope with her personal problems which may be affecting her work or her private life.

A Plan

(1) Confidentiality. This cannot be emphasised too much. The basis of the success of this interview is trust, and a breach of confidence is a breach of trust.
(2) Establish rapport.
(3) LISTEN – LISTEN – LISTEN. Let her state her problem; let her talk; give encouraging nods or grunts; sit relaxed and interested; only if she flags, ask her to expand on some point; redefine the problem if necessary.
(4) When you think she has really come to the end, look at each facet of the problem and endeavour to have HER formulate a plan of action. This is a real skill – the skill of enabling your subordinates to find their own answers to their problems. This is much more successful than telling them what they ought to do.
(5) You may, of course, put points where your knowledge will help guide your subordinate to a good course of action.
(6) Give an assurance of your continued help and support.
(7) Do not be afraid of advising a referral to a skilled specialist agency if you find you are out of your depth.

But I repeat – LISTEN. It will need great effort on your part not to jump in, but LISTEN – it will pay dividends.

The Grievance Interview

Aim

Remember – an arbitrator is always wrong in someone's eyes! With this in mind, you should aim to guide the aggrieved parties to reach their own solution within the Area policy.

Method

I do not know the answer to the thorny question of whether the manager should interview the two aggrieved parties together or if they should never meet. I have had success and failure with a variety of methods but currently I favour seeing each party separately and then bringing them together.

In the case of a single aggrieved party, remember the possibility of such things as an artificial grievance in order to gain the manager's attention for a personal problem; also the grievance may only be symptomatic of other deeper problems.

A Plan

(1) Get the facts. This sounds easy, but again in my experience getting the true facts is a difficult task often requiring tenacity and even some suspicion; and even then you may not get the whole story!

You will need to review the person's record, talk with the people concerned, elicit their opinions and feelings. You will need to decide what, if any, are the rules, customs or laws alleged to have been broken.

(2) Decide as far as possible the cause of the problem by considering all the available facts and their bearing on one another.

(3) Develop tentative solutions . . . work them through in your mind or on a colleague. What possible alternatives are there; what might be the result of applying any of these alternatives; how will they affect the person concerned or the ward team as a whole?

(4) Conduct the grievance interview, influencing the outcome indirectly so that the parties concerned come to their own solution which incidentally happens to be your solution!

As I have said before, indirect interviewing is a most difficult technique but can be achieved. The best hints are:
(a) listen;
(b) re-state the problem in your own words;
(c) establish areas of agreement — and you may have to circle through (a), (b) and (c) a number of times before you can go on to (d);
(d) summarise and gain agreement on action decided;
(e) express thanks for their help and cooperation.

(5) Take the action agreed — do this yourself, do not evade the issue.

(6) Review the results — after a period of time see how successful the exercise has been.

The Reprimand Interview

It is unavoidable, but the very title of this interview indicates a possibility of a prejudiced approach. Ideally we should have an open mind and define the true purpose of the interview in neutral and objective terms but in practice we have already decided that we are dealing with a person who has certain shortcomings.

Aims

(1) To improve performance.
(2) To prevent repetition of mistakes.
(3) To protect our patients against malpractice of any kind.

A Plan

(1) Preparation:
   (a) be sure of your facts (see above);
   (b) take time to fully investigate the circumstances;
   (c) take into account the personality and individuality of the person whom you are going to reprimand and plan the interview accordingly.
(2) The interview:
   (a) always reprimand in private; NEVER in front of other members of staff;
   (b) keep control of yourself — if you lose your temper you have lost the case;
   (c) state the case clearly and precisely;
   (d) avoid arguing;
   (e) give opportunity for the person to reply in full;
   (f) show the employee how to improve — this interview must be constructive and end on a positive note giving distinct advantages.
(3) Review the results:
   (a) mention the person's work, particularly the aspect which caused the problem in the first place;
   (b) do not continue to show antagonism toward the individual after you have dealt with the case.

N.B. If a formal reprimand is to be recorded as part of your Area Disciplinary procedure, then it could be that the person concerned is entitled to have her trade union/professional organisation representative or a friend present at the interview.

This does not materially alter the conduct of the interview except that you will need to be prepared for questions from the third party present.

The Termination Interview (Dismissal)

Aims

(1) To dismiss the employee from the Authority's service
(2) To remove any misunderstanding about the cause for dismissal.

A Plan

Much depends on whether the dismissal is for disciplinary reasons or for
matters such as redundancy or retirement when a person had automatically
anticipated an extension of service.

(1)   Do not take too long before coming to the point. If the person
       knows the reason for the interview, a long period of idle conversa-
       tion prolongs the agony; if she does not know, then she becomes
       suspicious and anxious which does not augur well for the remainder
       of the interview.
(2)   State the facts you are both facing and the reasons for this action.
(3)   Do not argue.
(4)   State what help and support is available to her and any right of
       appeal she may have.
(5)   Elicit what special areas of need the employee may have and
       ascertain what help can be arranged to meet it.

Again, the employee will probably be entitled to representation at this
interview.

The Exit Interview

These interviews are conducted either by the line manager or the
Personnel Department to monitor staff wastage in order to improve the
selection process and thus to reduce labour turnover.

Aims

(1)   To gain information about the job the person is leaving.
(2)   To ascertain as accurately as possible the reasons for the person
       leaving.

A Plan

(1)   Preparation
       (a) Review the Job Description and the job holder.
       (b) Discuss the job and person doing it with that person's immediate
            supervisor.
(2)   The interview
       (a) Make the purpose of the interview clear and stress the anony-
            mity of the conversation you are about to hold with her.
       (b) Elicit reasons for leaving – look for the 'hidden' reasons as
            well as the stated reasons.
       (c) Ascertain the strength and the weakness of the job/organisation
            and any areas for improvements.

(d) Correct errors of fact.

(e) Give appreciation and thanks for her contribution to the organisation and best wishes for her future.

These are difficult interviews for many reasons as these people are reluctant to be honest. They do not want to burn their boats behind them; they may need future references; they may not want to discredit former colleagues or possibly may just want to let a bad experience die a death. If you are aware of these difficulties you can develop your own approach to minimise these factors.

CONCLUSION

Skill in interviewing can only be developed by training and experience. It is essential that every manager makes a concentrated effort to improve her expertise in this area of human relationship management. Whatever the reason for the interview, each merits the same degree of concern for the individual and all require careful thought in their execution.

A good interview, and one which will ensure a high degree of success, is the one which becomes a free discussion between the interviewer and the interviewee.

CASE STUDY — WARD HOUSEKEEPER
Here are some further details on your Ward Housekeeper. List how each of them performed at interview, which one you would select for the job. Say why you have selected her. You might like to choose a first reserve also. I will let you know exactly what happened and whom we appointed at the end of Chapter 12.

At Interview
Mrs Day
A quiet-spoken lady with a confident manner. Although now a widow, she has worked for most of her adult life and is obviously anxious to continue work. She would prefer an occupation of the type she is used to and one in which she would have a measure of self-confidence. She has been in a supervisory post for 3 years, having under her control a number of staff who had a wide range of standards and experience. She feels, therefore, that she has the necessary experience in handling difficult situations caused by different work standards. The domestic work on board the liner, 'Cruise Queen', did to some extent overlap the kitchen work, but she enjoyed harmonious relations with the catering staff. When ashore she attended courses in the use of modern cleaning equipment and in supervisory techniques. She has limited experience of compiling staff rotas since these were always arranged before sailing. She thus had no absentee problems to contend with.

Mrs Terry
A bustling woman, 42 years of age, who is well known to you. She is married with a grown-up family of two sons and one daughter, all of

whom have done well educationally and are in good positions. She has worked with you off and on for 12 years at your previous hospital, the last 8 years being years of permanent full-time employment. A particularly loyal woman, she is a bit short-tempered, but she has decided organising ability. She became a forewoman at Bankfoot General Hospital soon after it opened and you noticed the cleanliness in 'E' section is well above average and absenteeism on the part of domestics is very low. Mrs Terry declares that she learned much from her attendance at a recent course for forewomen organised by the Regional Board, and is now undertaking an evening course of two evenings per week in cleaning science at one of the local technical colleges. She is happily married and is a devoted mother to her children. She confesses to being a 'Bingo addict', and says that this is her sole means of recreation since her husband will not allow a television in the house.

Mrs Freeman
A well dressed and well mannered lady, 42 years of age. Since leaving nursing she has not been employed but has concentrated on bringing up her children as she did not think that she could be an adequate mother and nurse, taking into consideration the often long and irregular hours she had to work. However, she now feels that her children are old enough to be left on their own for short periods and would like to return to day work. *She does not want to return to nursing* because she feels that she has been *out of touch* too long, methods and equipment having changed so much since she last worked. She *also wants to work regular hours* so that she can have free week-ends to spend time with her family.

Mrs Freeman appears to be a very sensible, capable and interesting person with an air of quiet authority. In her free time she has for many years been an active member of a local women's institute and served as secretary and treasurer to the WI for a period of 10 years. She once gave an interview on WI work to the BBC 'Woman's Hour' and has written several articles for the local paper on home nursing. Her husband is a representative for a local firm producing floor treatment materials. Both she and her husband are anxious for their two children (a boy and a girl) to proceed to University in fullness of time.

Miss Smithson
A dark well built young lady who looks capable and efficient. Full of enthusiasm for the course in cleaning technology just completed and would obviously be quite capable of demonstrating equipment and also of organising the work. Has experience of catering but prefers the domestic side and has obviously set her eyes on eventually becoming a Domestic Superintendent in the not too distant future, and will no doubt achieve her ambition after experience in the hospital field. In her present post she has overall charge of the training centre and it appears to have been run to the satisfaction of the firm, after a few clashes of personalities with the warden, whom she felt was questioning her ability and who tried to force his own ideas of running the centre which, in her opinion, were antiquated

211

and inefficient. She also felt that her training was being wasted and that more satisfaction could be obtained through working in a hospital where her type of training was vital and essential.

Miss Nelson-ggwynne

Telephoned shortly before the first date for interview to say that she would not attend. Attended at the second date. She is a tall commanding spinster, probably in her early fifties with a County accent and having a rather regal and imperious manner. She proved to be a poor listener and seemed to feel that the patients at the hospital were the recipients of some form of charity, though she did not say this in so many words. She did not listen to the details of the position offered so that it is difficult to say if she regards herself as competent to perform the duties. It seemed that she may move from her present address if the Bankfoot overspill takes place. She arrived in her own car, a Rover 3-litre.

CASE STUDY — SCRIPT FOR APPRAISAL INTERVIEW FOR 'ALICE JONES'

The following script is an example of the type of discussion that may take place during an appraisal interview.
Cast: Alice Jones, Charge Nurse; Brian Lemin, Nursing Officer.

NO   Hello Miss Jones.

AJ   Hello Mr Lemin.

NO   Let's go and sit over here; it's a bit more comfortable and we can spread any bits and pieces out on the coffee table.

AJ   Yes that's fine — I've got that form you asked me to fill in and my Job Description.

NO   I wonder if you felt the same as I did when I compared what I was actually doing with my Job Description — mine bore no resemblance to each other.

AJ   I did rather, but I've never seen the point of Job Descriptions — a Charge Nurse's job is a Charge Nurse's job and you just get on with it.

NO   That just about sums up what I thought too except when I went to Coldchurch Hospital in my second Charge Nurse's post. The Assistant Matron there was superb. She made me look at myself and the way I worked for the very first time in my life, and gave me an awful lot of help.
Anyway, enough about me — how about you; how have things gone for you these past 11 months?

AJ   Well, not so bad really. The Charge Nurse I took over from must have been a bit lax with her discipline. I found that the patients were doing just what they liked when I came on to the ward, and I found it rather difficult to get them to accept my authority.

NO   How did you achieve this in the end?

AJ   I jolly well cracked the whip and let them know who was the boss; and that went for the students too — they were just as bad.

NO   You are talking a bit in the past tense — does that mean that you've stopped cracking the whip?

AJ   Well, I think I may have mellowed a bit, but you should know the answer to that better than me; after all you interview all the students leaving your unit — what do they say?

NO   More or less what you've just told me. They seemed at first to regard you as a bit of a sergeant major type — in fact I did hear a patient say that he would rather jump on his ex-sergeant major's corns than let you catch him doing something wrong.

AJ   Oh dear, isn't that awful? I'm not as bad as that now am I?

NO   No, of course not; I would have told you before now if you were, as neither student nurses nor patients take kindly to regimentation these days.

AJ   When I look back I think I was a bit petrified running this ward in a somewhat unfamiliar speciality and with Mr Morgan breathing down my neck. I probably overdid it in the beginning.

NO   The fact that you recognise that possibility means you can go ahead and develop the kind of leadership which is more natural to you and probably more effective. It could be that you might like to consciously work towards improving your style of leadership in a systematic way over the next 6—12 months.

AJ   Yes, I think it would be a point which would bring about a better atmosphere and a more enjoyable working situation on the ward.

NO   Good — I tell you what I'll do. I'll let you borrow a super book on leadership which I have and we must make a point of discussing it together when you've had time to read it.

AJ   Right, that's fine.

NO   I'd say you'll do all right in that direction, just like you managed to get Mr Morgan eating out of your hand.

AJ   Oh yes — he's a dear really; he only seemed to want to be sure himself that he could trust me with his patients.

NO   Yes, I do like him a lot myself now I've got to know him. I think he has only a couple of years to go before he retires. By the way, have you seen the Hospital Activity Analysis? He pretty well consistently keeps his patients two or three days longer than other surgeons doing the same operations.

AJ   Does he? I must say I never realised that. Do I gather from that remark that you would like me to do something about it?

NO   Frankly YES, but it is a very dicey area to operate in; after all he is the surgeon and he does do the discharging and it is his responsibility.

AJ   Oh yes, I realise that; but to tell you the truth, many of the patients are champing at the bit to go home, and with the District Nurse liaison officer now pretty well established I think that he and I together could manage something.

NO   Well, if you did it would help reduce your waiting list and probably make the work on your ward a bit more interesting. Would you like to make that a goal to achieve in the coming year?

AJ   Yes I would. And while I think of it, I would like ours to be the

	ward used to evaluate those new dressing packs the Procedure Committee have had made up.
NO	Certainly that can be arranged; but I WOULD like to say one thing — when you write your report for the Committee I'd like to help you with it. Frankly, your report writing hasn't improved much over the months; your report on the colour coding of CSSD packs told me nothing even after I'd corrected the grammar.
AJ	I don't know why you keep on at me about these reports; after all, no one ever looks at them when they leave here. They're a waste of time.
NO	Well, there are two reasons why I 'keep on at you' as you say. The first one is that I have to rate you on the appraisal form in the area of written expression, and I want to give you the best possible chance to get a reasonable rating — but you must know that it is not going to be a good rating this year.
AJ	Well you can please yourself about that.
NO	That is not the point — you surely realise that this is not your strong point?
AJ	Yes I do, but it's not worth bothering about as I hate writing and besides they're not worth the effort.
NO	I know you're wrong there. They are useful and they are used by the teaching and senior administration, and with the new examination system they're going to be even more important.
AJ	And that's another thing — when am I going to an 'Art of Examining' course?
NO	Well, knowing your attitude on this particular subject, I didn't think you were interested; and in any case, you could have asked.
AJ	For the record, I am interested and I would like to go on the course.
NO	That's fine, then; it would seem to be advantageous to us all. It could show you how student nurse reports are being used and give a more meaningful purpose to them. They might well give you some tips on how to write them.
AJ	That seems fair to me.
NO	Let's recap what we've agreed up to now. Firstly, YOU have agreed to reappraise and try to improve your leadership function, and I am going to give you improved feedback in this area and lend you a book on the subject. Secondly, you are going to try to increase Mr Morgan's patient throughput without decreasing the quality of patient care; and you're on your own with that one! Thirdly, I'm going to do my best to get you on an 'Art of Examining' course (no promises, mind you, but now they're doing them as a two-day course it should be easier), and YOU are going to put your mind to improving your report writing — agreed?
AJ	Agreed. (*Pause*)
NO	I really must say that I liked your suggested shift rota that you sent in. I think it will be one accepted by the Chief Nursing Officer for implementation when we do go over to shifts.

AJ   Thank you. I did enjoy doing that — in fact, it made me think that if I did perhaps decide to leave bedside nursing I would like to do allocation. I enjoyed maths at school and I seem to be able to grasp a lot of the technical nature of my husband's job when he talks about it. I've seen some articles about it in the nursing press which I've found very interesting.

NO   That's useful to know. Allocation is not up everybody's street. I'm sure that if you had the time Jean Bell, the Group Allocation Officer, would be delighted to chat to you. I know her very well so give me a buzz when you would like to go and I'll fix it up.

AJ   Thanks, I will.

NO   By the way, you mentioned your husband just now. How is he enjoying this area and his job?

AJ   He likes both very much, especially now we've got the house more or less how we want it. He gets a car with his job and this enables us to get about the area very well when we are both off together. I can't speak for him, of course, but I've got a feeling he wouldn't mind settling here for a bit. It's about time we did settle down; four moves in five years of marriage is no fun.

NO   Does settle down mean 'family' as well?

AJ   Yes, I hope so; but I still think I'm a bit of a career woman, so I wouldn't want to be out of hospital long, perhaps start soon after with some part-time work. I don't really know, I haven't given that part of it much thought. One hurdle at a time, that's me.

NO   Well, that's a lovely plan; I look forward to your achieving that objective. Are there any difficulties within our new management set-up that you think I could help with?

AJ   No, not really.

NO   None! Perhaps I should have stayed a Charge Nurse; there seem to be fewer problems there. What about the domestic staff?

AJ   Oh yes — well, you asked for it; in my opinion those girls are coming it. I'm sure it was not intended that they should play the Domestic Supervisor off against the Charge Nurse; but believe me that's what's happening: 'I can't do this because the Supervisor says that . . .' and so on — it's hopeless and the Domestic Supervisor must be a part-timer because I can never find her. She's very nice when I do track her down — too nice, that's her trouble, and too nice to her women as well.

NO   Now we're back to leadership — yours as well as hers, but I will make a point of seeing her and try to get this straightened out.

AJ   Yes; when I do manage to have a word with the Supervisor, she informs me that I no longer have a complete say in how domestic work on my ward shall be done because they are all on a bonus scheme of some sort. Although the domestic work schedules were reorganised recently, I had no idea what effect any bonus scheme would have on them. Any chance of us having a meeting on this? Other Charge Nurses are in the same boat and we are all working in the dark.

NO   You have a very good point there. Perhaps a Study Day . . .

AJ   (*Interrupts*) Yes, That's it — a Study Day on this bonus scheme business would be ideal.

NO   OK. I'll have a chat with the Senior Nursing Officer and Principal Nursing Officer to see if we can lay it on. Anything else?

AJ   I'm still clutching this form and my Job Description; we started off on the subject of job description but didn't seem to get any further.

NO   My goodness, yes — I'd quite forgotten; and I think they are both so important, especially the pre-appraisal guide. Let's go through together. Over to you.

AJ   This first part is a bit elementary really and all tied up with job descriptions and suchlike, but I'd like to discuss this matter of accomplishments in the past year.
When I really looked at this I found it rather gratifying . . .

REFERENCES AND FURTHER READING

Fletcher, J. (1973). *The Interview at Work.* London, Duckworth.

Fraser, J. M. (1966). *Employment Interviewing,* 4th edn. London, Macdonald & Evans.

Harlow, E. and Compton, H. (1967). *Practical Communication,* Supervisory Series 2. Harlow, Essex, Longman.

Randell, G. A., Packard, P. M. A., Shaw, R. L. and Slater, A. J. (1972). *Staff Appraisal.* London, Institute of Personnel Management.

Singer, E. J. (1974). *Effective Management Coaching,* London. Institute of Personnel Management.

Chapter 12

Communication

I quote from the *Daily Mirror*, 1 May 1975.

'Every second was vital to the doctors toiling at the scene of the Moorgate Underground disaster.

'A doctor trying to ease the pain of trapped victims sent out the message — "I want Entonox" — a form of anaesthetic.

'But by the time the verbal message had been passed along the chain of rescuers, it had become — "The doctor wants an empty box".'

But for the seriousness of the situation, you would probably burst your sides with laughter. It is the classic example of the party game communications exercise where a message is whispered around the room and the distorted result is the source of a great deal of hilarity. I enjoy it — it is good fun — but at work it drives me silly.

Communications is the 'in' word at the moment and is likely to be for some time. It is at the receiving end of all our excuses, grouses and inefficiencies . . . and notice it is always 'the' communications, never 'my' communications or even 'our' communications but the great anonymous 'the'. The Communications = The Scapegoat.

I have one very simple, straightforward answer to this problem. It is not a technique, it is not a lecture, it is not a magic formulae that works by waving a wand. It is the simple statement that 'WHEN EACH OF US IN THE ORGANISATION MAKES IT OUR PERSONAL RESPONSI-BILITY TO COMMUNICATE EFFECTIVELY — THEN AND ONLY THEN WILL OUR COMMUNICATIONS PROBLEMS BEGIN TO BE SOLVED.'

It is no use blaming others, it is no use blaming communications for what YOU should have done. You are all nurse managers and are presumably literate and articulate, so there is not any excuse.

Having delivered a 'verbal' harangue with conviction and passion, I will happily take on a supportive and informative role which will, I hope, be of value to you as you take your communications function seriously.

A BRIEF THEORY OF COMMUNICATIONS

Definition

Various dictionaries use words such as 'impart', 'transmit', 'share' to describe the word 'communications'.

I find it a rather chameleon-like word which changes its meaning according to the situation. It seems to me that communication implies that not only do we transmit facts, ideas and opinions but also feelings, bias and prejudice (the latter group, albeit unknowingly). This complexity seems to be the problem. Whilst I place the responsibility of good communications on you as individuals, I must accept that the path to effective communication is fraught with good intentions and real difficulties.

Just look at the fairly standard model of the communications process shown in Fig. 12.1.

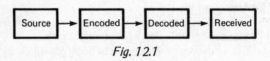

Fig. 12.1

What this model is saying is that we have an idea (source) that we put into words (encode), the receiver interprets the message (decodes) and thus receives it.

How simple it would all be if it were just like that. That model does not tell half the story. For a start, it is incomplete because I believe that no communication can be considered completed until we are sure it has been understood. This puts the model as in Fig. 12.2.

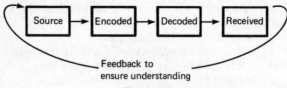

Fig. 12.2

Perhaps at this stage we should return briefly to the definition and offer a redefinition. It is that 'Communication is the process used in order to be understood.'

Some of you might well want to add to this 'and to provoke action' but this I am afraid is more to do with the sociological and psychological aspects of management.

The theory of communication is all very well but to be more practical the objective approach to communication would be that it is:

(1) To be heard.
(2) To be understood.
(3) To be accepted.
(4) To provoke action.

Each one of these objectives has its own problems which are commonly referred to as 'barriers to communication'.

BARRIERS

Barriers to Hearing

The most obvious barrier to hearing is NOISE; either the noise volume shuts out the communication or, more commonly in our situation, the noise distraction prevents us from hearing. I often find it difficult at a meeting to 'hear' what is being said because I have only half an ear for the speaker as I am trying to hear the comments and asides of others who may be (rudely) talking at the same time.

This perhaps has a bearing on the other barrier under this heading, that of POOR CONCENTRATION. Concentration itself relates to the degree of fatigue (mental or physical) the receiver is suffering from and the physical environment of the work-place.

To illustrate them both in one sentence, I would ask you to contrast your powers of concentration at the beginning of a lecture in a warm but well ventilated room and the last half of a lecture in a warm, stuffy, humid classroom. Even the most interesting speaker stands little chance of communicating effectively in the latter conditions.

Barriers to Understanding

Vocabulary

Are you using the right words, correctly arranged and appropriate to the person to whom you are talking? There are some hilarious lists of communication blunders circulating most offices. One which illustrates this point is purported to have been sent to the Social Security offices. It said 'In accordance with your instructions I have given birth to the twins in the enclosed envelope.'

It could be that the communicator or the receiver has a limited vocabulary; a defect in the ability of either will make communication difficult.

I am sure that the onus for communicating is on the communicator. Therefore consider the age, experience, intelligence, etc., of your listeners and adjust your language accordingly.

Accent

Accents are most acceptable in speech; however, if your accent is so broad as to prevent your being understood, then it is your responsibility to modify it.

Pitch

This means the level of understanding at which you are communicating. Whilst it is insulting to talk down to people, it is far more preferable than talking over the tops of their heads.

Misconceptions

Either deliberate or accidental misconceptions can occur. People sometimes have preconceived ideas which affect their understanding or they jump to conclusions and do not wait for the full communication to be given.

There is only one way of making sure you are understood and that is to invoke the feedback stage in communication and discover, by questioning, the level of understanding of the receiver.

Barriers to Acceptance

Status

The less status and authority you possess, the more difficult it will be for you to gain acceptance of your communication. This is unfortunately an axiom of working life.

Fear

Mainly this is in relation to change. People do not like the unknown which change always represents. They are happy in the known 'status quo' of the present. Their suspicions and fears lead to a high possibility of non-acceptance.

Prejudice

Prejudices have already been mentioned earlier in this book and, when they operate, acceptance becomes difficult.

Apathy

Even though your staff may receive and understand the message, if morale is low, the apathy it produces will lead to non-acceptance.

Barriers to Action

Much of this book has dealt with the complexities of man management and the behaviour of people at work; some of the more complex reasons why we often fail to provoke action have already been discussed. However, to look on the positive side of things and relate it purely to the problem of communication, I would suggest the following to help improve your communications in general and probable action in particular.

(1) Communicate in language which can be understood.
(2) Encourage two-way communication between you and the receiver.
(3) Exhibit enthusiasm in order to generate enthusiasm.

If we go back to our model on communication we can now add more to it, as in Fig. 12.3.

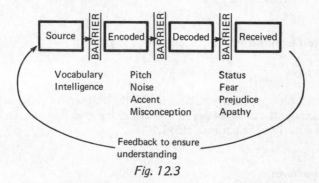

Fig. 12.3

The barriers shown can also be grouped under the three headings of Intellectual, Physical and Emotional.

CHOOSING THE MEANS OF COMMUNICATION

Basically there is a choice of two methods of communication:
(1) Verbal.
(2) Written.

Within each of these headings are a variety of communication techniques, and each of these techniques can be aided by a variety of other techniques (e.g. a talk is improved by a visual aid).

Your choice depends on your objective, the time available, the number of people involved, their availability, if a record has to be kept, etc., etc.

To help you decide, let me briefly review the advantages and disadvantages of each of these media.

Verbal Communication

Advantages

It is more personal; it enables you to adapt your message according to the feedback you are getting; it enables the receiver to ask questions; it is quicker.

Disadvantages

Different people may interpret your message in different ways; people may just not 'get the message'; it can be expensive getting a group of people together to talk to; poor or conflicting recall may be experienced by the receivers.

Written Communication

Advantages

It gives more opportunity to ponder over the best way of communicating the message; it can be re-read and/or checked; it gives a permanent record; it is less likely to be misunderstood.

Disadvantages

It is impersonal; gives one-way communication only; it can be 'lost'; there is no guarantee it will be read.

COMMUNICATING EFFECTIVELY VERBALLY

While we are taught the three Rs from childhood, it has taken men many years to realise that 99% of all our communications are by speech and it is only in recent years that educationalists have developed an education process which accepts this fact.

It is true we have had speech, drama and elocution available (often as optional extras) in our schools but often these only teach you how to say other people's words in a stereotyped manner. What we really need is training how to say our own words in a way which produces results.

Unfortunately a book lacks the essential qualification for teaching effective speech, as it is only a one-way communicator and also it requires YOU to practice. THE ONLY WAY TO LEARN TO COMMUNICATE VERBALLY IS TO DO IT.

You must accept every opportunity which is offered to you to get practice in communicating verbally in a number of different situations —

interviews, meetings, teaching, speeches, talks, etc.

The more you do it the less nervous you will become, and if you are suitably self-critical, then you will improve.

The lists of dos and don'ts for would-be 'speakers' are interminable so I have tried to keep my hints down to a minimum.

(1) A speaker must know her subject and approach it with both sincerity and conviction that her subject is worthwhile. She must also transmit her enthusiasm for the subject.

(2) Preparation and planning is essential. This is best done under three headings:

   (a) *The topic.* See that you are clearly briefed for your talk as to the subject and its scope; make it as specific as possible to suit both yourself and the person who is using you.

   (b) *The objective.* The various purposes which a talk may have can influence the way in which it is prepared. Some of the purposes could be:

   > To inform
   > To impress
   > To persuade
   > To recommend
   > To entertain

   Remember that to achieve your objective must be your prime consideration in both preparation and delivery.

   (c) *Consider your audience.* Find out as much about your audience as possible. This will enable you to prepare a talk most suitable to their needs. Here is a check-list which may help you.

   > How many are expected?
   > What age group?
   > What are their backgrounds?
   > How much do they already know of the subject?
   > What are their likely attitudes?
   > What are their interests?
   > What have they been told to expect?

Preparing your speech

(1) Consider your audience.

   (a) Are they likely to be interested, friendly, bored, indifferent? Are they intelligent, dull, young, old, mixed? These are some of the characteristics which might influence your speech.

   (b) What is their previous knowledge of the subject?

(2) Define your aim.

   (a) Teach (then they must remember certain things).

   (b) Convince (they should be influenced and interested).

   (c) Make a proposal (they must be clear as to what is required of them).

(d) Give background (a general idea will do).
(3) Subject matter.
    (a) Collect all ideas, no matter how insignificant, in any sort of order; write them down on separate slips of paper and mark the most important points.
    (b) Sort these ideas into related 'piles' then put these 'piles' in a logical sequence.
    (c) Start the process off, throwing out material not strictly useful. (This happens at all stages from now on, but remember you have marked the most important points already.)
(4) Prepare speech (see below).
(5) Check-list.
    (a) How can I make it more interesting for my audience? (Anecdotes? Visual aids? Alter structure?)
    (b) Time it (best with tape recorder — silent reading of it is hopeless).
    (c) Try it on someone.
    (d) Memorise first and last paragraphs.

Notes for a Speech

(1) Introduction.
    (a) Get the attention of the audience.
    (b) Give proposed plan of speech.
(2) Development: this is fairly obvious.
(3) Conclusion.
    (a) Summarise or re-state the various points which you have made.
    (b) Explain or justify or point out to the listener the value of carrying out the ideas in your speech. Obviously the conclusion is determined by the purpose of the speech but it should have finality and never a weak ending.

Note 1 — Never apologise for speaking! Begin with a bang! small or otherwise, but arouse the interest and arrest the attention of the audience.

Note 2 — Speak from notes, not the full text.

Note 3 — Even if you know your speech inside out, still take notes with you.

Using Notes

There is nothing wrong in using notes — there is a lot wrong in speaking from material that has been prepared for reading purposes. The two forms of communication are very different. When writing material which is to be read you can be literally prosaic; this material, when used as a talk, would sound pompous and unnatural.

When we speak we do so very imperfectly compared with the way we write, but it is the very nature of the two media.

Speech is fleeting — once spoken it is gone . . . lost forever.

Writing is permanent — you can re-read it over and over again.

People listening to a talk are either listening, thinking, dreaming or catching up.

Readers read at their own pace according to their own understanding.

Because of these differences we have developed a special way of talking which overcomes many of the difficulties I have pointed out.

Let us take time to analyse a piece of spoken English. Imagine that these are two Health Visitors talking about a client over coffee. 'Oh I had a terrible time this morning. I went and visited Mrs Smith — poor woman — do you know her? She's so hard to talk to. She's aaa withdrawn as though she's in mmm a world of her own, there's a barrier between her and reality'.

It reads badly, doesn't it? If I were writing that I would say quite simply 'I had a difficult time interviewing Mrs Smith this morning' (or words to that effect).

Here then is the first difference — we use more words when we talk than when we write. Why? Well because speech is so fleeting we have developed a way of repeating ourselves in different ways. In our example we have said that Mrs Smith:

is withdrawn;

is in a world of her own;

has erected a barrier.

This repetition makes sure our message gets across.

Now let us look at the phrase 'Do you know her?'. This is called an 'echo-sounding device'. In other words we say something, see the reaction it brings and adapt our speech accordingly. If her colleague had nodded or said 'yes', the conversation would probably have ended something like this — 'Well then you know just how difficult it is to get her to talk'.

The whole of speech is an echo-sounding device — everything you say provokes an action for you to read, be it interest, yawning, fidgeting and looking at their watch. Note what is coming back to you and try to do something about it.

And what about your ers, aas and mms? They too have a name — it is 'stabilisers'. They are an almost acceptable form of speech as they allow you a pause to think of what you will say next and allow your audience to catch up with you.

This is the very reason why a person reading a paper at a seminar is not as enjoyable as a 'speaker' who just uses headline notes. The paper reader:

(1) Goes too quickly.

(2) Does not repeat herself.

(3) Has no stabilisers.

Mind you, whilst I say 'stabilisers' are necessary, if you mumble and stumble along using them all the time they become known as 'fillers' and these are just NOT acceptable.

225

To apply these points to notes:

(1) Write out your talk as naturally as possible.
(2) Make headline and subline notes and talk to these.
(3) Write them on convenient sized cards, as in Fig. 12.4.

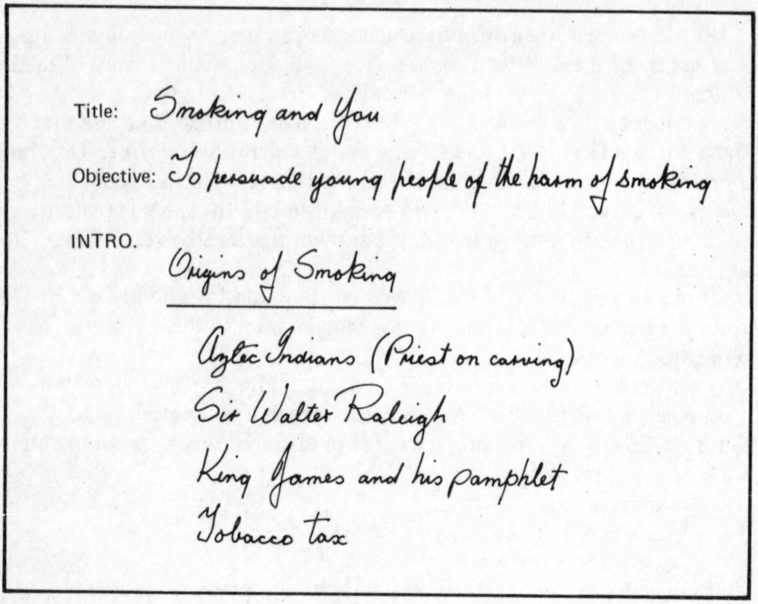

Title: *Smoking and You*

Objective: *To persuade young people of the harm of smoking*

INTRO.

Origins of Smoking

Aztec Indians (Priest on carving)
Sir Walter Raleigh
King James and his pamphlet
Tobacco tax

Fig. 12.4

Timing

Timing is a most difficult thing to teach. You just get to know. I know that four pages of A4 of my writing takes me 25 minutes to deliver — but that has come from a great deal of experience.

Do not time it by reading it to yourself. Ten minutes of silent reading can equal at least 20 minutes of talking, if not a great deal more. The only way is to tape it or deliver it as normally as possible and time yourself ... I would do this a number of times as it is excellent rehearsal.

Nervousness

I still get nervous! The trouble is I don't show it. What happens is that I break out in a bath of bodily perspiration!

I think it is good not to be blasé about talking in public. It gives an edge to your performance and keeps reminding you of the standards you desire to keep.

You should know that, if you have done your homework well and know your subject, you will soon settle down and warm to your subject.

226

A few very deep breaths seem to help before you get started, but best of all is when you get into your talk, you will feel a lot better.

Remember . . . you can improve your ability and self-confidence in speaking by taking every opportunity to practise. Preparation and practice are the keynotes.

Giving a Talk in Various Situations

Vote of Thanks

(1)   Express pleasure at being asked to perform this function.
(2)   Why? Because the person is in some way an exceptional speaker or has exceptional knowledge of his subject.
(3)   Comment on the part of the speech which particularly interested you and reinforce the point. This shows courtesy as a good listener.
(4)   Use a personal experience related to the talk if possible.
(5)   Comment on the effect the speech will have, maybe to increase activity on behalf of Oxfam, etc.
(6)   'And therefore, on behalf of us all,' or some similar expression, 'I should like to thank you very much indeed.'
(7)   Lead the applause, if appreciation is to be shown in this way.

Present a Gift

Function. To recall his achievements in the past; to wish him happiness in the future; to present the gift.
(1)   Refer to the occasion: say that you feel it is an honour to have been asked to make this presentation.
(2)   Refer to the past: number of years he has been associated with you; some remember him from his early days.
(3)   Refer to the present: esteem in which he is held; any personal or humorous incident.
(4)   Describe the gift: say why this particular choice was made.
(5)   Present the gift: wish him health and happiness; express pleasure and hand him the gift.

Accept the Presentation of a Gift

Function. To express appreciation; to acknowledge any help that you may have received from other people; to thank those who have contributed to the gift.
(1)   Express delight in the gift: look delighted when you say this.
(2)   Refer to your early days as a member of staff: refer to early friendships made and new interests found in the group.
(3)   Acknowledge the help of others.

(4)   The gift (useful or decorative) will keep alive happy memories of your association with the group: describe the gift; not all members will know what the gift is even though they subscribed to it.

(5)   Thank the person making the presentation on behalf of the group and ask her to accept your gratitude to all: thank the person by name and give the full name of the group.

Chairmanship

Chairmanship is an art. A Chairman should have:
(1)   A calm and friendly disposition.
(2)   The ability to think quickly and objectively.
(3)   A sound knowledge of procedure.
(4)   A sense of humour and absolute control of temper.

The duties of a Chairman are fivefold and should follow a set design.
(1)   Opening remarks should be addressed to the audience, welcoming those present, establishing a pleasant, friendly atmosphere and outlining the purpose of the occasion.
(2)   The subject of the talk having been introduced, reference should be made to the reasons why this should be of special interest to the audience.
(3)   To encourage deeper interest, it should be announced that the Speaker will be prepared to consider questions arising from his talk.
(4)   The introduction of the Speaker to the audience should include all his titles and qualifications, emphasising his knowledge of the subject and establishing his right to be recognised as an authority.
(5)   Finally, the Chairman must express general appreciation of the Speaker's willingness to address the audience, concluding with a clear repetition of his name and the title of his talk.

N.B. Opening and concluding sentences should be carefully prepared and memorised but should thereafter be delivered as if impromptu.

MEETINGS AND GROUP DISCUSSIONS

Nothing is more frustrating nor gives rise to greater indignation than aimless, interminable meetings.

We are living in an era of meetings. The principles of participation and consultation require meetings. The dissemination and discussion of complex material and issues require meetings. Our right to be heard on matters affecting our working life requires meetings. Effective up and down communication requires meetings. Far from being apologetic about them, I must state firmly that I believe they are an effective channel for getting things done.

Unfortunately, these meetings are not automatically effective because they are necessary. Neither are they effective just because the members of the group are intelligent, well meaning or indeed senior in grade.

To be effective, a meeting makes considerable demands on the skills of both the leaders and members. To help you, here are some guidelines for before, during and after the meeting.

Before the Meeting

(1) Be sure of the aims of the meeting.
(2) Plan how you will communicate these aims and the topics to the meeting.
(3) Plan to cover the agenda in the time available.
(4) Prepare supporting material (charts, graphs, etc.) and have it ready in the order of the agenda so that you will be able to produce it quickly and unfussily at the time required.

During the Meeting

(1) Introduce the meeting and the subjects clearly and offer a suggestion as to how the meeting should tackle it.
(2) Listen, summarise, re-state, clarify, support, challenge.
(3) Involve all members of the group — ask them questions if they are not forthcoming.
(4) Depersonalise attacks; divert and control irrelevancies.
(5) Seek out areas of agreement.
(6) Talk through areas of disagreement.
(7) Summarise conclusions and agree action points.

After the Meeting (Review)

(1) How did it go?
(2) How did I do?/we do?
(3) What went well? (Can we repeat it?)
(4) What went badly? (How can we overcome these difficulties in the future?)
(5) Did we achieve the aims?

After the Meeting (Action)

(1) Circulate minutes/notes as appropriate.
(2) Implement action agreed at the meeting.

PROCEDURE FOR COMMITTEES

I. The Committee

(1)   Must have terms of reference, i.e. its purpose. It often seems to be the case that people set up a committee at the drop of a hat to discuss anything and everything often seemingly without knowing why they are discussing it. Again we return to the principle of the objective; unless a committee really knows what it should be doing it cannot possible work effectively.

(2)   Must have a 'duration', e.g.
(a) Permanent. This means ongoing. The committee perpetuates itself, as long as the reason for it being called together continues. Of course, members may change regularly either on an annual basis or according to the specific rules of that committee. Although the members change, the committee which is the constituted body of members remains.

(b) For a specific purpose, i.e. until their task is complete. Probably the most famous committee of recent years is the Salmon Committee. Their specific purpose was to look at the management structure of nursing and to make recommendations as to how the nursing services can best be administered. They deliberated and came to their conclusions, after which they disbanded. No doubt you can think of other committees also, Brigg's and Mayston being two which readily come to mind. Each of these had a specific purpose and was only constituted to complete a specific task.

(3)   Must have rules, either
(a) Written. If written they must be strictly adhered to. The name given to these written rules vary and some of the more frequent ones which you may come across are Standing Orders, or Articles of Association. If you are a new member of the Committee one of your first questions should be whether or not there are these Standing Orders in existence. If there are, then these Standing Orders will probably indicate all the rules for conducting the meetings of that committee and as a new member you should make yourself familiar with them.

(b) Verbal. If rules are verbal then Common Law rules apply. Within Common Law there is enough precedent to enable anyone to run an orderly meeting either of a private committee or a public meeting. Much of the advice I will be giving in this section is based on Common Law.

(4)   Must have officers, i.e.
    Chairman   *Secretary*
    Vice-Chairman   *Treasurer*

The rules should include how officers are elected and the length of term of office for each of them. The committee which changes all of its members once a year has an inherent weakness inasmuch as it lacks continuity. If you have any say in the setting up of any committee, the practice of having one-third of the members retire each year can be recommended. This means that each person is elected to a committee initially for a period of one, two or three years. Thereafter one-third of the committee automatically retires and those who are elected in their place therefore serve for three years.

These officers of the committee can also be members. In fact they usually are; it is only in big company meetings that there is a professional secretary who is not actually a member of the committee. The implication of this is that each of the officers of the committee, if elected from members of the committee, has a vote. If they are professional officers they do not have this right of voting.

A committee need not have all of these officers either, there is no point in having a Treasurer if there is no money involved. Likewise a Vice-Chairman is not necessary for small, comparatively informal committee as if, say, the Chairman is not present, it is a very simple matter of electing a Chairman for that meeting only. I do think it is a good idea to have a Secretary. If it is worth having a committee and worth having meetings, then it is well worth having the meeting arranged and run as efficiently as possible and having good minutes recorded of that meeting.

II. Officers — Their Duties and Powers

(1) Chairman. Most of his powers and responsibilities are Common Law powers.
(a) To see that the meeting is duly convened and properly constituted. This means that the requisite amount of notice is given to all entitled to receive notice of the meeting. It is generally accepted that seven days' notice is a good rule. Normally the Secretary does this but none the less it remains the Chairman's responsibility to see that this is done. You will often see in newspapers official notices of committees and/or meetings being held. Undoubtedly this notice, being published in such a manner, is one of the Standing Orders of that Committee. (In my own experience, failure to give the requisite amount of notice caused chaos in a small new society of which I was a member. We were called to London for our first Annual General Meeting and the first point of order the Chairman had to deal with was that this meeting was not duly convened. The proposer of that motion went on to point that according to the rules the proper amount of notice had not been given and therefore the whole of the meeting was null and void. The end result of this was that he was shown to be correct and the meeting broke up in some disarray and, I might add, at great personal cost to those who had travelled some distance to be

present at that meeting.)

That a meeting is properly constituted is that the Chairman or a Chairman is present and that there is a quorum.

If the Chairman of the committee is not present then any member can propose the name of another member present to act as Chairman; provided he is seconded and the committee accept this nomination then that person will act as Chairman for the whole of the meeting.

A quorum is the minimum number of members that can make binding decisions for that committee. If you have rules then the quorum will undoubtedly be contained within them; if you have no rules then it would be at your discretion. I suggest that at least half the membership present is ideal; you may reduce that number but I would certainly recommend that it never be less than one-third of the membership of that committee. The quorum must be maintained throughout the duration of that meeting. I will be dealing below with what happens if a quorum is not maintained.

(b) Preserve order. This means physical order as well as the order of debate. The Chairman under Common Law has a great deal of power, including the power to physically eject a person from a committee who has given just grounds for his ejection by causing a great deal of trouble. The Chairman cannot obviously eject a person just because he disagrees with him, or the rest of the committee; they can only do this if the person is creating a nuisance or consistently breaking the Standing Orders of that committee.

(c) Conduct proceedings regularly. This means that the Chairman must see that decisions are properly taken and, again, that the order of debate is preserved.

(d) Ascertain the sense of the meeting. This has relevance to (b) and (c) above inasmuch as the order of debate is applied in order that the Chairman can ascertain the sense of the meeting.

It is here that one of the great merits of committee meetings can be emphasised. Its strength is that at every step the will of the majority is acted upon. The Chairman must always see that the opinions of the majority are given by seeing that motions are 'put', seconded, discussed, amendments discussed and a proper vote taken.

(e) Decide on points of order. A member can raise a point of order at any time — it infers an irregularity in the proceedings and it must be dealt with immediately.

The member makes his point by interjecting at any time the phrase 'point of order, Mister (or Madam) Chairman'. At this stage the Chairman must stop all the proceedings and ask the person who has made the point of order to make their point. Having heard the case the Chairman will decide whether he should sustain that point of order or reject it. Whatever the Chairman then decides, his decision, once taken, is irrevocable. Therefore, if you are a Chairman your responsibility for knowing the rules and regulations of the committee is a great one. Normally the Chairman and the Secretary put their heads together and between them they will make a decision. But I must emphasise that even if he makes the wrong decision there is no procedure to have that decision reversed. He is rather like a referee at a football match saying that a particular shot resulted in a goal not being scored. No matter how many times the TV cameras replay it and show that the ball actually went over the line the result remains unaltered. The referee said it was no goal and it is no goal.

(f) To see that all business is transacted within the scope of the meeting, i.e. the Chairman must make sure that things brought to that committee are within its terms of reference. Additionally, he will often need to decide whether or not he can accept an item for discussion under Any Other Business. A minor item may be discussed under this heading but if a member raises a matter of such significance that the Chairman feels that the members ought to have time to go away and study the matter and perhaps even ask questions of those they may be representing then he could rule that it is not within the scope of this meeting and suggest that it be put on the agenda for the next meeting.

Possibly under this heading I could mention that it is a general rule that members other than the proposer of a motion should speak only once on each motion. This I find personally a rather stifling rule but I can see how important it is when it comes to handling large public meetings where one person could continually be on his feet and not giving others the chance to speak.

If I can give a hint here. If you are faced with being Chairman of a large meeting and a number of people want to speak on a motion, it is a good idea to have the 'pros' and the 'cons' lined up and then invite a 'pro' then a 'con' to come to the microphone alternately. I have seen this done in a meeting of more than 300 people and it resulted in a very orderly and interesting discussion.

(g) See that business is conducted in the order laid down in the agenda. Again this has reference to (b) and (c) above. The Chairman cannot by himself alter the order of the items of the agenda. Only the meeting can change this order of the agenda.

It seems to me to be a very useful protective rule inasmuch as some people (in my opinion, rather rudely) look at the agenda rather as they look at the sales catalogue at an auction. They say to themselves that they will not bother with the first six to eight items on the agenda and will turn up just in time to discuss a particular item in which they have an interest. If that member arrives and finds the Chairman has dealt with that item before he arrived he

*can, despite his own rudeness, be justifiably aggrieved if it was
dealt with on the arbitrary motion of the Chairman.*

*The order of debate can be changed if the Chairman or member
proposes that an item be taken out of turn, is seconded and a
majority vote recorded on it. Then our rude man could be told very
clearly that it was the will of the meeting that that agenda item
be taken out of turn and he has no redress on that decision.*

*(h) Only allow discussion where there is a motion. If there is an
intention to take a decision at the meeting then a motion must be
'put'.*

*A motion is a sentence in definite terms preceded by the word
'that'. It is very wise to spend a great deal of time phrasing your
motions so that they actually reflect the decision which you
require taken. Many motions containing 'ifs' and 'buts' and 'maybes'
and 'eithers' and 'ors' are really not acceptable. They must be
definite statements. (The motion that was regularly put and
discussed at the Staff College where I worked was that the tutors to
the staff college wear mini kilts. A motion, which I may add, was
frequently carried and resulted in my knobbly knees being exposed
very frequently at the end-of-course parties!)*

*As Chairman you must make sure that the motion, clearly and
without ambiguity, can serve as a focal point for discussion.*

*When the motion has been decided upon and has been passed
by the committee that same sentence becomes a resolution. You
will also see sentences in the minutes which read 'it was resolved
that . . .' (tutors to the staff college . . . wear mini kilts).*

*(i) Ensure no irrelevant discussion. This is very clearly a difficult
duty of a Chairman. It means purely and simply that the Chairman
must stop people for deviating from the subject and going on to a
lot of irrelevant discussion. As Chairman you must be firm, but
tactful, in the way in which you exercise this control.*

*If you do exercise this function effectively then you will rapidly
gain for yourself a reputation of being an excellent Chairman.*

*(j) That all motions are put to the vote. The Chairman must make
sure that the pros, the cons and the abstainers are recorded. Usually
this is done by a show of hands, but sometimes the Chairman can
judge the sense of the meeting and the shouts of 'ayes' and 'nos'. If
the latter is done then the Chairman will have to use his inbuilt
clapometer; if he has any doubt then he must put the motion to the
vote by show of hands. It is also possible to have a secret ballot
where each member puts her mark on a piece of paper and the
Chairman and Secretary count these and announce the result.*

*The matter of abstainers should not be overlooked inasmuch as
the number of abstainers can often indicate the tenor of the meeting.
For example, if half the members present abstain from voting I*

would view the decision made by that committee with a great deal of reservation.

(k) To adjourn the meeting subject to the consent of the meeting itself. The meeting can only be adjourned if a motion for adjournment is put, seconded and the vote carried. The only time a meeting may adjourn without the consent of the members is on a point of order that 'there is not a quorum present'. Whenever the number of members present at a meeting falls below the stated quorum and a member makes a point of order on the matter the Chairman must rule that the meeting has adjourned. If a qualifying member has only left the room temporarily then the Chairman may suspend proceedings until the member returns.

(2)   Secretary

Before Meeting
(a) Accommodation for meeting arranged.

(b) Notice of meeting is sent correctly and on proper authority.

(c) Ensure agenda is sent out, having been agreed by the Chairman and including reports from any sub-committees.

(d) Send the minutes with the notice.

(e) Enclose a proxy form. A proxy form is where a member is allowed to sign a form which will enable another member of that committee to cast her vote for her. Quite a few societies have this rule and if you are faced with the question of whether or not you should fill in a proxy form may I ask you to consider very carefully the person to whom you will entrust your vote. The reason for this note of caution is that you have no power to tell that person how to vote. She may use your vote entirely as she wishes.

At Meeting
(f) To see (with the Chairman) that the meeting is properly convened. I have already discussed this point under 1(a) above.

(g) To assist the Chairman in conducting the meeting. In practice the Secretary does a great deal of the work prior, during and after the meeting. The Secretary's role during the meeting is to guide the Chairman on all matters of procedure, feed him the relevant papers and documents at the appropriate time, tactfully remind the Chairman of various matters as appropriate to the items being discussed, and take notes of the meeting in order that the minutes may be produced.

235

(h) To produce minutes.

(i) To guide Chairman in matters of order. This has been discussed under 2(g).

(j) To ensure that the appointment of Chairman and members is quite in order. It will be up to the Secretary to make sure that all the rules of appointing Chairman and members of the committee have been followed. For example, that nomination forms are received in time and properly seconded, and that at the meeting when various names have been proposed the voting is done in a proper manner.

It is usual for the Secretary to take over the meeting for a very short time when the Chairman has to be elected. Usually the Chairman symbolically or actually leaves the Chair. Then the Secretary reads the nominations that have been submitted together with the names of those who have seconded the nominations, or calls for nominations from the committee (whichever is appropriate to the rules). The Secretary then calls for a show of hands on the nominations which have been put before the committee, counts the number of votes and announces the Chairman. At this stage the new Chairman takes the Chair and takes over the running of the rest of the meeting.

(3) Treasurer
    (a) To check expenditure and see that it does not exceed income.
    (b) To collect subscriptions.
    (c) To pay accounts.
    (d) To keep proper accounts.
    (e) To raise funds for special projects.
    (f) To ensure that the society's funds are invested as instructed by the committee.

III. Procedure at Meetings

(1)   *The Chairman will take the Chair. Should the nominated Chairman not be present the Vice-Chairman may automatically take the chair. If neither is present then a Chairman may be voted in according to the proper procedure for the duration of the meeting.*
(2)   *The Chairman will see that a quorum is present.*
(3)   *Apologies will be received.*
(4)   *Notice convening the meeting will be read. This is to assure all members that proper notice was given according to the rules of that committee.*
(5)   *Deal with the minutes of the previous meeting, and if all are agreed the Chairman will sign them as being a proper and correct record of the previous meeting.*
(6)   *Deal with matters arising from the previous minutes.*
(7)   *Deal with items as shown on the agenda.*

(8)   Any other business.
(9)   Fix date of the next meeting.

IV. Discussion Rules

(1)   As per standing orders. If there are no standing orders then the following rules will be useful guidelines for you.

(2)   Business must be dealt with in the order as it appears on the agenda.

(3)   All speakers must address the Chairman. In very formal meetings they stand when they do this. You should observe the conventions of that committee and follow them.

(4)   Members should not address other members direct. The correct way of addressing another member is by gaining the permission of the Chairman by a phrase such as 'through you Mister (or Madam) Chairman may I say . . . '.

(5)   Only one person should speak at a time. The Chairman has the prerogative to select the person who has the floor. If you are Chairman you should do this in a positive manner so that the person you have selected clearly knows that she has the floor.

(6)   Members may speak only once. As I have already said, this can be rather a stifling rule in small committees where discussion is welcome but a useful rule in very large meetings.

(7)   Discussion must be kept to the motion at all times.

(8)   Motions and amendments must be in definite terms. Sometimes motions have to be in writing. All motions must be seconded or else they die. The only motions which do not have to be seconded are those put by the Chairman of a subcommittee on the subject pertaining to the work of that committee.

(9)   Motions once proposed should not be withdrawn. The only way a motion can be withdrawn is by the committee accepting a motion to that effect. A person cannot say, 'Oh, I will withdraw the motion'; that must be a proposal which is seconded and voted on.

(10)   Motions once discussed should not be discussed a second time. The same motion can of course be brought up at another meeting and very often this is done quite successfully. In the intervening period people have obviously been buttonholed or the climate for discussion has changed. However, it is hoped that the member who monotonously raises the same motion meeting after meeting is not a person who would be re-elected to that committee.

(11)   When an amendment is proposed, discussion must centre on the amendment and a decision taken on that before the meeting returns to discuss the original motion. An amendment is only a minor alteration of the motion by leaving out words, adding or changing words. It is essential that the alteration be minor and this, incidentally, excludes the introduction of the word 'not' into a motion, for that would completely alter the motion and could not be classed as a minor alteration.

The procedure for proposing an amendment is to wait until the motion has been put and seconded, then at any time during the discussion a member may propose an amendment. Provided the proposal is seconded then the meeting turns its attention to whether or not it is going to accept the proposed amendment. After full discussion, a vote is taken on the amendment, and if it is accepted the wording of the motion is changed accordingly and discussion then centres on the now amended motion (the substantive motion).

Any number of amendments may be proposed to an original motion but I suggest that the Chairman accept only one amendment at a time and deal with that; otherwise things can become very confusing.

(12) Points of order can be raised at any time.
(13) Voting is normally by show of hands. Unless it is in the standing orders the Chairman does not have a casting vote. What this means is that, unless the rules say otherwise, the Chairman has only one vote which he can cast on any motion. If he uses his vote in the original show of hands then he may not vote a second time to break a deadlock. The Chairman can, however, refrain from voting in the original show of hands on a motion; then if a deadlock is discovered, he may use his vote to break it.

A piece of advice which I think would be useful to any Chairman is never to use his casting vote to alter the status quo. The reason for this is that if the Chairman by his vote changes the status quo by his single vote, it virtually has become his individual decision to change the order of things. This leaves him open to a great deal of criticism . . . a very unwise position to be in.

V. To Terminate Discussion

These rules are probably amongst the most important things I have to say about committee procedure as those skilled in committee work can, with a willing accomplice, bamboozle a committee into making decisions before they are ready to do so. Both the Chairman and the Secretary, as well as the members of course, should make themselves very familiar with the methods of terminating discussion.

(1) After all have spoken, put the motion to the vote. This, of course, is the normal way.
(2) Guillotine motion. This is when a member proposes that discussion will cease after a set period of time and that, regardless of how many people there are left to speak, the meeting must vote on the motion and the discussion.
(3) By the proposal and seconding of the motion 'that the question now be put' and having it carried. This is a means of stopping discussion on a motion and getting the vote taken then and there. Again, this is regardless of any other people who may have wished to speak on the motion.
(4) By the proposal and seconding of one of the following motions:
(a) 'that the question not be put', or

(b) 'that we proceed to the next item of business'.
In both these cases there is no vote on the motion and the meeting has to proceed to the next item on the agenda. While this is a legitimate means of terminating discussion it is rather rarely used. (A motion so dealt with dies and will have to be put and seconded at a further meeting should the matter need to be raised again.)

(5) To refer. The motion to refer a motion means basically that while the committee wants to toss out the motion they do not reject it out of hand. The procedure for referring a report is to propose and have seconded the motion 'that we refer the report back to the committee of its inception'.

By doing this the committee is saying, 'Now you have heard what we think and feel, take this motion back, perhaps reword it and amend it in the light of what you have heard and then re-submit to us at another time.

(6) That the matter 'lie on the table'. When there is not enough information available this is a very useful device for delaying making a decision; members can then make their own enquiries and the Secretary can produce facts and figures which may be required in order that the committee may make a more useful and informed decision at a later date. Once a motion is lying on the table it can be brought up at a subsequent meeting without having it proposed and seconded. The procedure for doing this is for the Chairman to say 'Ladies and gentlemen we have the motion that . . . lying on the table; the floor is open for discussion'.

VI. Meeting Adjourned

As already mentioned, the meeting can only be adjourned on the proposal for adjournment being seconded and the meeting carrying it by a vote.

WRITTEN COMMUNICATIONS

In this section I will confine myself to the very important topic of report writing for management. . . though my first point applies equally to all kinds of written communication. It is that effective communications:
(1) Have impact — gain and hold the reader's attention.
(2) Convey meaning — i.e. the writer's meaning!
(3) Stimulate the desired action or response.

Introduction

The writing of reports on management topics is a common and essential feature of management in health care organisations. The technique for writing these reports differs a great deal from the reports that nurses are familiar with, i.e. patients' reports or student nurse reports. The purpose of this section is therefore to suggest guidelines and presents some conventions for writing effective management reports.

Purpose of Management Reports

The purposes for which reports can be written fall into three general categories. These are to persuade, to inform and to confirm.

(1) Persuasive. In this report the writer has the objective of influencing or persuading the reader to take some specific action. To be effective, the report must show that the advice given is correct and also that it is superior to any other alternative course of action.
(2) Informative.
    (a) to communicate new facts to the reader;
    (b) to interpret facts with a significance to management;
    (c) to relate cause and effect of facts revealed by investigation.
(3) Confirmative. This report places some important factor on record.

A report, whilst conforming for the most part to one of the above categories, will quite frequently contain some element of some of the others.

Principles of Report Writing

In all writing it must be remembered that it is the READER (not the writer) who is important and that you have only fulfilled the purpose of writing the report when it has been acted on in the way you intended. To achieve this a report should be BRIEF, ACCURATE AND CLEAR.

Brevity

The report should be as brief as the purpose will allow. Keep the report RELEVANT by not including material which does not contribute to the points required to be made to achieve action. Do not repeat in detail what the reader already knows except to confirm figures relative to the report. Use the minimum words and ideas to express the meaning clearly.

Accuracy

In report writing you must be careful to distinguish matters of fact from assumptions. When you use figures make sure they are complete and arithmetically correct. A slip-up in any factual information you may write can adversely colour the reader against your report even though the rest of it may be totally accurate.

Clarity

There should be no doubt about the meaning your words are intending to convey. Avoid ambiguity or vagueness and only use jargon and abbreviations if you know that all your readers will fully understand the language of the situation.

Writing the Report

The American Bureau of Naval Weapons kept reminding its report writers, in typical American style, to KISS! And what a great idea it was when you learn that the word stands for Keep It Simple, Stupid!

Although I am going to discuss a number of headings frequently found in reports, I am a firm believer that a report should have only a beginning, a middle and an end. You may call it an introduction, the central sections and conclusion if you like!

However, as a reader as well as a writer of reports, you may find useful the following list and explanation of various headings frequently found in reports.

1. *Headings.* They are used to:
(a) enable you to find your place quickly (signposts),
(b) enable you to pick out the relevant parts of the report,
(c) act as quick reference after you have read it.

2. *Introduction.* It should be short, stating briefly the terms of reference, its purpose and any other matters which will place the report in its setting for the reader.

3. *Definition of terms and symbols.* This heading is self-evident but an example would be 'In this report the term 'she' should be interpreted as applying to nurses of both sexes'.

4. *Conclusion.* This is a summary of the discussion in the main text, including its findings and references drawn from them. It should not contain any new material not included in the text.

5. *Recommendations.* These arise from the conclusions or results of the work. Sometimes they are included in the conclusion.

6. *Summary.* A brief survey of the ground covered in the main text and the objectives achieved. This is usually written to give the reader a quick answer to her problem rather than reading the whole report! Be careful about including a summary because, if a report is written to persuade, the summary might prejudice its outcome by giving the results before the reader has been subjected to your arguments.

Include it only if it will help your point to succeed.

7. *Bibliography.* Strictly speaking, this is a complete list of all material written on the subject. Better to list your books under a heading of 'Further reading'.

8. *References.* In medical literature, the most common system is the shortened Harvard system.

References should be listed at the end of the report in alphabetical order of the author's name. In the text of the report they should be referred to in parentheses by the name(s) of the author(s) and the year of publication.

If you have to quote more than one paper by the same author(s) in the same year, you should add the letters (a) (b) (c) and so on to the year in the text and in the reference list (e.g. 1976(a), 1976(b) etc.).

The references to articles should be listed in the following order:
> Surname and initials of author(s);
> Year of publication (in parentheses);
> Name of journal (underlined), using the appropriate abbreviation from the *World List of Scientific Publications*;
> Volume number (in arabic numerals);
> First page number.

Here is a mythical example:
> Bloggs, J. (1976). *Br. med. J.*, 3, 99.

For books, the full title, city of publication and publisher must be included, as follows:
> Bloggs, J. (1976). *Diseases of Report Writers.* London, Pitman Medical.

9. *Division of Text.* There are many systems in use. Here are some examples.

(a) Section Headings

Main Headings:	roman numerals (upper case), e.g. I, II, III
subheadings:	arabic numerals, e.g. 1, 2, 3
followed by:	lower case letters, e.g. a, b, c
followed by:	lower case roman numerals, e.g. i, ii, iii

(b) Paragraph Numbering

The most widely used system is:
Chapter and paragraph, e.g. '6.3' which is 'chapter 6 paragraph 3'.
Others are:
Straight paragraph numbering throughout
Page and paragraph, e.g. '99.3' which is 'page 99 paragraph 3'.
Page/chapter, paragraph and line, e.g. '18.3.1' which is 'page (or chapter) 18 paragraph 3 line 1'.

10. *Appendices.* These are for the presentation of detailed material which would have been out of place in the main body of the text (i.e. it would have spoilt the smooth flow).

11. *Abstract.* This is a somewhat more detailed summary. It is a section

of the report which can stand by itself somewhat like a very shortened version of the whole document.

If you really are ambitious in your report writing, then here is a suggested structure from which you could select to meet your needs.
(1)   Title (short, informative and unambiguous).
(2)   Abstract.
(3)   Summary.
(4)   Contents (a list of main headings and page numbers).
(5)   Introduction.
(6)   Discussion (the main body of the report).
(7)   Conclusions.
(8)   Appendix.

Perhaps if you are less ambitious then the following check-list might be of value to you.
(1)   Who is my reader?
(2)   What will she want to know?
(3)   What use will my reader make of the report?
(4)   What am I trying to say?
(5)   What words will express it?
(6)   What image or idiom will make it clearer?
(7)   Is this image fresh enough to have an effect?
(8)   Could I put it more concisely?
(9)   Have I said anything that is avoidably ugly?

COMMUNICATION CHANNELS

I suppose the most basic channels of communication are One-way and Two-way Communication.

Communication Game

There is a game you can play which demonstrates the uses of each of these techniques very effectively.

The game requires two members of a group to describe a pattern of squares verbally so that those listening can draw them. The first member is allowed to give her instructions once only and the group cannot ask any questions (i.e. one-way communication).

The second member may repeat her instructions by request from the group and answer any questions they may ask (i.e. two-way communication). Add to these two rules that the person describing the pattern must not 'draw' in the air or in any other way, indicating only by speech the pattern of squares. Any pattern will do — something like this perhaps?

243

Fig. 12.5

Fig. 12.6

Just make sure that all squares touch at the corners or half-way mark and that no odd angles are chosen, just 90 and 45 degrees.

Results

I have played this a large number of times and the results I am about to describe are fairly typical.

(1) One-way communication:
   (a) it is done quicker;
   (b) it is carried out less accurately (i.e. drawn badly);
   (c) the communicator does not feel too badly about the way she did her job and blames any mistake on the receiver.

(2) Two-way communication
   (a) it is slower
   (b) it is noisier and more chaotic;
   (c) the communicator feels threatened by the remarks and questions asked by the group;
   (d) it is drawn very much more accurately.

The lessons we can learn from this game are numerous.

(1) One-way is APPARENTLY more efficient to an outside observer − though knowledge of the results disproves this.
(2) One-way is a quicker method initially but what about rectifying mistakes.
(3) One-way is easier for the communicator.
(4) Two-way is slower but more efficient.
(5) Two-way is more difficult for the communicator.
(6) Two-way does not offer APPARENT efficiency.

Translating this into management terms − If you want to appear efficient by getting an inferior job done poorly and then be in a position to blame others then be a one-way, autocratic, non-consultative leader. If, on the other hand, you don't mind what people say as long as you get good results, then be a two-way, consultative, discussive leader.

Play the game for yourself and you will find even more lessons to be learnt from it than I have outlined.

Up and Down Communications

The other basic communication channel is up and down communications.
It is my experience that downward communications are very much

more effective than those at the top of the structure realise, but upward communications have to be consciously worked on and organised well if they are to be effective.

I think that the reason for this is the perception of human kind whereby subordinates develop a sixth sense relating to the character, personality and true motives of their bosses; probably in order to survive.

It results in subordinates reacting more favourably to those things which they judge to be of the greatest personal concern of their boss and put their greatest effort into these areas. (This phenomenon also accounts for the fact that some communications sent by the superior never get acted upon!)

In this up and down communications channel, there must be a focal point for communications exchange and this unhappy lot falls on the shoulders of middle management.

Analysis of communication in hospital by actual observations and by simulating management in exercises on courses, always reveals that the volume of communications handled by the middle managers is twice as much as either their superiors or subordinates.

If you believe in the saying 'knowledge is power' then it is easy to see who is the most powerful group in the organisation, The middle managers are the group who interpret senior managers' policies, filter the communications which they receive from above and below, and decide how much they keep to themselves and how much they pass on.

The effectiveness of the organisation depends a great deal on both the integrity of the middle manager and her communications ability.

COMMUNICATION PATTERNS

The results of a very interesting management exercise which we developed at the William Rathbone Staff College, entitled Bavelas Squares, told us a lot about the effectiveness of various management structures.

We did a puzzle in different groups each using a different communication pattern. These patterns are shown in Fig. 12.7.

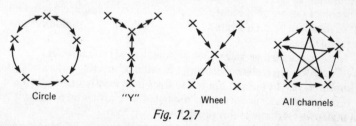

Circle   "Y"   Wheel   All channels

Fig. 12.7

While we labelled them with these names they were equivalent to various management and communication structures as shown in Figs. 12.8 to 12.10.

245

Circle = Lateral communication

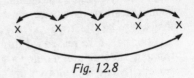

Fig. 12.8

Y = The old management structure

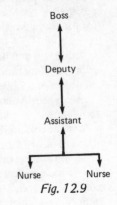

Fig. 12.9

Wheel = Our current structure

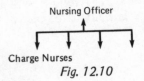

Fig. 12.10

All channel = Group discussion or meetings

Our results invariably showed that the Wheel was the most efficient means of communication except when there was a large amount of communication as there is during a time of CHANGE in an organisation. Then it becomes the worst (because one person cannot handle, analyse and make decisions at such a rate as the sheer volume of communications required).

In a time of change when the communications volume was high then the Circle was first, always proving the value of meetings when deciding complex issues. In normal times also the Circle mostly came second.

Consistently at the bottom of the list was 'Y'. We always knew it was an inefficient structure; this proved it.

Incidentally, we also did crude measures of morale in these various groups. All Channel came top and 'Y' came last!

All in all, I am convinced that the underlying reasons for our management structures and our pattern of meetings is very sound. If there is a failure then it is in the people who communicate, not the organisation in which they are communicating.

HOW TO IMPROVE YOUR COMMUNICATIONS

(1) Accept YOUR responsibility for communicating efficiently and conscientiously.
(2) Think clearly – clarify your ideas (know your objective) before you communicate.
(3) Analyse the problem – accept that communicating has its problems, try to anticipate where problems may occur and devise strategies to overcome them.
(4) Consult with others in planning your communication.
(5) Ask questions.
(6) Try to see the matter from the other side.
(7) Follow up your communications.
(8) Be a good listener – you should want not only to be understood but also to understand.

CASE STUDY – CAN YOU STATE A CASE
Imagine yourself in the position of Mrs Ryan, Personal Secretary to Mr Hardy who is the Director of Education for a large Area School of Nursing. For the past 2 years you have had to do your work in an office with four other typists, three of whom are serving the doctors. There is one internal telephone and one external telephone between the five of you.

The room is rather small and stuffy and the girls are much younger than you and inclined to be chattery and somewhat noisy. There is also the problem that the office faces a main road and consequently there is a great deal of traffic noise. Some of the girls smoke and you find this an irritation, especially with the fact that if you open a window the traffic noise becomes almost unbearable.

A small room has become vacant directly opposite Mr Hardy's office. You would very much like to have this room as your office. You know that you will have to speak to Mr Hardy about it.

What would be the most effective way for you to put your case to Mr Hardy?

Prepare and write down a detailed plan of action.

WARD HOUSEKEEPER – RESULT OF APPOINTMENT
I said that I would let you know whom we appointed as Ward Housekeeper. We chose Miss Smithson and it was a disastrous appointment. There was no doubt she was a young, bright person but her interpersonal relationships in a line management position were quite appalling. However, she was an excellent teacher and if the staff respected her for

247

anything it was for her technical knowhow.

After a period of time it became apparent that the Unit could not function effectively with her in charge. We had a need for someone to undertake a training role within the Area so we took a deep breath and appointed Miss Smithson to this job. She was a great success at it; need I say more.

In fact, we very soon had Mrs Terry working in her old position and she worked out very well.

REFERENCES AND FURTHER READING

Bagley, W. A. (1964). *Facts and How to Find Them.* London, Pitman.

British Association for Commercial and Industrial Education (1960). *Tips on Talking*, 2nd edn. London, BACIE.

Citrine, Lord (1968). *ABC of Chairmanship.* London, NCLC Publishing Society.

Compton, H. and Bennett, W. (1967). *Communication in Supervisory Management.* London, Nelson.

Cooper, B. (1964). *Writing Technical Reports.* Harmondsworth, Essex, Penguin.

Appendix
Staff Appraisal

At the time of writing, the Health Service appraisal system is under review. The objectives remain fundamentally the same but there are some significant changes proposed.

In outline, the new scheme envisages:

(1) An annual written appraisal of performance carried out by the nurse to whom the appraised is accountable followed by an appraisal interview, again normally carried out by the immediate superior of the appraised.

(2) The completion by the appraised and the appraiser (together, if necessary, with other members of staff who can make a positive contribution) of a Development Action Plan.

   A Development Action Plan is a 'simple statement in writing of objectives agreed between a senior nurse and a member of her staff for the development of the latter'.

   Development includes clinical skills as well as personal development and the development of potential for more responsible work.

(3) A countersigning nurse will scrutinise the form for both accuracy and fairness. This person is usually the appraiser's immediate superior.

(4) The appraised will have an opportunity to read and record in writing on the form itself any remarks she might want to make following the appraisal.

There are also clear recommendations for the safe custody of the forms, with the actual appraisal form being kept secure from unauthorised scrutiny. The Development Action forms, being of a different nature, will be retained by both the appraised and the appraiser for each to monitor progress.

The forms are to be retained for five years and then destroyed.

A copy of the forms proposed is reproduced below. You will note that it is a six-point rating scale with each point represented by a letter, the interpretation of which is:

A — Outstanding; exceptionally effective. Performance is ALWAYS well above the normal standard. An 'A' assessment should be supported by reference to specific occurrences.*

B — Above the standard required; more than generally effective but not positively outstanding.

C — Well up to the standard required; generally effective; shortcomings in some areas are offset by good performance elsewhere.

D — Up to the standard required; performs duties moderately well and without serious shortcomings. Although performance could be improved, this is in no sense an adverse marking.

E — Below the standard required; definite weaknesses make her barely good enough to 'get by'. This marking is likely to be a transitional one in that it sounds a warning note which should result in some positive action by all concerned; e.g. further training, special help and advice or change of duties. Unless performance improves it is probable that it will, for one reason, or another deteriorate further.

F — Unsatisfactory; definitely not up to the duties. This rating should be supported by reference to specific occurences.* It should never happen that you give an 'F' assessment without having previously drawn the nurse's attention to her shortcomings, and where these are serious, without having told the Countersigning Nurse that you have done so.

CRITERIA

Throughout the assessment keep in mind the following criteria adapted as necessary to meet the varied circumstances as between, say, the hospital or community nurse, the tutor or health visitor.

Organisation and Management

Consider her working methods and the organisation of her own time and activities; the assessment of priorities; ability to work under pressure; and the handling of emergencies. Also her ability to plan ahead and to co-ordinate other services and personnel in relation to the needs of the patient; ability to match staff to fluctuating demands of work to be done; use of resources; and the delegation of work to juniors.

Supervision of Staff and Leadership

Consider her ability to bring out the best in her staff; to appraise performance; to identify development needs and to counsel accordingly. Is

* The assessment should of course reflect performance over the whole period of the report and not be unduly influenced by one or two outstandingly good or bad occurrences.

she supportive to her staff? Does she handle disciplinary matters with
confidence, firmness and understanding?

Relationships

Consider her ability to establish and maintain good relationships with
patients, clients, their relatives, and the other groups of staff and organisations listed; to deal with 'difficult' personalities; and, generally, to handle
inter-relationship situations with confidence and perception.

Ability to Communicate

Consider how effective the nurse is both orally and in writing in making
herself understood to her patients/clients, her staff, her learners, her
seniors and others. Are written communications always relevant, clear
and well set out? Does she speak clearly and put her points across
convincingly and concisely?

Teaching and Training

Consider her skill in identifying and satisfying the training needs of
patients/clients and their relatives (in health education, etc.) and/or
qualified staff and learners. If the appraised is a Tutor, consider her
general effectiveness in formal teaching, informal teaching and personal
tuition. Does she have a good knowledge of educational techniques?
Does she keep herself up to date with advances in nursing and medical
knowledge?

Ability to Contribute/Develop/Carry out New Ideas and Methods

Consider her ability to see useful possibilities and alternatives which are
not always obvious to others; willingness constructively to question
established practices and procedures; and ability to provide fresh insight
and broaden perspectives.

Analysis of Problems; their Solution; and Decision Making

Consider her capacity to transform, break down or reformulate an
apparently complicated problem into workable terms; to draw sound
conclusions from an analysis of a problem and produce practicable suggestions for its solution. Where the solution of a problem is entirely the
responsibility of the nurse being appraised, consider the decisions made

and their consequences, e.g. the use made of resources and its effect on the quality of service provided.

Other Relevant Skills not Covered

This section has been provided for an assessment of skills not covered under other headings of the form. It might also be used to comment in more detail on some of the skills used by nurses engaged in capital project work; service planning; management services; and personnel policy; etc.

Summary of Performance Over All

Use this section to add in your own words a word picture of the appraised. Include qualifying remarks if overall performance is affected by health, experience, available resources or organisational problems. Add remarks also if there are particular failings, which it is within the nurse's power to correct; e.g. poor relationships with medical, administrative and other groups of staff; supervision of staff.

I must say that while I may have a few niggardly criticisms of the form, this new appraisal scheme is a tremendous improvement on the old scheme and offers a great deal for both the development of the individual and the nursing profession.

....Authority

Review for the period from...................... to..

PART I

Mr/Mrs/Miss (Forenames).................................Surname ....

Date of Birth ....

Professional qualifications ....

Present grade and post...

Service in present Authority commenced... (Please show any
significant break(s) in service (e.g. 3 months or more) during the period under review

....

Service in present grade commenced ....

Service in present post commenced ....

Service with present appraiser commenced ....

Service with countersigning nurse commenced ....

PART II

Key Tasks
(Set down here an agreed list of the key tasks and responsibilities during the period under review — see paragraph
4 of the Notes for Guidance of Appraisers and Countersigners.

PART III(a)

ASPECTS OF PERFORMANCE

In this part of the form you consider the skills required to carry out the duties described in Part II. You should
make as much use as possible of the spaces for comment so as to provide as full a picture as possible but PLEASE
READ THE NOTES FOR GUIDANCE OF APPRAISERS AND COUNTERSIGNERS BEFORE COMPLETING
THE APPRAISAL AND THROUGHOUT ITS COMPLETION.

ASPECT	I		A	B	C	D	E	F		COMMENT*
1. ORGANISATION AND MANAGEMENT OF WORK										
2. SUPERVISION OF STAFF AND LEADERSHIP										
3. RELATIONSHIPS (a) Patients/Clients, their relatives, etc.										
(b) Immediate colleagues, medical, administrative, ancillary and other groups of staff										
(c) Social Service Departments, schools and supportive agencies										
(d) Nursing management										
(e) Learners, visiting lecturers and other visitors										
4. ABILITY TO COMMUNICATE (a) Orally										
(b) In writing										
5. TEACHING AND TRAINING (a) Patients, their relatives, etc. (e.g. health education)										
(b) Qualified staff (e.g. in ongoing on-the-job development)										
(c) On-the-job training of students, pupils, etc.										
(d) Education of students/pupils in formal and informal settings.										
6. ABILITY TO CONTRIBUTE/ DEVELOP/CARRY OUT NEW IDEAS AND METHODS										
7. ANALYSIS OF PROBLEMS; THEIR SOLUTION; AND DECISION MAKING										
8. OTHER RELEVANT SKILLS NOT COVERED ABOVE (a)										
(b)										

* If the space provided for comment in this and other parts of the form is insufficient use another sheet of paper
and attach to the form.

PART III(b)

SUMMARY OF PERFORMANCE OVER ALL

PART IV

TRAINING NEEDS AND DEVELOPMENT OF POTENTIAL

1. Has the appraised been the subject of any form of development/action during the past year? If so, please comment giving, if possible, an assessment of any effect on performance/confidence.

2. Would she benefit from and be suitable for any form of development action during the coming year? If so, please specify; state briefly the aim of the action proposed; and complete a 'Development Action Plan' form, copies of which should be held by those principally concerned.

3. Does the appraised have any special aptitudes or inclinations? Could these be better used than at present for the benefit of the Service and the nurse herself? If so, please give your recommendations.

4. To what extent are your comments based on personal knowledge of the nurse and her work?

Signature of Appraiser . . . . Grade. . . . . Date. . . . .

PART V

REMARKS OF COUNTERSIGNING NURSE

1. Is the appraised satisfied that this appraisal is both accurate and fair?   YES/NO

2. If the answer to 1. is 'NO' what action is called for?

3. I note the assessment made above and the Development Action Plan. I have the following additional comments to make, all of which I have discussed with the nurse and her appraiser:

4. (To be completed where no Development Action is proposed.) I have the following comments to make in respect of the appraisee's training and development needs:

5. To what extent are your comments based on personal knowledge of the nurse and her work?

Signature of countersigning nurse. . . . . .Grade. . . . . Date. . . . .

PART VI

I have seen the above assessment of my performance and have discussed it at an appraisal interview. I would like to add the following remarks:

Signature of appraised. . . . . Date. . . . .

Development Action Plan

NOTES
1. A Development Action Plan is a simple statement in writing of objectives agreed between a nurse and a member of her staff for the development of the latter. It should be subject to review.
2. The term 'development' should, in this context, be interpreted broadly to include the development of clinical skills as well as personal development and the development of potential for more responsible work.
3. The plan should be practicable and where it involves action, or support, on the part of others – particularly, for example, the appraiser's own seniors – their prior commitment should be secured. It should concentrate on one or two important areas which call for some extra effort or an improvement in methods.
4. If you need further help or advice on drawing up a plan, your seniors or the Personnel Department will be able to advise you.

DEVELOPMENT ACTION PLAN AGREED BETWEEN:

. . . . (Appraised) and

. . . . (Appraisee)

for the period. . . . .

Action to be taken by appraisee:

Action to be taken by appraiser (and/or other senior staff):

Date for review. . . . .

INDEX

259